The Challenge of Educational Innovation and National Development in Southern Africa

American University Studies

Series XIV
Education

Vol. 36

PETER LANG
New York • San Francisco • Bern
Frankfurt am Main • Paris • London

Dickson A. Mungazi

The Challenge
of Educational Innovation
and National Development
in Southern Africa

PETER LANG
New York • San Francisco • Bern
Frankfurt am Main • Paris • London

Library of Congress Cataloging-in-Publication Data

Mungazi, Dickson A.
   The challenge of educational innovation and
national development in Southern Africa / Dickson
A. Mungazi.
      p. cm. — (American university studies. Series
XIV, Education ; vol. 36)
      Includes bibliographical references (p.   ) and
index.
      1. Educational innovations—Africa, Southern.
I. Title.   II. Series.
LB1027.M864   1991   370'.968—dc20   91-38677
ISBN 0-8204-1713-0   CIP
ISSN 0740-4565

Die Deutsche Bibliothek-CIP-Einheitsaufnahme

Mungazi, Dickson A.:
The challenge of educational innovation and national
development in southern Africa / Dickson A.
Mungazi.—New York; Berlin; Bern; Frankfurt/M.;
Paris; Wien: Lang, 1991
   (American university studies : Ser. 14, Education ;
Vol. 36)
   ISBN 0-8204-1713-0
NE: American university studies / 14

Innovation in education has an important role to play in building a new society. Brian Carlson, Headmaster, South Africa, 1988

The thrust for national development in Southern Africa cannot be undertaken without meeting the challenge of educational innovation . A Zimbabwean Educator, August 10, 1989.

*To the Memory of Gaylord Smith, humanitarian,
teacher, and friend, whose life was an example of
the greatness of humanity.*

Contents

Acknowledgments

In the process of writing a book that discusses highly critical aspects of a critical region, one needs to exercise great care in obtaining original materials and documents that enable one to interpret events and policies in an accurate manner and logical fashion. It is for this reason that the author wishes to express his profound gratitude and appreciation to the embassies of the countries of Southern Africa in the U.S.A. for allowing him access to some of these materials. He also wishes to thank the leaders of the countries of Southern Africa which he visited in 1983 and 1989 for their willingness to offer him some important insights into the problems that they are experiencing.

The author particularly wishes to express his appreciation to the Zimbabwe National Archives, the Ministry of Information and the Ministry of Education and Culture, for allowing him access to original documents and materials he needed as part of the data required to produce the study. His special appreciation goes to Mr E.C. Makunike, the Director of the Ministry of Information, and Mr E. C. Chikwanha and Mr E. Mutiti, his deputies, for their assistance in obtaining the materials he needed and for the interest they showed in the project.

The author wishes to record his special appreciation to Betty Russell, Marge Maston and Ed Bulinski, all of the Center for Excellence in Education at Northern Arizona University, for their assistance in programming the computer so that the manuscript could be produced more efficiently. In a similar fashion, he wishes to thank Dr. Sam Minner, former director of the office of research and faculty developmentand interim executive director in the Center for Excellence in Education, Dr. Robert Holloway and Dr. Arnold Danzig for their support and encouragement. The author wishes to extend his special appreciation to Mary Reed, also of the Center for Excellence in Education, for preliminary editing of the manuscript. To Carla Duran, also of the Center for Excellence in Education, the author wishes to extend his special appreciation for typography and to Linda Gregonis, indexer and proofreader. He also wishes to thank Jeannette Weatherby and Jill Talley of the Faculty Services Office in the Center for their assistance in dispatching the proofs to the publisher.

In a similar fashion, the author wishes to thank his nephew, Clifford Mungazi, for allowing him the use of his car while he was in Zimbabwe in 1983 and 1989 , and Mr. and Mrs. William Kodzai for their hospitality and other forms of assistance, as well as a number of individuals who granted him interviews while he was in Southern Africa in 1989.

Finally, the author wishes to thank the members of his family, his wife Della, his daughter, Marcia, and his sons, Alan and Gaylord, for giving him constant support and encouragement without which the study could not have been completed.

SOME FACTS ABOUT SOUTHERN AFRICA, 1990

	Angola	Botswana	Mozambique	Namibia	South Africa	Tanzania	Zaire	Zambia	Zimbabwe
Pop.	8,971,000	1,220,000	15,250,00	1,400,000	34,000,000	24,746,000	33,991,000	7,770,000	8,987,000
Area in Sq.Mile	481,353	231,804	308,261	318,261	435,868	364,886	905,063	290,586	150,873
Date of Col.	1575	1889	1575	1885	1835	1885	1885	1891	1890
Col.Nat.	Portugal	Britain	Portugal	Germany	Britain	Germany	Belgium	Britain	Britain
Capital City	Luanda	Gaberone	Maputo	Windhoek	Cape Town	Dar es Salaam	Kinshasa	Lusaka	Harare
Curre.	Kwanza K29=US$1	Pula P2.20=US$1	Metical M403=US$1	Rand R1=US$1	Rand R1=US$1	Shilling S134=US$1	Zaire Z6.50=US$1	Kwacha K1.20=US$1	Dollar $2.10=US$1
GNP in B$	4.5	0.930	0.640	--------	60	7.20	6.50	7.40	5.30
Literacy Rate	30%	35%	14%	16%	75%	86%	55%	54%	50%
Type of Govt.	Socialist	Democratic	Socialist	Democratic	One-party	One-party	One-party	One-party	Democratic
Current Leader	Edwardo de Santos,1979	Quett Masire,1980	Joachim Chissano,1986	Sam Nujoma,1990	F.de Klerk,1988	A.Mwinyi,1985	Sese Seko,1965	K.Kaunda,1964	R.Mugabe,1980
Official Lang.	Portuguese	English	Portuguese	English	Afrikaans English	English	French	English	English
% of GNP spent on Ed.	14%	4.1%	3.8%		39%	31%	30%	25%	30.1%
Date of Inden.	1975	1966	1975	1990	1910	1962	1960	1964	1980

Preface

Introduction: The Concept of National Development

This is a study of the effect of educational innovation on national development in Southern Africa, that part of Africa south of the Equator. The term *innovation* means change, not for change's sake, but to ensure improvement. Therefore, educational innovation calls for change in the educational system in order to improve it. The thrust for educational innovation in Southern Africa must be seen in the context of the enormous political and economic problems that this critical region of Africa is experiencing and from the point of view of the fact that change in human existence is an imperative to the development of society itself.

Two questions are critically important to this study. The first is: Why is it important for the nations of Southern Africa to initiate educational innovation? The second question is: What does successful educational innovation involve? The answers to these questions lie in the character of Southern Africa itself. Before discussing that character, the expression *national development* must be defined. Flowery as it sounds, the expression *national development* is not fully understood by the leaders of the nations of Southern Africa. However, it carries the definitive meaning of embracing a program of action designed to improve the essential features of national institutions. These include efforts to ensure fundamental freedoms of the people, such as self-expression, the right to participate in national politics, to earn a decent income, social association, freedom of religion. A nation that denies its citizens these freedoms cannot be regarded as progressive, and any thrust for its own definition of national development is void of any real meaning.

In the context of contemporary terminology, national development means affording all the citizens basic freedoms to pursue goals and objectives that are consistent with their interests and purposes. These include the right to pursue careers without restrictions, to participate in the political process, to run for public office, to exercise freedom of self-expression, to own property, to exercise, to criticize the government without any reprisals, to belong to a political party of one's choice, and to earn a decent living and live where one wishes. In short, national development means setting goals that citizens can pursue to improve the conditions of living so that they are better than they were in the past. This allows citizens to identify with national purposes. These are the elements that combine to create a national social climate that brings happiness and security to the citizens. National development has its basis in this climate.

The Concept of Educational Innovation and National Development

Now, an answer to the first question to the first question must be provided, why it is important for nations of Southern Africa to initiate educational innovation. The character of Southern Africa itself demands that nations initiate educational innovation because that is one viable way of finding solutions to the problems of national development. The release of Nelson Mandela on February 10, 199 from life imprisonment life imprisonment following his 1964 conviction on charges of attempting to overthrow the government of South Africa, was a dramatic turn of tragic events that began to unfold with the victory of the Nationalist Party led by Daniel Malan in the elections of 1948. Can one define Mandela's release as an element of national development without making an effort to dismantle apartheid? The answer is no because apartheid does not allow the components previously identified to combine and operate in the manner that would translate subsequent events into a thrust for national development.

The enactment of the infamous Bantu Education Act in 1953 was an event that set South Africa on a deadly national conflict. When Malan retired from active politics in 1958, he was succeeded by Hendrik Verwoerd, a man of uncompromising belief in the supremacy of apartheid, the superiority of the Afrikaners, and the assumed inferiority of the Africans. As the director of Bantu Administration in the Malan government, Verwoerd became the principal architect of apartheid as he systematically applied it to reduce the Africans to the status of bare existence. To accomplish this objective, Verwoerd used provisions of the Bantu Education Act to elevate the Afrikaners to the pedestal of absolute political supremacy enshrined in their invincibility and infallibility.

Verwoerd assassination in 1966 brought John Vorster to the seat of power from where he directed apartheid to new unprecedented heights. The decision of his government to enforce new provisions of the Bantu Education Act created a national climate that led to the explosion that was heard around the world from Soweto in June, 1976. Facing a barrage of outcry and criticism from the international community, Vorster decided to resign in 1978 on grounds of poor health, rather than face the reality that apartheid was setting South Africa on a course of self-destruction. Indeed, apartheid was rolling with a vengeance.

Vorster's successor, Pieter Botha, approached the problems created by apartheid in Southern Africa, not just in South Africa, with a new determination to ignore the protest from the international community and to make apartheid the sacred shrine that both the Afrikaners and the Africans must worship with total supplication. The intensification of the armed struggle, spearheaded by the African National Congress (ANC), along with a series of bomb explosions throughout South Africa killing many and injuring many more and the imposition of economic sanctions combined to force Botha to urge his fellow diehard Afrikaners to *adopt or die*. However, Botha did not have the courage to face up to the reality that apartheid had gone too far. Instead, he warned the world, "Don't push us too far." When

Frederick W. de Klerk succeeded Botha in 1988, he recognized the critical nature of the South African society as a victim of apartheid. This is why he called for change.

It is not surprising that Mandela's response to de Klerk's call was his own call to innovate the system of education on the basis of initiating nothing less than dismantling apartheid in order to transform the character of the South African society. de Klerk and his fellow Afrikaners must realize that while the recognition that maintaining a political status quo cannot be done forever, it is equally an elusive task to initiate change in the social structure without accepting the challenge of educational innovation. Therefore, the challenge to de Klerk is to respond to the call to end apartheid in order to change the system of education so that a thrust for national development can be made.

This is the only way solutions to the problems of national development can be found This is the reason why the Africans have demanded an end to apartheid as a condition of that development. This would bring the people of South Africa, both black and white, closer to understanding each other for the benefit of their country. This is what Mandela saw when he said on February 13, 1990, that education under apartheid was a crime against humanity. The recognition of this truth constitutes a prerequisite of the challenge of educational innovation in South Africa . That the Africans do not vote in national elections; that they are not allowed to run for national public office because they not regarded as citizens of South Africa, are, indeed, forms of the ultimate crime against humanity that apartheid has instituted. Indeed, the first order of business for de Klerk and his government should be to dismantle the Bantu Education Act to convince the Africans that its leaders meant well. That they did not do this raised some serious doubt about their sincerity to bring about genuine change. The action taken by the South African parliament on June 5, 1991, to repeal provisions of the apartheid law did not constitute the final act to remove the last vestiges of of an oppressive system because the black people were still second class citizens and foreigners in the land of their birth.

The character of other countries of Southern Africa also shows that educational innovation is critical to reshaping their societies. In Mozambique, a country with a literacy rate of 14% in 1987, and Angola with 30%, the brutal civil wars have left the people without hope for the future and without purpose or direction. The plundering and brutality with which Jonas Savimbi's UNITA in Angola and Afonzo Dhlamini's Renamo in Mozambique wage the struggle for their respective causes lead to the conclusion that education would help the warring parties to understand the destructive nature of the conflict that these two former Portuguese colonies have endured since they gained independence in 1975. Conventional wisdom would suggest that investing in education would make it possible for Mozambique and Angola to recognize the critical nature of national unity. Once people are educated sufficiently, they understand the need to restructure national programs to ensure the happiness and security of all. This cannot be done in the context of existing conditions. Without adequate education it is not possible to recognize this reality.

Instead of directing their resources towards the destruction of each other, the people of these countries could direct them toward the development of dynamic societies with a potential for greatness. Observers have concluded that the economic, the physical, and the psychological damage that the people of both countries have endured will take years to repair. If there is a need to make a new thrust for educational innovation anywhere in Africa, that need is greater in these two countries than anywhere else on the continent.

Following a bitter fifteen - year war that led to the independence in April 1980, Zimbabwe, the former British colony of Southern Rhodesia recognized that its first priority in its efforts to rebuild the devastated country was to make a fresh start in education because its leaders realized that it was crucial to other aspects of its national endeavors. Therefore, as soon as it was instituted, the new government of Zimbabwe accepted the challenge of national development by initiating a new thrust in educational innovation.

But, in 1980, the conflict between the government and dissident elements culminated with the announcement by the government of its intent to turn Zimbabwe into a one-party state. That this announcement derailed the educational program that the government had put in place is seen in the general decline in the economy, a lack of confidence in the future among the people, and the periodic wave of violence that has marked most of Zimbabwe's first decade of independence. When a new conflict broke out in 1989 between the government and university students over the question of corruption by some government officials, there was a widespread feeling that the government itself had become the problem because in its desire to institute a one-party system, it had lost sight of the national objectives that it had identified at its inception.

However, the efforts that Zimbabwe had made since independence in initiating educational innovation to improve its literacy rate of 40% in 1983 had, by 1991, been recognized as having a stabilizing influence in shaping the course of national development. By 1988 that rate had increased to 50%. If Zimbabwe can overcome the temptation to turn the country into a one-party state, then it can stand on the verge of a great nation enshrined in the priceless potential that has been acknowledged as the basis of a truly happy and progressive nation. The road to this greatness lies on Zimbabwe's ability to meet the challenge of educational innovation within the national climate of political freedom and individual liberty.

The granting of independence to Malawi and Zambia in October, 1964, was an occasion that raised new hopes among the Africans of these countries of a brighter future than the past. But, when Hastings Kamuzu Banda of Malawi and Kenneth Kaunda of Zambia converted their countries into a one-party government system, the euphoria of a brighter future turned into an abyss of despair. The efforts that these two countries made in changing the system of education to reflect the needs of the people as a basis of a brighter future than the past fell into the background of things as every activity by their national leaders focused on strengthening the notion of a one-party rule. Both Banda and Kaunda have been in power since that time, but are not willing to admit that they have become the major problem that their countries are facing. By 1990 Malawi had a literacy rate of 25% and Zambia of 54%.[1] Indeed,

---

[1] *The World Almanac and Book of Facts*, 1990

both countries have endured the agony of underdevelopment as a result of the action of their leaders.

This pattern of one-party government has been persistent in Southern Africa. When Mobuto Sese Seko staged a military coup in Zaire on November 25, 1965, it was the beginning of the road to a military dictatorship that has entrenched itself deeper than in 1965. Seko himself has shown no mercy towards those who hold different political views from his own and the direction that Zaire must take. Over the years Seko has been reported to have a personal fortune estimated in billions of dollars while the people have been enduring grinding poverty. Instead of directing his efforts towards the development of the people through educational innovation, Seko has designed a strategy to keep himself in office for life, just like Banda and Kaunda. The literacy rate of 55% in Zaire in 1989 could have been better if national resources had been directed towards educational development of the people.

Botswana is the only country in Southern Africa whose government and people seem to understand and appreciate the importance of casting the educational process in the national framework of democratic principles. Although its literacy rate of 35% out of the total population of 1.2 million in 1990 is comparatively low, its people are among the happiest in all of Southern Africa because they enjoy all the fundamental freedoms that are essential to national endeavors as we have defined them in this study. While this author was there in 1983 and 1989, he was pleased to see that a multi-party democracy is well and alive. There was no government control of the media, no restrictions on the people's right to belong to political parties of their choice, no massive nationalization of major industries. The National Commission on Education of 1977 seemed to understand the importance of accepting the challenge of initiating educational innovation to sustain these democratic values and practices. This study discusses its findings and the implications of its recommendations.

Since Botswana achieved independence from Britain on September 30, 1966, under the leadership of Seretse Khama, it has never wavered in its commitment to democracy. When Quett Masire assumed the office of President on July 13, 1980, following Khama's death, there was no fear that the democratic principles that were established at the inception of independence would be in danger. The people and their government fully cooperated in a new endeavor to ensure national development based upon a new thrust for educational innovation. Botswana's efforts in this national thrust are also discussed in this study as an example of what nations of Southern Africa can do to promote national development through educational innovation.

The problems that these examples show are the reasons why nations of Southern Africa, more than other countries of the *Dark Continent*, with possible exception of the *Horn of Africa*, must initiate educational innovation. Conventional wisdom seems to suggest that problems of national development cannot be resolved in isolation to those of education. Because change in education is necessary to initiate change in society, the concept of innovation becomes an imperative to acquiring ability to face other problems.

The Thrust for Educational Innovation

Now the second question must be answered: What does educational innovation involve? What has been discussed concerning the national character of the countries of Southern Africa leads to the conclusion that the thrust for educational innovation involves two basic components. The first is to ensure the development of the individual to make national development possible. The second component is to consider the outcome of educational innovation. This will help nations of Southern Africa focus on why such innovation is important. In order to discuss the importance of educational innovation in Southern Africa, this study begins by discussing its influence on the structure of society itself. In doing so it underscores the need for innovation in general and suggests its structure, purpose, and outcome. It also discusses the problems that have placed this region at the crossroads.Chapter 2 discusses the need for educational innovation from the perspective of its role in helping shape the character of society during the colonial period. The discussion of the educational objective, the educational policy and the educational process during the colonial period leads to the conclusion that the need for educational innovation is an imperative to political independence and to breaking away from past systems that were designed to serve the interests of the colonial society.

Having established in the first chapter that the educational system during the colonial period was designed to serve the interests of the colonial society, the study moves on to discuss in subsequent chapters how educational innovation can help solve the problems left behind by the colonial governments. Chapter 5 relates to the conditions of educational innovation and what nations of Southern Africa can do to improve them to have it serve the needs of the people. Chapter 6 considers some strategies of educational innovation

The outcomes of educational innovation is the focus of Chapter 7. Outcomes as a product of educational innovation entails important considerations. Among these outcomes are the freedom of students to choose their own course of study and to pursue career objectives consistent with their interests. This is an important way of ensuring the fullest opportunity for all students to plan their future in an unrestricted manner This suggests the conclusion that a nation enjoys a greater degree of freedom as a result of educational innovation than before. These components are summarized in Chapter 8.

Conclusions and Implications

Nations of Southern Africa must remember that as critically important as it is, educational innovation must be initiated within the environment of fundamental change that must take place in the social system. This means that the political system has to change to embrace the general concept of change itself. The elections held in Namibia in November, 1989; to pave way for independence scheduled for March 21, 1990, the change of socioeconomic system in Mozambique announced by President Joaquim Chissano in August, 1989, the efforts made towards a negotiated settlement between the warring parties in Angola, and de Klerk's peace overtures towards ANC, and other formerly outlawed political parties, all combine to create a climate of regional peace so desperately needed to place Southern Africa on the road to a new society and prosperity.

To initiate change is an enormous task, but it is a task that must be accomplished because while the risk of failure is there, the consequences of not trying are devastating. The relationship between social change and educational innovation are two pillars of development the nations of Southern Africa need to cooperate to ensure the success of national development. For that cooperation to come about, South Africa must first recognize that apartheid has to go so that a new non-racial society is created. Meaningful educational innovation can take place only in this kind of setting. This is the challenge before Southern Africa.

SOUTHERN AFRICA

1

SOUTHERN AFRICA AT THE CROSSROADS:
A REGION IN NEED OF INNOVATION

Innovation in education has an important role to play in building a new society .
Brian Carlson, 1988.

Apartheid is on a rampage in all of Southern Africa in immoral defence of itself.
Robert Mugabe, July, 1980.

Introduction: The Setting

The massive demonstrations staged in July, 1990, in Lusaka, Zambia, carried
four clear messages for all of Southern Africa.[1] The first was that the region's old
guard had been in office far too long and that it was time for change in national
leadership. The second was the one-party system of government must give way to
a multi-party democracy as a prerequisite of a new thrust for national development.
The third was that mismanagement, corruption by government officials,[2] and their
unwillingness and the inability to see the need for change combined to constitute a
cancer that was destroying the vital tissue of national life. The fourth was that
innovation in education must become a critical factor of political, social, and
economic change to ensure national development. That in 1990 every country in
Southern Africa was going through a very difficult period as a result of a popular
demand for fundamental social change underscores the need for innovation in
education. The problems of Southern Africa are many and varied, ranging from the
one-party system of government to the oppression of apartheid. This study
discusses how educational innovation can help resolve these problems.

Speaking to the Organization of African Unity (OAU) on the problems of
national and regional development in Southern Africa at the summit conference
held in Freetown, Sierra Leone on July 2, 1980, President Robert Mugabe of
Zimbabwe used unprecedented clarity to present the critical nature of how
apartheid, the internationally notorious racial policy of South Africa, had become a
major problem in the region. Mugabe stated:

---

[1]The geographical definition of Southern Africa is: that part of Africa south of the Equator,
including Angola, Botswana, Lesotho, Mozambique, Namibia, South Africa, Swaziland,
Tanzania, Zaire, Zambia, and Zimbabwe. These countries are the focus of this study.
[2]*The New York Times,* July 15, 1990.

> Apartheid is on the rampage in all of Southern Africa in immoral defence of itself. In Mozambique, it is actively sponsoring acts of sabotage. In Zambia, it is not only deploying its own troops in open attacks upon that country, but it is also promoting the Mshala gang. In Angola, it has been committing mass murders of civilians, financing Unita and directing numerous acts of sabotage. In Swaziland and Lesotho, it has conducted incursions. In Zimbabwe it has attempted to disrupt independence celebrations and has recruited some five thousand persons for military training to defend itself in Namibia.3

Indeed, it is true that, with a possible exception of the *Horn of Africa*, no region of Africa has experienced the agony of conflict between efforts to maintain the social and political status quo and endeavors to initiate meaningful change. It is equally true that the continuation of the major problems of Southern Africa can be traced to apartheid. From its inception unofficially in 1652[4] and officially in 1948, apartheid has become identified as the principal cause of problems of change in all of Southern Africa. All the people of Southern Africa are victims of it.

This is the reality of the situation that Nelson Mandela took into account when he said on May 4, 1990, "When I went to prison (in 1964) I could not vote. Twenty-seven years later, I still cannot vote. We are all victims of apartheid."[5] The conviction and sentencing of Winnie Mandela, his wife, to six years in prison on April 14, 1991, on charges of kidnap and conspiracy against a black youth in Johannesburg, is one of the continuing tragic legacies of apartheid. There is no question that the white judge who tried and sentenced her was part and parcel of the system of apartheid that both Nelson and Winnie have vigorously opposed and that he wanted maximum negative publicity to tarnish their reputation. In spite of de Klerk's claim to the contrary, apartheid was well and alive in South Africa and beyond as of 1991.

Although apartheid has been a major problem in all of Southern Africa, one must see it in the context of an array of other problems it creates. These are the problems that pose a challenge to the countries of the region in their struggle for meaningful change or innovation. One of these problems is how to make education relevant to the conditions of the times. One must also understand that education helps to determine the direction that nations take in their developmental efforts. The fact of the matter is that education, to serve its intended purpose, must be related to other national aspects such as political and socioeconomic factors. That the application of apartheid makes it virtually impossible to initiate such change suggests the conclusion that if apartheid is dismantled, then it is quite possible that

---

3Robert Mugabe, Zimbabwe: *For the Record, Number 2:* An Address to the OAU, Freetown, Sierra Leone, July 2, 1980. By courtesy of the Zimbabwe Ministry of Information.

4For the evidence to substantiate this conclusion ,see Dickson A. Mungazi, *The Struggle for Social Change in Southern Africa: Visions of Liberty.* New York: Taylor and Francis, 1989, p. 93.

5Harold Dow, CBS-TV Evening News, May 4, 1990.

other problems can be resolved. The continuing saga of ethnic violence in South Africa and the claim by the government that it is unable to stop it undercuts the very essence of what a nation is and destroys the fabric of national development.

The Purpose of the Study

To fully understand how apartheid affects all of Southern Africa, one needs to understand how, over many years, South Africa has created an economic system which forces all other countries in the region to depend on it. The purpose of this study, then, is to show that educational innovation is critical to both national and regional development. Without educational innovation, any effort to initiate change in the national and regional character in order to meet the needs of all the people becomes elusive. The study will also show that without fully understanding the nature of educational innovation, nations of Southern Africa will always be handicapped by underdevelopment. The study therefore examines a number of critical factors that are related to educational innovation in this critical region of Africa. It offers some theoretical considerations of innovation as well as forces that must influence it.

The Extent of the Problems

In discussing the need for educational innovation in Southern Africa, one must have a complete comprehension of the extent of the problems that exist in the region. Because of its past, Southern Africa is experiencing enormous economic and political problems that must be resolved if the future is to be meaningful for all. This is why this study takes the position that a viable method of resolving these problems is initiating educational innovation. The economic system and the system of education were two major institutional structures that the colonial governments created to sustain their own position of power. A brief discussion of a few examples and how they have been a factor of development of the region as a whole follows.

The Political Situation

Mozambique: Every country in Southern Africa is experiencing serious political problems. In Mozambique a brutal civil war has been raging for fourteen years inflicting an incalculable loss of human life and national programs.[6] The Mozambique National Resistance (Renamo) led by Afonzo Dhlakama had been engaging in rebel and terrorist activities that defy comprehension. That Renamo did not define its objectives in launching a campaign of destruction and killing suggests the tragic nature of the political situation in Southern Africa. It is a well known fact that Renamo has been utilizing the military assistance it has been receiving from

---

[6]ABC-TV, *20/20*, March 2, 1990

South Africa[7] to carry out raids into Mozambique and Zimbabwe, killing at least 100,000 and maiming many more in 1989 alone.[8]

The fact that most Renamo rebels were indiscriminate in their killing suggests a lack of understanding of the value of the human being. South Africa's decision in 1975 to support Renamo and Renamo's willingness to accept military assistance to further its own objectives in the region suggests vulnerability of a group that has no cause and demonstrates the absence of any rationality in its behavior so critical to human thought process and national endeavors. What Renamo fails to appreciate is that it is destroying the country for the benefit of no one. Renamo's action also suggests complicity with South Africa to destabilize the region. The decision by de Klerk in February, 1990, to cut off aid to Renamo as part of the policy of his government in seeking dialogue with ANC was an action that President Joaquim Chissano took into consideration in deciding to initiate dialogue with Renamo.

Above every thing else, Renamo's action indicates a dire need for education to help its members appreciate the essentials of a society struggling for survival and development. With only 30% literacy in 1990,[9] Mozambique's future hangs perilously on the cliff of self-destruction and will depend on a national effort to educate its people so that they all understand the essential elements needed to build a new nation. Renamo's activity must therefore be viewed from the perspective of enormous political problems that Mozambique has been facing since its independence in 1975. In August, 1989, Chissano recognized the seriousness of the political problems that Renamo was creating for the country and cited some figures to substantiate his conclusion that it had no cause but to kill for the sake of killing. From 1978 to 1989, nearly 700,00 people had been killed in the civil war in the country, over 1.6 million people had been left homeless, over 2,600 schools and over 800 health clinics had been destroyed or closed down, and more than 40 factories and 1,000 shops had been destroyed.[10]

A question now arises; how long could Mozambique continue to walk down the road of this political agony and self-destruction without losing the vital human resources needed for national development? As of the time of writing Mozambique's fifteen million people are yearning for an answer to the question so that they can redirect their efforts toward the development of their country. The knowledge that the political crisis in Mozambique poses serious implications for the region as a whole is why, in August, 1989, the Organization of African Unity (OAU) appointed President Daniel arap Moi of Keny[11] and President Robert Mugabe of Zimbabwe co-chairmen of a commission to find answers to the political

---

[7]On February 15, 1990 this author wrote a letter to President de Klerk advising him that his overtures of peace to ANC in South Africa would be futile if he did not stop supporting UNITA and Renamo activities.

[8]*The Washington Post*, August 1, 1989

[9]*World Almanac and Book Facts*, 1990.

[10]*The New York Times*, August 6, 1989.

[11]Indeed, in July, 1990, Kenya was rocked by violent demonstrations against the Moi government. That the demonstrators demanded an end to one-party rule, which Moi instituted in 1982, suggests a critical need for innovation in Kenya itself.

problems of Mozambique. It is not surprising that the two leaders fully shared OAU's conclusion that Mozambique's commitment to educational innovation would place the country on the road to national reconstruction and development.

In a communique issued in Nairobi on August 8, 1989, OAU stated,

> The aim of the mission is to put an end to this inhuman situation. The first action is to stop all terrorist action. The acceptance of these principles could lead to a dialogue for ending the violence that has destroyed Mozambique and to establish peace for normal life so that national developmental programs can be reinitiated. Unless the scourge of violence in terminated, all other forms of national development cannot take place.12

Chissano's decision in January, 1990 to introduce " a draft constitution that embraces universal suffrage, a secret ballot, a direct election of both the President and the parliament and the reintroduction of private ownership of land"13 constitutes essential elements of much needed change in Mozambique. But Mozambique will need a fundamental educational innovation to implement the changes that Chissano outlined for the transformation of Mozambique.

Zimbabwe: While Mugabe was on mission to find a formula for peace for Mozambique, political events in his own country suggested a potential for a major confrontation. These developments began to unfold in 1988 when Edgar Tekere, a leading member of the ruling ZANU-PF, resigned from the party in protest against the possibility of the introduction of a one-party state, which the Mugabe administration had been saying since 1980 that it would prefer to a multi-party system currently in operation. Tekere was also protesting against what he said to be wide-spread corruption among top government officials. In April, 1989, when a commission of inquiry appointed by the government under the chairmanship of Justice Sandura uncovered wide-spread corruption by six senior government officials,14 Zimbabwe was poised for the most serious political crisis since it gained independence on April 18, 1980.

The fact that this scandal had far deeper political implications than appeared on the surface suggests the critical nature of the politics of Southern Africa and the need for innovation in education. Recognizing the political damage the scandal had inflicted on his ability to discharge his responsibility to the country, Maurice Nyagumbo, veteran politician and a respected nationalist, one of the six officials and a close associate of President Mugabe, took his own life to spare his family further embarrassment and national disgrace. President Mugabe was saddened by both the extent of the damage the scandal had done and the death of a man who had done so much during the struggle for independence.

12OAU, *A Communique on Mozambique.* Nairobi, Kenya, August 8, 1989.
13*Time,* March 5, 1989, p. 27.
14For the names of these officials and the extent of their involvement in the scandal, see *The Herald,* April 13, 1989.

This was not all. When, on August 4, 1989, Dzingai Mutumbuka, Minister of Education and Culture, was fined $105,000 for his part in the corruption, events edged much closer to a major national political crisis.[15] Indeed, a new wave of political tension in Zimbabwe emerged from an unlikely place, the University of Zimbabwe itself. In August, 1989, professors at the university issued a statement criticizing government action which they said "is making it impossible for the institution to discharge its proper constitutional responsibilities and functions as a university."[16] The arrest and detention of law professor Kempton Makamure appeared to be a culmination of incidents the professors believed constituted harassment due to their opposition to what was widely reported to be government corruption and degenerating political and economic programs.

That these developments were a sequel to the demonstrations staged by students at the university in September, 1987, against reports of continued corruption by some government officials suggests the critical nature of the crisis. When "the students called for academic freedom and their inalienable rights and demanded the university administration to lift its tacit ban on the student magazine, *Focus*,"[17] relations between the university and the government became more seriously strained, even though, by provisions of the national constitution, the national president is also the chancellor of the university.

The conclusion that in 1989 the national political climate in Zimbabwe was deteriorating rapidly is substantiated by a series of events that took place in quick succession. Displeased with the efforts the government was making to restore the confidence of the public, students at the university engaged in a variety of activities that the government concluded hovered on defiance of the law. On August 9, Joshua Nkomo, senior government minister, and Faye Chung,[18] Minister of Education, went to the university in an effort to defuse the situation. They held a meeting with the students and tried to establish dialogue. In an impassioned and emotional appeal, Nkomo pleaded with the students, saying:

> We do not want a confrontation with our children. We have gone gray because we have a heritage to protect, and that heritage is yourself. Therefore, dialogue must be started. You cannot solve problems by shouting. Knowledge is not just shouting. Some of your behavior is not Zimbabwean.[19]

When 2,000 students responded by demanding that Nkomo make assurances that the government would not turn the country into a one-party state and that Zimbabwe Unity Movement (ZUM), which had been recently formed under the

---

[15]Zimbabwe, *The Herald,* August 4, 1989.

[16]Zimbabwe, *Parade News Magazine,* August, 1989, p. 44.

[17]*Ibid.* p. 45

[18]Faye Chung became Minister of Education on August 4, 1989, when Dzingai Mutumbuka was forced to resign from the government following his conviction on charges of gross corruption.

[19]Zimbabwe, *The Herald,* August 11, 1989.

leadership of Edgar Tekere, be allowed a platform to express its political views, Chung's patience ran out as she responded: "Senior Minister Nkomo has been invited here not to be insulted. If this is what we call our future leaders, then I must say that this university is full of rubbish, and the government will not waste money on rubbish."[20] This exchange of views created a situation with a new potential for explosive outcome.

However, when the government refused to grant ZUM leaders permission to hold political meetings at the university, the students were once more in a restive mood. Fearing a general breakdown of law and order, the government temporarily closed the university for two weeks in October, 1989. A few weeks later the government granted ZUM permission to hold political meetings throughout the country, easing the political tension that was disrupting national programs. For a period of time in 1989, the entire country was held in suspense over what the future held politically. The political crisis in Zimbabwe furnishes yet another piece of evidence to substantiate the conclusion that Southern Africa needs a fundamental educational innovation to create a climate of national development different from what the past offered.

The elections held on March 24, 1990, show that the desire of the government to turn the country into a one-party state was not shared by many people. Not only did seven parties contest the elections, but throughout the country various forms of violence were reported related to the question of a one-party state. In a statement issued on the day of the elections, the Catholic Church's Justice and Peace Commission criticized the government's move to install a one-party state, saying, "The use of firearms against political opponents is a shocking development. The rising incidence of violence and intimidation is already calling into question the freeness and fairness of the elections."[21] Mugabe considered the elections so crucial that he did not find time to attend the independence celebration for Namibia on March 21. By June, the increasing demands on teachers combined with rapidly rising enrollments, inadequate salaries and declining conditions of service to force teachers to go on strike, threatening to derail the course of national development that Zimbabwe had charted. Indeed, as 1990 came to an end, Zimbabwe faced the ultimate challenge to its national developmental efforts.

Zambia In Zambia, the violent clashes that erupted between the people and the police in June, 1990, came as a surprise to no one. This was a result of the government of Kenneth Kaunda's decision to raise the cost of cornmeal, the staple diet of the people, from $0.05 to $0.12 per pound as part of the austerity measures to halt further decline of the economy. For Zambians, whose average monthly income was $20.00, the rise imposed new severe economic difficulties. Demonstrations against the government led to riots which in turn led to clashes with the police, causing 45 deaths and 153 serious injuries.[22]

---

[20]*Ibid.*

[21]Karl Maier, "Opponent May Thwart Mugabe's Bid for One-Party System," in *The Washington Post*, March 29, 1990.

[22]*Time*, July 9, 1990. p. 38.

Charges of corruption by government officials, and the mismanagement of the government itself along with a decline in the price of copper, and the introduction of a one-party system caused an erosion in public confidence in the government . This is why the people demanded the resignation of the government and the restoration of a multi-party system. Even though Kaunda promised to hold a national referendum in October, 1990, to determine whether to restore the multi-party system since it was abolished in 1972, relations between the people and the government had been damaged beyond repair. Kaunda, who assumed office at the inception of independence from Britain in October, 1964, was at a loss to understand why Zambians were in a state of rebellion against his government. Like many other African leaders, he could not understand the political implications of a one-party rule. Indeed, like other countries of Southern Africa, Zambia was poised for a major national conflict unless changes were made in the educational system to make social change possible.

Namibia In Namibia the odyssey of political conflict began with the inception of the German colonial system in 1885, and shows that educational innovation is a prerequisite of national development. A disturbing aspect of the political conflict began to form as a result of the action of the Berlin Conference in 1885.[23] Otto von Bismarch (1815-1898), the flamboyant chancellor of Germany from 1871 to 1888, used the influence and the power he had secured as a result of the Franco-Prussian war from 1870 to 1871 to launch a campaign, not only to create a new German empire in Africa, but also to put into practice his idea of *blood and iron* to extend German power in both Europe and Africa.

The establishment of a colony in Namibia meant, in the words of Paul Rohrback, one of the architects of the German colonial policy, "the Native tribes would have to give up their lands on which they have previously grazed their stock in order that the white man might have the land for the grazing of his stock."[24] General von Trotha outlined further conditions for the Africans that led inevitably to conflict that left wounds that would not be healed. In warning the Africans, "The Herero people must depart from the land. If they do not, I shall force them to do so with large cannons. I shall drive them out. I shall order shots to be fired at them,"[25] von Trotha created an environment of conflict of major proportions.

Indeed, by 1904 German colonial rule of Namibia had become so oppressive that the Africans found themselves in a state of open rebellion. Von Trotha's response was to issue extermination orders to subdue them. As a result, by the time the rebellion was crashed in 1905, the Herero population had been reduced

---

[23]Dickson A. Mungazi, *The Struggle for Social Change in Southern Africa: Visions of Liberty.* New York: Taylor and Francis, 1989, p. 25.

[24]Ronald Segai and Ruth First, *Southwest Africa: Travesty of Trust.* London: Deutsche, 1967, p.180.

[25]John Dugard, *The Southwest Africa/Namibia Dispute.* Berkeley: The University of California Press, 1973, p. 26.

from 80,000 to 16,000, and the Namas population from 20,000 to 9,000.[26] When South African forces seized Namibia in 1915 on orders of the Allied Forces to foil German strategy to win the war, the Africans hoped that their oppression would soon be over. But to their dismay, they soon found that they had substituted one oppressive system for another. South Africa moved in to institute a system that was so oppressive that a new dangerous situation was created.

When Britain transferred the mandate the League of Nations had given it to administer Namibia to South Africa, a perilous course to conflict had been mapped out. On November 27, 1918, the South African Defence Forces issued a proclamation demanding to annex Namibia and incorporate it as the fifth province of South Africa[27] "to take all measures to make such laws and to issue regulations and orders to enforce the government of the Protectorate while it remains in military occupation by the Defence Forces of South Africa."[28] The League of Nations, fearing to endanger its fragile existence, merely gave a rubber stamp approval of South Africa's administration of Namibia but at a great cost. General J. C. Smuts argued the case for the South African position when he said:

> The German colonies in the Pacific and Africa are inhabited by barbarians who not only cannot possibly govern themselves, but to whom it would be impracticable to apply any ideas of political self-determination in the European sense.[29]

That Smuts was actually expressing disappointment with the League's basic principle that stated:

> To those colonies and territories not yet able to stand by themselves under the strenuous conditions of the modern world there should be applied the principle that the well-being and development of such people form a sacred trust of civilization and that this trust be embodied in this Covenant,[30]

suggests the extent of the conflict that emerged between the League and South Africa over the future of Namibia. It was Article 5 of the Mandate, however, that became a cause of conflict between the League and South Africa because the latter

[26]Marion O'Callaghan, *Namibia: The Effects of Apartheid on Culture and Education.* Paris: Unesco, 1977, p. 18.

[27]At the inception of independence in 1910, South Africa incorporated four provinces to form the Union of South Africa. These were: the Cape Province, Natal, the Orange Free State, and the Transvaal.

[28]The Union of South Africa, *Proclamation over Southwest Africa*, November 27, 1918.

[29]J. C. Smuts, *The League of Nations: A Practical Suggestion,* 1918. By courtesy of the U.N.

[30]The League of Nations Covenant, Article 22, January 20,1920. By courtesy of the U.N.

simply refused to observe a critical provision of the Covenant that "the mandatory shall ensure the freedom of conscience and free exercise of all forms of rights."[31]

When the United Nations was drafting its charter in San Francisco in 1945, South Africa once again vigorously sought its approval to incorporate Namibia into its own territory and went on to argue,

> For twenty-five years, the Union of South Africa has governed and administered the territory as an integral part of its own territory and has promoted to the utmost the material and moral well-being and social progress of the inhabitants. There is no prospect of the territory ever existing as a separate state and the ultimate objective of the principle of the mandate is therefore impossible to achieve.[32]

From this disagreement the U.N. knew clearly that South Africa had been working hard to foil the U.N. plan for Namibia so that it would make a case for Namibia's incorporation into its own territory. That South Africa interpreted the U.N. Charter as compatible with its policy of *apartheid* forced the U.N. to launch a campaign to deprive South Africa of its trusteeship of Namibia. This was the beginning of a struggle that lasted till November, 1989.

As part of this campaign the U.N. asked the International Court of Justice at the Hague in 1960 to rule on the legality of the U.N. demand for South Africa to withdraw from Namibia. In the same year Ethiopia and Liberia sponsored a joint resolution in the General Assembly calling on South Africa to withdraw from Namibia. But when South Africa refused to abide by both the ruling of the International Court of Justice and the resolution of the General Assembly, a new stage was set for a new level of conflict to emerge. The formation of the Southwest Africa People Organization (SWAPO) in 1954, its recognition by OAU in 1965 and by the General Assembly in 1973 as the official representative of the people of Namibia[33] led to an increase in dissention. That from 1976 to 1988 SWAPO waged an armed struggle against South Africa is indicative of the raising conflict between the parties.

When, on September 29, 1981, the Security Council adopted Resolution 385 asking South Africa to withdraw from Namibia, there were related events that showed that South Africa must accept the U.N.'s policy or face increased isolation. By 1989 a delicate agreement was reached to hold elections in Namibia as the first step towards achieving sovereign independence on March 21, 1990, seventy-four years after South Africa had occupied it. This was a new day for all Namibians. "Despite a hard-fought campaign and major ideological differences, the seven parties represented in the 72-member national assembly worked out

---

[31]The League of Nations, *The Mandate for Southwest Africa*, May 7, 1920. By courtesy of the U.N.

[32]John Dugard, *Southwest Africa/Namibia Dispute*, p. 89.

[33]TransAfrica, *Namibia: The Crisis in United States Policy Towards Southern Africa*. Washington, D.C., 1983, p. 7

compromises quickly after beginning negotiations November 21, 1989."[34] Although SWAPO won 41 seats, it fell short of a two-thirds majority of 48 seats needed to carry out its programs. With the Democratic Turnhalle Alliance, a multiracial coalition that favors an economic system similar to that of South Africa, winning 21 seats, and the remaining five parties with a total of 10 seats, the problems of reconstruction in Namibia seem enormous, and Sam Nujoma's task as the first president must be understood as a complex one. The light at the end of the tunnel would show the extent of the problems that Namibia has since encountered in its efforts to innovate its educational systems so that national development can take place.

Angola: In Angola the bloody civil war that broke out at the time of independence in 1975 has felled and destroyed beyond repair national installations - hospitals, factories, schools, etc - and killed or seriously injured thousands of people. The road to conflict in Angola parallels that of Namibia and Mozambique. The ascendance of Antonio Salazar (1889-1970) to power in 1932 set the stage for one of Africa's bitterest conflicts to emerge. Salazar's revitalization of the colonial policy of *Estado Novo* (New State)[35] created conditions which the Africans could no longer tolerate by 1960. When in 1959, the Africans expressed anti-Portuguese sentiments, Salazar responded by ordering massive arrest of those suspected of instigating the African displeasure with the colonial conditions which controlled their life. Using the so-called International Police for the Defence of the State (PIDE), Salazar instituted a brutal oppression of the Africans. Under it he subjected the entire African population to a level of suffering never before known in both Angola and Mozambique. Indeed, Salazar had become the von Trotha of the Portuguese colonies in Africa as hundreds of Africans suspected of apposition to colonial domination were rounded up and shot.

However, by March, 1961, bands of African guerrillas responded by attacking colonial installations in rapid and relentless succession. When he discovered that *assimilados,* constituting less than 3% of the Africans and whom he considered educated enough to claim Portuguese citizenship rights, constituted the core of the leadership among the Africans, Salazar turned his anger towards the schools and ordered their systematic destruction or closure as a strategy to turn the African masses against the guerrilla leaders. But when the strategy backfired, the conflict took a perilous turn as a full scale war between colonial forces and the Africans broke out.

By 1967, nearly seven years following the outbreak of the war of liberation, in 1960, Portugal was putting nearly 40% of its national budget into its wars against guerrillas in its colonies in Africa. The Portuguese tax payers were being asked to make sacrifices in a futile effort to sustain the colonial status quo. By the time that Salazar suffered a massive stroke in 1968, he had drained the Portuguese economy to the extent that his successor, Marcello Caetano, had no means of

---

[34]*The New York Times*, December 21, 1989

[35]For detailed discussion of the effect of the application of this policy to both Angola and Mozambique as colonies, see, for example, Dickson Mungazi, *The Struggle for Social Change in Southern Africa: Visions of Liberty*. New York: Taylor and Francis, 1989.

sustaining the military forces in Africa. On April 25, 1974, Portuguese military forces removed Caetano from office because they were disillusioned with Portuguese colonial policy and mounting casualties among their ranks.

On October 22, 1974, Portugal and the three liberation organizations that were fighting against it , UNITA, MPLA, FNLA, signed a cease-fire agreement and hurriedly worked out constitutional arrangements for independence scheduled for November 11, 1975. In a tragic twist of events, the leaders of the three parties, Holden Roberto of FNLA, Jonas Savimbi of UNITA, and Agostinho Neto of MPLA, began to vie for power and ignored the interim arrangements of collective responsibility pending the outcome of elections. A few minutes after mid-night on that day, MPLA declared itself the government of Angola and Neto became president. With this action Angola entered a new phase of bitterness and conflict. Jonas Savimbi immediately requested and received substantial financial aid and weapons from South Africa and the Reagan Administration in the U.S.A. to wage a new guerilla war that has almost destroyed Angola.

The action of both the Reagan Administration and South Africa in giving Savimbi financial aid and weapons to fight the MPLA government and that of the MPLA itself in inviting Cuban military personnel to defend itself accentuated the bitterness and elevated the conflict and struggle to a new tragic height. While this was happening, the thrust for national reconstruction and development so necessary after fifteen years of a brutal war of independence was tragically brought to a halt. All the people of Angola, like those of Mozambique, have reaped is the grapes of wrath and an unprecedented national disaster. The educational process so critically essential to national endeavors has been rendered meaningless in the wake senseless brutality that recognizes no limits.

By August, 1988, when the civil war in Angola had reached a stalemate, the Reagan Administration, having come under considerable criticism both at home and in Africa, for supporting Savimbi and the *Contras* in Nicaragua, decided to play the role of peace broker. After announcing on February 18, 1986, that the U.S.A. would provide the financial and military aid Savimbi had requested, Chester Crocker, Reagan's special envoy to Southern Africa, met in Geneva on July 31, 1988, with South African and Cuban officials to explore ways of initiating a cease-fire in Angola. In a statement issued August 8, 1988, the U.S.A., Cuba, MPLA government, and South Africa issued a communique stating,

> We reiterate our decision to subscribe to a bilateral agreement which will include a timetable acceptable to all parties for the staged and total withdrawal of Cuban forces from Angola. The parties have undertaken to reach agreement on this timetable by September 1, 1988.[36]

---

[36]*Prospects of a Settlement in Angola and Namibia*, a statement issued by the parties involved, August 8, 1988. By courtesy of the U.N.

However, Savimbi, still confident that he would continue to receive the aid he would request from both South Africa and the U.S.A., reacted, "It would be most unwise for us to stop fighting just because there is a joint statement."[37]

By November, 1989, when Namibians were getting ready to participate in elections to prepare for independence on March 21, 1990, Angola entered a new phase of national conflict. That Savimbi made periodic visits to Washington where he was always received as if he were a head of state, and that he had been an honored guest at the House House, suggest a tragic outcome whose dimensions neither Savimbi nor the Reagan Administration appeared to understand. Savimbi's claim of fighting against Communism in Angola was, in essence, a strategy that he knew would always have the U.S. react favorably. Who said that the era of the cold war was over? Mikhail Gorbachev and George Bush might as well need a second Malta[38] summit to sort this sordid affair out. *Glasnost* is no substitute for the hard realities that Angola was facing in this dark hour.

South Africa: The drama of national conflict and the agony of social change have been played out in more painful ways in South Africa than any other country in all of Southern Africa. Since the official introduction of the notorious policy of apartheid in 1948, South Africa has been steadily edging perilously close to the brink of a major national disaster. When, on January 25, 1944, Daniel Malan (1874-1959), an ordained minister in the Dutch Reformed Church and active member in the Nationalist Party politics, expressed his political philosophy relative to the future of South Africa as intended "to ensure the safety of the white race by maintaining the principle of apartheid,"[39] he was expressing the prevailing thinking among the die-hard Afrikaners. Unaware of the extent of the national conflict that would emerge as a result of this policy, Malan and the Nationalist Party which he led exploited this prevailing thinking to win the elections of 1948.

It was not surprising that as a government, the Nationalist Party 's first priority was to make apartheid the law of the land. Taking into consideration the report of the Fagan Commission of 1947, which recommended that the Africans be controlled more effectively, the Nationalist Party government enacted a law to give legal effect to the views Malan had expressed in 1944. In a quick succession, the Nationalist government enacted a series of laws that made it and the Afrikaners supreme in every way possible. This is the reason why, in 1951, the government named the Tomlinson Commission to study and recommend new ways of making apartheid more effective. Accepting the recommendations of the Tomlinson Commission in 1952 that separate areas be established for different races, the Nationalist government introduced a new system of controlling the Africans, the so-called Bantustan Homelands. It is a tragic fact that the Afrikaners have refused

[37]*The News York Times,* August 8, 1988.
[38]The first Malta conference was held in January, 1978, between the British Foreign Secretary, David Owen, U.S. Ambassador to the U.N., Andrew Young, and Joshua Nkomo and Robert Mugabe in an effort to revive the Anglo-American peace proposals for Zimbabwe
[39]Brian Bunting, "The Origins of Apartheid: in Alex La Guma [Ed.], *Apartheid: A Collection of Writings in South African Racism by South Africans.* New York: International Publishers, 1971, p. 24.

to acknowledge that the Bantustan Homelands, more than any other component of the policy of apartheid, is not only one of the greatest tragedies in human existence, but also the major conflict in Southern Africa as a whole. The enactment of the Group Areas Act in 1950, the Native Passes Act, 1952, and the Bantu Education Act, 1953, ushered in the beginning of an unprecedented suffering to which apartheid has subjected the Africans. It is for this reason that in 1976 the Soweto uprising captured the news headlines around the world.

However, before and after the Soweto tragedy, the Africans of South Africa were constantly reminded that every moment of their life, from sunrise to sunset, from birth to death, were, indeed, a conquered and enslaved people and that forgetting this basic fact constituted a criminal offense. The meeting held between Nelson Mandela and Pieter Botha (President from 1978 to 1989) in July, 1989, and the one between Mandela and F.W. de Klerk in December, 1989, came as a painful reminder of the supremacy of apartheid. The tragic truth of apartheid is that the Afrikaners have been guided by the views that Paul Kruger (1825-1904), president of the ill-fated Transvaal Republic from 1883 to 1900 expressed in the statement that "The black man must be taught that he belongs to an inferior class of people who must learn to obey."[40]

The truth of the matter is that the Afrikaners have not wavered from this principle. When de Klerk announced on February 2, 1990, that Mandela would be released unconditionally and that the ban on ANC would be lifted, many people responded with measured skepticism and disbelief because de Klerk himself subscribed to the principle that apartheid must rule supreme. Where would such a policy lead the country? However, the fact that de Klerk recognized the imperative of change in the structure of apartheid suggests a critical need to begin all over again.

The announcement that de Klerk made on June 7, 1990, in the South African parliament that his government was lifting the state of emergency except in Natal constituted a condition that ANC had specified as necessary to hold negotiations over the future of the country. But the world was held in suspense as to what the next step would be in the saga of the South African drama of conflict between the struggle for change and efforts to maintain the status quo. de Klerk's announcement appeared to show that at last the Afrikaners had come to accept the reality that they must recognize the fact that they must accord the Africans the status of equal partners in this elusive African *perestroika*. The important thing for the Afrikaners to remember in the situation in which choices are few is that the transformation of the South African political system can best be accomplished in the context of educational innovation. This is the line of thinking that Brian Carlson, Headmaster of St. Andrew's Preparatory School in Grahamstown, South Africa, took into consideration when he wrote in 1988, "Education is a powerful

---

[40]*Ibid.* p. 35

instrument of social change. Innovation in it has an important role to play in building a new society."[41]

Up to now, the government of South Africa has defied the voice of the international community calling for fundamental social change, it would spare the country the agony of this inevitable change to listen to one of its own people. The advertisement that was placed in *The Chronicle of Higher Education* of May 16, 1990, by the University of Cape Town inviting researchers from the international community to go there and help establish a new process of change is in line with Carlson's call. The call for a new thrust for national development in South Africa has now acquired an international dimension.

The Economic Situation

The action taken by the U.S. House of Representatives on August 12, 1988 to ban nearly all trade with South Africa in protest against apartheid, signified a growing global determination to let the Nationalist government know that it faced an increasing isolation from the world community as long as it maintained apartheid. When James Baker, U.S. Secretary of State, visited South Africa March 22, 1990, after attending an independence celebration for Namibia the previous day, he reminded de Klerk of that fact and that South Africa must commit itself to move towards an irreversible course to end apartheid as a condition of peaceful social change. The abandonment of the so-called Sullivan principles as a means to improve the economic plight of the Africans means that other alternatives must be explored to achieve an end to the apartheid system. What the world has readily recognized as a painful fact of apartheid is that it really does not matter how well educated Africans are, they are still subjected to the socioeconomic humiliation due to the color of their skin.

Action on the economy in South Africa is a refection of the rapidly deteriorating economic and social crisis in all of Southern Africa. For example, in Mozambique in 1988 the urgent need for famine relief that put 640,000 people in refugee camps shows how bad the economic situation has become. When, in 1989, that number had risen to 780,000, the U.N. Food Program sounded an alarm of desperation and called for an educational innovation that would help the people of Mozambique to understand and utilize new agricultural technology, study weather conditions and make a collective effort to resolve this problem.[42]

In a similar manner, the civil war in Angola has created a shortage of food production to the extent that the country needed more than 258,000 metric tones of food shipments.[43] The announcement made in July, 1989 by the government of Mozambique that it was abandoning its Marxist economic principles could have well been made in Angola, where a lack of trained personnel and a stagnation in

---

[41]Brian Carlson, "American Education: A South African Perspective in the Process of Desegregation," in *Kappa Delta Phi*, September, 1988, p. 99.
[42]*The Christian Science Monitor*, July 26, 1988.
[43]*Ibid.*

economic development have combined to place heavy demands on socioeconomic change in conjunction with innovation in education. The warring parties in Angola have yet to realize that this much needed development can only take place when the country is at peace. With an unemployment rate of 40% in 1989, both Mozambique and Angola are slowly but steadily edging closer to a major tragic economic fate.

In Zambia the government of Kenneth Kaunda was forced to close its borders in August, 1989 in order to introduce a new system of currency in an effort to revive the sagging economy. If the Zambian government had recognized the need for educational innovation soon after attaining independence in October, 1964, this crisis could have been averted. When, in May, 1987, Kaunda broke relations with the International Monetary Fund (IMF), he thought that his government would initiate viable economic self-sufficiency programs not only to give Zambia the greater degree of economic independence it needed for national development but also to serve as a model for other countries in Southern Africa. But Kaunda was unaware that the decline in the monetary value of copper would force him and his government to devalue the *kwacha* to a point where it was no longer able to compete with other monetary systems on the world market. This forced the production of copper to decline from 700,000 tons in 1979 to 417,00 in 1989.[44] There is no question that this economic crisis was caused primarily by an inability that is so common among African nations to relate education to other important national programs.

Zambia's economic problems must be seen in the context of the rapidly declining political system as well. This is apparent in the letter that Henry Kalenga, a member of the banned ANC, wrote in March, 1990, from his political prison in Kitwe to Amnesty International to say, " I write as one of the victims of Zambia's injustice and oppression, especially the draconian laws on detention without trial that the government has introduced as part of its standard operation. At a time when human rights are being internationalized, it is disheartening to note that Zambia violates human rights with impunity."[45]

In Malawi, assassination arrest and detention without trial of those opposed to the policies of Hastings Banda have become the ultimate manifestation of his repressive and oppressive rule. From the time that Henry Chipembere was arrested in 1965 to the time of that of Jack Mapanja and Osborne Mkandawire in 1987, Banda has recognized no limits in seeking to silence his political opponents. While he is doing this, the economy has suffered an irreparable damage and the suffering of the people has reached new heights. When in March, 1990, Mobuto Sese Seko of Zaire argued, "Zaire has no need for *perestroika* because its one-party state system is the most elaborate form of democracy in Africa,"[46] he neglected to say that the rapid decline in the economy was a direct result of the fallacy of a one-party system as a democracy.

---

[44]*The Economist*, September 30, 1989.
[45]George Ayittey, "In Africa Independence is far cry from Freedom," in *The Wall Street Journal*, March 28, 1990.
[46]*Ibid.*

Although Zimbabwe was recognized in 1988 by the Hunger Project as leading Africa in food production as a basis of economic development,[47] Zimbabwe's economy was considered fragile because the rapid decline of the dollar threatened national infrastructures that are essential to national development. The lack of trained personnel needed to initiate innovative strategies poses problems that make it necessary for Zimbabwe to brace itself for possible serious economic difficulties unless the government does something to halt the rapid decline of the dollar which in itself causes a rapidly rising inflation, which in turn causes rising unemployment. The twin problems of rapidly rising inflation and rising population have combined to create a set of socioeconomic and political problems that Zimbabwe may find hard to solve unless it makes a new effort to innovate its educational system to make it relevant to the needs of the times.

In South Africa the economic situation is as critical as that of other countries of the region. In 1989 *South Scan, Facts and Reports*, a private organization which is based in Cape Town, released some disturbing information about the economic conditions. This information had not been published, and the author obtained it from a friend while he was in southern Africa in 1989. Here is a summary of that information as it relates to South Africa. More than half the black population lives in abject poverty. In the so-called Bantustan Homelands, 80% of the people live below poverty line. In the region of Southern Africa as a whole, South Africa has the largest gap between the rich, who are white, and the poor, who are black. Under apartheid laws, this gap is maintained in order to control the black population. The release of Nelson Mandela on March 11, 1990, was partly due to international pressure to ease the economic suffering to which apartheid has subjected the Africans. As a result of poverty more than two million black children suffer from physical defects due to lack of proper nutrition and conditions of living. In many black townships twenty people live in single three-room houses, and sixty-six share bathroom facilities.

Between 1983 and 1888 a total of 175,000 houses were built for whites. This resulted in a surplus of 37,000 houses. But during the same period 40,000 were built for blacks. This resulted in a shortage of 590,000. Only 3.9% of all graduates from medical schools were black. Of the 708 students who qualified to be medical doctors in 1988, 575 were white, 89 were Indian, 16 were Colored, and only 2 were African. South Africa has 14 ministries of health, one for each of the Bantustan Homelands and one for whites, Coloreds and Indians each. Sixty per cent of the health budget is spent on administration, which is an amount that would be sufficient to build 100 hospitals with 50,000 beds for the black population. The announcement that de Klerk made on May 14, 1990, that hospitals in South Africa would be disegregated and the campaign he launched in Western capitols for support of his initiative to hold talks with ANC did nothing to indicate a plan of action to dismantle apartheid. Returning to South Africa on May 26, 1990, de Klerk received cheers and jeers when he claimed, "No one can stop

---

[47]*New York Times*, September 16, 1988.

the creation of the new South Africa."[48] But Mandela's response, "We cannot allow de Klerk to continue telling the world that apartheid is dead when we have no vote"[49] shows the ultimate challenge that the people of South Africa face. While de Klerk was claiming that his government was making an effort to create a new South Africa, starvation in the Bantustan Homelands was widespread, and infant mortality was higher in South Africa than in any other country in Southern Africa.[50]

In 1975, 27,000 children under the age of 5 died of starvation. But in the first half of the decade of the 1980's only twelve out of a thousand white children died before the age of 5. These figures compare unfavorably with other countries of Southern Africa. For example, in South Africa 72 black children died of starvation before they reached age of 5. In Zimbabwe the figure was 66. *South Scan* concludes that $5.3 billion was needed to fight poverty in the Bantustan Homelands and that the reason why the Afrikaners wanted to maintain apartheid is that they want to maintain their economic control of the Africans.[51] The effect of resisting change in both the political system and the economic system is that South Africa will continue to deteriorate to a point where a major national disaster will become inevitable. The action taken by the South African parliament on June 5, 1991, to repeal provisions of the apartheid law did not constitute the final act to remove the last vestiges of an oppressive system because the black people were still second class citizens and foreigners in the land of their birth. de Klerk and his government had to do more to create a climate of confidence so that negotiations would begin for the creation of a new South Africa.

Summary and Conclusion

What has been discussed in this chapter leads to two basic conclusions. The first is that political problems in all of Southern Africa have become so complex that they require something of a much better standard and far more viable a national resource than conventional wisdom would suggest. In all practical realities, education has often been regarded as a means to resolve national problems. However, the situation in all of Southern Africa would lead to the conclusion that the current educational process is far too inadequate to help solve these problems. What is therefore needed is a fundamental change in education to meet the needs of a rising and complex situation.

The fact of the matter is that in human experience education provides that needed catalyst to understand national problems in their proper context. This is the only way in which solutions can be found. Therefore, for Southern Africa educational innovation is the most viable basis of finding solutions to the political

---

[48]F. W. de Klerk, an address to South Africans on returning from a tour of Europe, May 26, 1990

[49]Nelson Mandela, responding to de Klerk's statement, May 26, 1990.

[50]South Scan, *Facts and Reports,Race Relations Survey, 1989.*

[51]*Ibid.*

and socioeconomic problems that exist there. Initiating educational innovation is an imperative of seeking solutions to the problems of Southern Africa as a whole because it would help nations see the situations they face from their proper perspective. No matter how much effort is made in seeking solutions to problems of national development, it is bound to fail if it is not related in practical ways to making an effort to innovate the educational process. The various aspects of that innovation is the subject of this study.

The second conclusion is that like politics, socioeconomic development helps shape a national character. Therefore, efforts made toward national development are possible only if individual citizens are able to advance themselves economically. In Southern Africa, more than any other region of the world, the more citizens are educated, the more they contribute to both their own development and that of their nation. This suggests the conclusion that because of the delicate nature of the economy, all countries in Southern Africa need education not only to sustain it, but also to strengthen it in order to reshape the emergence of a new national character.

An important consideration for the countries of Southern Africa to keep in mind is that "It is important to ascertain that the limited resources at the disposal of the persons or institutions who make educational input are utilized in the most effective way possible in pursuing national objectives."[52] To achieve this objective education must be innovated. This suggests the conclusion that it would be very difficult to introduce a new political and socioeconomic system without introducing a new system of education. With a clamor for fundamental social change in Eastern Europe in 1989, the call for fundamental change in political and socioeconomic spheres of national life, especially in Africa, goes out much louder now than it has been in the past. The existence of the system of one-party governments in Southern Africa has no place in the region of the future. It is in this kind of environment that educational innovation becomes a critical factor of an endeavor for national development.

---

52 J. C. Eicher, *Educational Costing and Financing in Developing Countries: Focus on Sub-Sahara Africa.* Washington, D.C., World Bank, 1984, p. 3.

2

THE NEED FOR EDUCATIONAL INNOVATION: A HISTORICAL PERSPECTIVE

In his traditional society the African was given all the education which he needed to function in his culture. Today, he has fallen away because Western education does not prepare him to function in Western culture. F.G. Loveridge, Education Officer in colonial Zimbabwe, March 13, 1965.

Before the coming of the Europeans to our country, no aspect of life, no boy or girl was ever neglected by our educational system because it was constantly being innovated to make it relevant to the needs of all students. An elderly African in Zimbabwe, May 15, 1974.

Introduction: The Universal Purpose of Education

When Jean Piaget discusses the purpose of education, he says,

> The principal goal of education is to create men and women who are capable of doing new things, not simply of reflecting what other generations have done, men and women who are creative, inventive, and who are discoveries.[1]

Piaget seems to underscore the thinking that the universality of the purpose of education is to prepare students to live and function efficiently in a changed social environment. In the twentieth century change, not for its own sake but in human existence, has been understood and accepted as an important factor or condition of development, and that any nation or society which does not seem to accept the concept of change denies itself an opportunity for its own advancement.

---

[1]William van Til, *Education: A Beginning*. Boston; Houghton Mifflin Company, 1974, p. 417.

This is the line of thinking that Immanuel Kant seems to take when he argues:

> The purpose of education is to train children, not only with reference to their success in the present state of society, but also to a better possible state in accordance with an ideal conception of humanity.[2]

In a similar manner Theodore Roosevelt captured the imperative nature of educational innovation in a universal sense when he argued:

> Education must light the path for social change. The political, social, and economic problems confronting us are growing in complexity. The more complex and difficult these problems become, the more essential it is to provide a broad and complete education to all students.[3]

What Piaget, Kant, and Roosevelt said seems to suggest two things about the purpose of education in a universal sense. The first is that from the most advanced societies to the least developed, from ancient times to modern times, human society has sought change, not for change's sake, but in order to improve the quality of human life. Therefore, any society, such as South Africa, that refuses to acknowledge the importance of change handicaps itself in any effort it might make to initiate its own development. Refusal to accept change as an important condition of human and social development inhibits the ability of all people to critically examine their society and appraise the essential components that constitute its very existence. In this kind of setting the thrust for national development loses its meaning, and the citizens are subjected to the agony of underdevelopment.

The second thing is that any social change that fails to relate effectively to educational innovation also loses the purpose for which it is initiated. Educational innovation is different from social change in some very important respects: it is often intended to improve the quality of life of the people; it enables the students to set individual goals and objectives consistent with political and socioeconomic principles; it promotes the development of a nation by developing the individual potential; it seeks to promote and manifest individual endeavors and it helps initiate the formation of a new national character so critical to national development. It helps define national purpose and objectives in a way that translates into collective action that shows demonstrated results.

The Need for Educational Innovation in Southern Africa Today

Indeed, if these elements of social change and components of educational innovation are universal in their application, one would have to say that they are far more critical to Southern Africa than any other region of Africa and the world because the problems discussed in Chapter 1 demand its special application to solve. This is why, with reference to the Third World situation in general, Paulo Freire of Brazil

---

[2]*Ibid.* p. 418.
[3]*Ibid.* p. 419

suggests that educational innovation involves much more than is implied in the search for a new meaning in an effort to resolve the contradiction that exists between the powerful and the dispossessed.[4] Therefore, educational innovation must, in effect, be initiated in a national climate that seeks to create an environment of collective understanding so that national goals can be defined only in terms of human need and individual goals. These are the elements that make educational innovation important in all of Southern Africa.

Failure to realize the importance of these elements and make a decision to accept them as imperative to national endeavors mean that the region would still languish in the mire of underdevelopment. To understand the importance of educational innovation in Southern Africa, one needs to understand the character of education in traditional African society as it is related to the purpose of education during the colonial period. A brief discussion on how educational innovation contributed to an effort for national development in Southern Africa today follows.

The Structure of Education in Traditional African Society

In traditional African society in Southern Africa the educational process began as soon as the child was able to understand the importance of relating to his environment, both physical and social. Instruction was given in the knowledge that society would have changed by the time the learner was ready to take his place in society. Therefore the concept of relevance and relativity of education constituted important principles in the process of providing education to the student. This means that the educational process was adopted to changing conditions to make it more applicable and effective to the needs of the learner.

Contrary to Western perception that education in traditional African society was irrelevant because it lacked a structured and formal curricular content, the fact of the matter is that education in traditional African society, as designed and understood by the Africans themselves, was more effective and meaningful than Western education was meant to be for Africans in the Western cultural context. As soon as the child could walk, his education began to take a definite form. First, he was taught the basic components of his culture and society and how to function in them. Those in position to influence his development, such as members of his immediate family, often taught him by both example and precept. His society taught him "that some things are right and others are wrong."[5]

Emphasis on this form of education suggests that coming early in the life of the student as it did, the teaching of moral values held a specially important place in the educational process. The underlying consideration in stressing the importance of moral values was that as an adult person the student needed to embrace valued moral principles in order to have meaningful relationships with other people, either in business activity or in personal association. Therefore, any person whose conduct or social behavior manifested a lack of these fundamental moral and social values was

---

[4]Paulo Freire, *Pedagogy of the Oppressed* (translated by Myra Bergman Ramos), New York: Continuum, 1983, p. 132.

[5]Michael Gelfand, *Growing up in Shona Society*. Gweru: Mambo Press, 1985, p. 11.

considered to have missed some essential aspects of his or her education.[6] It therefore became very difficult for such a person to have any meaningful relationships with other people unless he or she demonstrated a desire to learn the importance of moral values.

That education in traditional African society stressed the importance of learning moral and social values was also undertaken in the knowledge that as an adult, the learner was expected to demonstrate understanding of the value of the human person as an indispensable component of society itself because the character of society was made what it was by the thought process and behavior patterns of its individual members. That understanding was often measured in terms of a concerted effort to uphold and embrace a universal definition of human dignity and worth as a central *modus operandi*. This means that the teaching of religious values was not separated from the teaching of moral values.

Therefore, the Western concept of separation between church and state was not an applicable norm to social behavior in the traditional African context because the king and his subjects were considered equal before the law as their conduct or behavior were assessed by how they demonstrated commitment to sustain moral and social values as fundamental tenets of the success of their educational endeavors.[7] In this social setting, the educational process in traditional African society was more effective than Western educational and social settings in sustaining that universally proclaimed principle: *Society must be governed by law, not by man.* The practice of double standard which often characterize Western society today did not exist in traditional African society until the advent of the colonial systems in the nineteen century.

As the child grew and gained new experiences, his education began to embrace more advanced principles. The inclusive nature of the educational process also embraced critical components of diversity and individuality, not only in the educational process itself, but also as forms of instructional strategy. Its guided development, to conform to the developmental process of the learner, was intended to enable him to relate to human conditions which included the physical, the emotional, the spiritual and the mental characteristics, all considered essential to human existence.

The structure of this educational system suggests that education in traditional African society had relevance and application to human life far beyond itself because it was designed to train individuals to become capable of exercising social responsibility and to discharge duty in a much larger social order in order to uphold social institutional values. One must conclude that the only reason why the white man regarded this educational process as being a product of a primitive culture is that he wanted to justify his colonial intentions.

Another serious misconception that formed the basis of attitudes and policies among Westerners toward the Africans is that their society was distinctly marked by the absence of democratic principles, because, they argued, it consisted of

---

[6]Dickson A. Mungazi, *The Struggle for Social Change in Southern Africa: Visions of Liberty.* New York: Taylor and Francis, 1989, p. 53.
[7]*Ibid.* p. 54.

fragmented units of unstructured communities. But a study of government operations in traditional African society in Southern Africa furnishes clear evidence to prove that the contrary was, in fact, the case. To understand how education was structured to sustain democratic values, one needs to understand the structure of society itself and how its members embraced democratic principles. At the head of the African society was the king.[8] That the king "symbolized the unity of the whole society structured to sustain its collective values"[9] suggests a demonstrated commitment to democratic principles.

Although the king was a hereditary leader and was not elected, as is the practice in Western societies, people knew who was next in line of succession, he operated under a set of values distinctly different from those of Western societies. He was not at liberty to issue executive orders, as is the case in Western societies. Rather, he was required to consult members of the council before he could make decisions or take action on any matter. In this context, the king represented justice, equality before the law, fairness and freedom of all people in all aspects of life. In carrying out his duties the king "ruled by consent of his people and therefore enjoyed popular loyalty born of genuine patriotism."[10]

Yet another feature which demonstrates that the Africans in traditional society applied democratic principles in their social and political behavior is that society itself was divided into two levels, the ward of district, and the village. Over each ward was a ward head, and over each village was a village head. Their duties and functions included coordinating activities designed to promote and protect the interests of all the people. A team of councillors assisted both the ward head and the village head in discharging their responsibilities to the people. There was no room for even a powerful individual to resort to dictatorial power to have his own way prevail because the major restraints were the bonds that existed between leaders and the people and that came into being as a result of cultural traditions and the knowledge that leaders had an obligation to respect the wishes of the people they represented. Meetings were always open to the public.

There is no doubt that the king, the ward head, and the village head and their respective councils deliberated on issues and made decisions based upon the collective belief that they were in the best interests of the people. This practice evinces the observance of democratic principles.[11] That the Africans understood the importance of observing democratic principles is why the educational process itself acquired elements that were critical to the sustenance of the vitality and integrity of

---

[8]The European governments which instituted colonies in Africa refused to accept the concept of kings and decided to refer to them as chiefs in order to make a case to substantiate their claim that African society was primitive. For them to recognize African leaders as kings would be to place them at the same level as kings in Europe. If they did this, then they would not be able to justify their colonial intentions.

[9]V. W. Turner, *Schism and Continuity in an African Society.*. Manchester: University of Manchester Press, 1957, p. 318.

[10]Lawrence Vambe, *An Ill-Fated People: Zimbabwe Before and After Rhodes.* Pittsburgh: Pittsburgh University Press, 1957, p. 317.

[11]W. Raynor, *The Tribe and Its Successors: An Account of African Traditional Life and European Settlement in Southern Rhodesia.* New York: Frederick Praeger, 1962, p. 49.

their society. Therefore, the educational process was quite complete and relevant to the needs of the students. Indeed, the colonial governments themselves recognized this completeness and relevance. For example, in 1965, speaking to Rotary Club International in Harare, Zimbabwe, F. G. Loveridge, who was a senior education officer in colonial Zimbabwe with responsibility for African education, observed on the character of education in traditional African cultural society in comparison to Western education saying:

> In his traditional society the African was given all the education which he needed to function in his culture. Today, he has fallen away because Western education does not prepare him to function in Western culture. At the same time it does not prepare him to function in his own culture. Therefore, the African who goes to school in a Western cultural setting is placed in a socioeconomic limbo.[12]

Yet another misconception that Westerners had about education in traditional African society was that it lacked a defined curricular content. An examination of what was learned would furnish clear evidence to prove that what was learned was comprehensive because it included components that were essential to human conditions. Because the educational process entailed utilitarian characteristics, it required that learners demonstrate competencies in whatever they learned. Michael Gelfand describes the comprehensive character of education in traditional African society as he saw it in Zimbabwe:

> The son watches his father make a circular hole in the ground and places in it some charcoal. Air is forced through a tunnel into the hole. The charcoal is lit with lighted sticks and embers to a high temperature. When the iron in the fire turns red, the father uses a source-shaped implement to grip the top. His son holds it firmly while he hits it with a hammer to fashion the molten iron into a desired object.[13]

One can see that among other things, this form of education instilled in the learner a character that was essential to the sustenance of diverse components of society and individuality that made such diversity a critical element of human existence every where. Therefore, to conclude that the learning process helped transform the individual from being merely a person into being a finished product because the educational process was comprehensive is to acknowledge it completeness. Therefore, for Westerners to conclude that education in traditional African society had no definite curricular content furnishes yet another evidence to suggest that they had no clear understanding of the African culture itself.

One must be aware that a discussion of education in traditional African society would be incomplete if it did not address the question of how components of what was learned were related to the totality of life in the community itself. In concluding that education in traditional African society meant nothing more than a practice of superstitious beliefs, Westerners, including the nineteenth century missionaries to

---

[12]F.G. Loveridge, Senior Education Officer in Colonial Zimbabwe, "Disturbing Reality of Western Education in Southern Africa," an address to the Rotary Club International, Harare, Zimbabwe, March 13, 1965. Quoted by permission of the Old Mutare Methodist Archives.

[13]Michael Gelfand, *Diet and Tradition in African Culture*. London: E.S. Livingstone, 1971, p. 45.

Southern Africa, missed a critically important aspect of their claimed knowledge of the Africans and their culture. B.A. Powers concludes that the fact that education in traditional African culture, like that of any culture, was designed to place emphasis on cultural values that were considered essential to the well-being of society and its members, must be understood in the context of a universal purpose of education.[14]

Because the Africans had a tremendous respect for human life, learning to show respect of elders and children, to say prayers before a journey, to feed children or give them a bath, to celebrate the harvest, to clean the house, to fetch water from the village well, or to dig the ground, all entailed the observance of religious principles and social values that had to be learned fully and acquired carefully. In a similar manner, learning to embrace human qualities, such as integrity, honesty, truthfulness, and faithfulness was considered an essential component of the educational process and must never be taken for granted. For this reason the educational process was being constantly innovated to make it relevant to the needs of the students.

The completeness of education in traditional African society was described in 1974 to the author by an elderly African who observed:

> Before the coming of Europeans to our country, no aspect of our life, no boy or girl was ever neglected by our educational system because it was constantly being innovated to make it relevant to the needs of all students. Every person had an opportunity for education. Today, we are told that only so many can go to school. Why so many only and not all? Neither the missionaries nor the colonial government succeeded in convincing us of the wisdom of accepting both Western education and Christianity. Do you fail to see the intent of the colonial government in the education of our children today?[15]

Michael Gelfand agrees with this view of the completeness of education in traditional African society and goes further to add that the educational process covered all aspects of life, including law, religion, medicine, trade and commerce, agriculture, social ethics, language and music.[16] They all formed essential components of the learning process so critical to successful life. The absence of formal education, as it is understood in the West, did not in any way diminish its quality. Gelfand explains why, saying:

> There were no professional schools or teachers in the traditional African society. But the child learned from various members of the family and community as he grew. He learned from his grandparents, parents, and members of the community. Yet, his entire education was as complete as it is in Western culture. Whether it was agricultural pursuit or taking part in games.[17]

---

[14]B. A. Powers, *Religion and Education in Tswana Chiefdom*. London: Oxford University Press, 1961, p. 29.

[15]An elderly African, during an interview with the author in Mutare, Zimbabwe, May 15, 1974, in Dickson A. Mungazi, *The Change of Black Attitudes Towards Education in Rhodesia, 1900-1975*, a dissertation, the University of Nebraska, Lincoln, 1977, p. 80

[16]Michael Gelfand, *Growing up in Shona Society*. p. 217.

[17]*Ibid.* p. 220

What has just been discussed relative to the educational process in traditional African society leads to two basic conclusions. The first is that because the Africans themselves found it complete to meet their needs, there was no reason for them to abandon it simply because the white man constantly told them to do just that because he said it was designed to sustain a primitive culture. The second conclusion is that as long as the white man used the argument that both the education and the African culture in which it was cast were primitive, he was unable to see the need to utilize the positive attributes inherent in the African society to initiate a new relationship with Africans based on mutual trust. This is why the colonial governments introduced educational systems of their own to train the Africans to serve their own purposes. The purpose of the introduction of Western education to Southern Africa is now discussed in order to indicate how it created problems that demanded educational innovation of the region today.

The Purpose of Western Education for Africans in Southern Africa

When the Portuguese established colonies in Angola and Mozambique in 1575, they faced a situation which they had not anticipated; the strength of African culture and the viability of the educational system within it and its relevance to the life-style of the Africans. It was the combination of the cultural viability, institutional structure and the educational process that presented the Portuguese with a problem of how to break the Africans in order to subject them to colonial rule. During the next forty years the Africans resisted, not only the colonization of their land, but also the form of education the Portuguese were pressuring them to accept.[18]

By the time Brazil declared itself independent in 1822, the Portuguese had succeeded in creating an environment which forced the Africans to need some form of Portuguese education. This gave the Portuguese an opportunity to define its purpose of education as acquiring an ability to speak the Portuguese language. In this manner, the process of acculturation had begun and the life-style the Africans had known for centuries was altered permanently. From the very start the purpose of Portuguese education in Angola and Mozambique was to maintain distinctions between the level of development for Africans and for Portuguese nationals.[19] This was done because the Portuguese colonial government feared that education for Africans in the context of Portuguese culture would have on them the same effect that it had had on the people of Brazil; an increase in the level of their consciousness.

But, through the efforts of one determined and brilliant African, Antonio de Miranda, who had taught himself how to read and write the Portuguese language, the Africans in Angola began to believe that the Portuguese colonial officials were afraid that their form of education would enable the Africans to see the injustice of the colonial system itself. Therefore, the consciousness that the Portuguese colonial officials feared education would help raise among the Africans became a new reality through trying to deny it to them.

---

[18]Lawrence Henderson, *Angola: Five Centuries of Conflict*. Ithaca: Cornell University Press, 1979, p. 15.
[19]*Ibid*. p. 18

By the time the Berlin conference concluded its deliberations on the colonization of Africa in February, 1885, its participants had outlined strategies of training the Africans to function as laborers in accordance with the Victorian perceptions of the Africans and in order to gain profit in the wake of the magnanimous expectations envisaged by the Great Industrial Revolution. The new established colonial governments began to formulate new theories and philosophies of education for Africans consistent with the purposes they wished to accomplish. In this way the spokesmen of the colonial establishments sharpened the cause and the strategies that the colonial governments had designed to ensure that the Africans were trained to fulfill stated purposes. There is space in this study to discuss briefly a few specific examples of the various purposes that the colonial governments established for African education

In the German colony of Namibia the responsibility for formulating a colonial policy, known as *Deutsche Kolonialbund*, fell on the shoulders of General von Trotha. His appointment as commander-in-chief of the colonial armed forces was not made lightly; it was the result of a carefully calculated and seriously considered policy because he had a distinguished military record greatly admired by Erwin Rommel (1891-1944), who was nicknamed the *Desert Fox*. A brilliant German general who commanded German forces in the Second World War, Rommel's military strategy almost paralyzed Allied operations in North Africa. His tragic death in 1944 spelled the demise of Adolf Hitler and his Third Reich.

That von Trotha, mystic and flamboyant as he was, was a classic example of colonial contradiction in the purpose in the policy the German colonial government formulated is evinced by what he did. First, he ordered the Africans to move from their land to make room for German settlers. Then, after the African rebellion was crashed in 1907, he demanded that the Africans be trained as laborers.[20] That von Trotha pursued this colonial educational purpose for Africans with the same intensity as the level of brutality he had used to crash the rebellion shows the extent to which the German colonial officials were committed to it. In order to train the Africans as laborers, the German colonial officials forced the Namas and the Hereros to amalgamate in order to facilitate the implementation of their policy which included the recruiting and training of laborers.

When, in 1894, the German colonial government allowed the missionaries to open schools for Africans, it stipulated a condition that the major curricular component be practical training and basic literacy to ensure the adequate supply of labor.[21] It also reserved the right to inspect those schools to ensure compliance with its requirements. That the missionaries wanted to emphasize the teaching of religion suggests that the education of the Africans was placed in a conflicting position created by two colonial institutions. This was the situation which placed the Africans at an educational disadvantage. as their education was so manipulated that it could not accrue real social benefits to them but to the German nationals themselves. That the colonial officials, at the urging of von Trotha, concluded that this was the only

---

[20]Marion O'Callaghan, *Namibia: The Effects of Apartheid on Culture and Education.* Paris: Unesco, 1977, p. 19.
[21]*Ibid.* p. 96.

form of education from which the Africans could benefit because they were considered inferior to the white man suggests the strength of the Victorian misconception that characterized the attitudes of the colonial governments toward them.

The implementation of this policy and the fact that the Africans had been subjected to colonial domination combined to create a damaging doubt among them about the value of their culture and their worth as human beings. This is why four Africans were considered to be equal in social status to one white person. The notion that Germans were superior to Africans was carried to dangerous limits by Adolf Hitler. Until German forces were defeated in Namibia by Allied forces in 1915, German colonial officials pursued this policy with impunity.

The Legacy of Cecil John Rhodes: Treating the Africans as a Subject Race

In British colonial system the purpose of education for Africans took similar lines as in German colonies. As soon as he arrived in Southern Africa in 1870 in search of fortune, Cecil John Rhodes (1853-1902) began to formulate his own philosophy and policy towards the Africans. Although the British had been in control of South Africa since the Boer migration of 1835, the formulation of a policy towards the Africans became the exclusive domain of Rhodes and his associates. Using the massive wealth he rapidly acquired on arriving in South Africa to pave his way to the top rung of the political ladder, Rhodes, as prime minister of the Cape Province in 1896, felt ready to enunciate his own philosophy of both the place and education of the Africans, saying,

> I say that the Natives are like children. They are just emerging from barbarism. If I may venture a comparison, I should compare the Natives with regard to European civilization to the tribes of the Druids. I think that we have been extremely liberal in granting barbarism forty or fifty years of training what we ourselves obtained only after many hundreds of civilization.[22]

In constantly reminding the Africans that they and their culture represented barbarism, Rhodes and the British colonial establishment subjected them to what Canaan Banana concludes to be a confused state of *cultural dualism* which forced them to doubt the values of their own without being accepted into that of the white man.[23] This is precisely what F. G. Loveridge meant when he said in March, 1965, that the African who was educated in a Western cultural context was placed in a political and socioeconomic limbo. If this was not a deliberate educational purpose for Africans, it certainly was the effect it had on them.

Rhodes' political behavior and policy toward the Africans manifested a classic example of colonial contradiction. Speaking on June 23, 1887 in the Cape

---

[22]Stanlake Samkange, *What Rhodes Really Said About Africans*. Harare: Harare Publishing House, 1982, p. 14.

[23]Canaan Banana, *Theology of Promise: The Dynamics of Self-reliance*. Harare: The College Press, 1982, p. 53

Parliament on the second reading of the Native Registration Bill, Rhodes received a standing ovation when he argued:

> I will lay down my own policy on the Native question. Either you receive them on equal footing as citizens, or you call them a subject race. I have made up my mind that there must be a class legislation, and that we have got to treat the Natives where they are, in a state of barbarism. We are to be lords over them. We will continue to treat them as a subject race as long as they remain in a state of barbarism. What is civilized man? It is a person with sufficient education to enable him to write his name. The Natives should be a source of assistance to the white man as laborers. This must be the main purpose of his education.[24]

It is therefore not surprising that during and after his life Rhodes remained the crown prince of British colonial policy towards the development of the Africans. He had become the unquestioned mentor to future colonial officials who followed his footprints as logical disciples seeking not only to sustain the presumed wisdom of a man they revered and regarded as infallible in the process of human thought and action, but also to elevate the ideals he represented to a new height of the white man's power over the Africans.

It is for this reason that Rhodes' influence on educational policy for Africans in the British colonies in Southern Africa became profound. By the time of the Boer War of 1899 in South Africa, Paul Kruger (1825-1904) had been president of the ill-fated Boer Republic of the Transvaal since 1883 and remained in office till 1900. A complicating factor was that Rhodes and Kruger were bitter political enemies. However, they had one philosophical belief in common about the place of the Africans in colonial society. Kruger, a poorly educated man but an uncompromising believer in the Boer myth of white superiority, repeatedly urged the Africans to be so trained that they would fulfill tasks appropriate to their presumed intellectual and social inferiority. This is why he stated his own philosophy of education for Africans, saying, "The black man must be taught to understand that he belongs to an inferior class and that his function in society is to serve as a laborer."[25]

By the time that the policy of apartheid was officially introduced following the elections of 1948, from which the Nationalist Party was returned to power, the need to sustain the notion of white superiority through education had become so strong that it exerted a major influence in the enactment of the Bantu Education Act of 1953. In that same year, Hendrik Verwoerd (1902-1966), then Minister of Bantu Affairs which was responsible for African education, explained the purpose of education provided for them in the Bantu Education Act, saying,

> Native education must be controlled in such a way that it should be in accord with the policy of the state. If the Native is being taught to expect that he will live his adult life under a policy of equal rights, he is making a big mistake. The Native who attends school must know that he must be the laborer in the country.[26]

---

[24]*Ibid.* p. 26
[25]Alex La Guma, *Apartheid,* p. 13.
[26]Hilda Bernstein, "Schools for Servitude", in Alex La Guma, *Apartheid,* p. 43.

By the time of the Soweto uprising in June, 1976, it had been recognized that the education of the Africans was "being perverted to create bondage out of a racial setting and to restrict the productivity of the Africans to local and subservient tasks."[27] One can only conclude that in defying a call for innovation, such a system of education is bound to lead to a major national catastrophe.

The pattern of this policy and purpose for African education was quite consistent with the rest of the other countries of Southern Africa during the colonial period. For example, in Zimbabwe the colonial officials designed an educational policy that was quite consistent with Rhodes' philosophy. This is precisely why Earl Grey (1851-1917), who served as administrator from April 12, 1896 to December 4, 1898, argued in 1898 when he introduced an education bill that the purpose of education for Africans was to train them as laborers, adding, "I am convinced that the very first step towards civilizing the Natives lies in a course of industrial training and manual labor which must precede the teaching of religious dogma."[28]

To conclude that the colonial government in Zimbabwe formulated an educational policy for Africans to serve its own political and socioeconomic purposes is to acknowledge that it could not be designed along any other line of thinking. The sad aspect of the attitude of the colonial government towards the Africans is that they concluded that it was uncivilized simply because it was different. Once this attitude became a basic operative principle of their action, colonial officials were not likely to see the positive side of the African culture. This is exactly why the chief native commissioner argued in 1905:

> It is cheap labor which we need in this country, and it has yet to be proved that the Native who can read and write turns out to be a good laborer. As far as we can determine, the Native who can read and write will not work on farms and in mines.[29]

To give effect to this line of thinking, the colonial government enacted ordinance Number 133 in 1907 to provide for manual labor as a viable form of education for Africans. There is no question that the strategy that the colonial government in Zimbabwe designed to reduce the education of the Africans to a level where it helped serve the labor needs of the colonial society was synonymous with its desire to have it prepare the Africans to serve its own political and socioeconomic purposes.

This is the reason why a senior colonial government official wrote a letter to the editor of the *The Rhodesia Herald* in June, 1912, to state what he believed must be the purpose of African education as he saw it, saying, "I do not consider it right that we should educate the Native in any way that will unfit him for service. The Native

[27]*Ibid.* p. 44.
[28]British South Africa Company Records: Earl Grey, 1896-1898: Folio AV/1/11/:GR/1/1/11:547-548. By permission of the Zimbabwe National Archives.
[29]Southern Rhodesia: The Annual Report of the Chief Native Commissioner for Moshonaland, 1905. By permission of the Zimbabwe National Archives.

is and should always be the hewer of wood and the drawer of water for his white master."[30]

This is also why, Ethel Tawse Jollie (1874-1950), one of a very few women to be elected to the colonial legislature, was quite candid in arguing that the Africans must be educated differently to prepare them to function as laborers,saying during a debate in the legislature in 1927,

> We do not intend to hand over this country to the Natives, or to admit them to the same political and social position as we ourselves enjoy. Let us therefore make no pretense of educating them in the same way we educate whites.[31]

> In supporting Jollie's argument, Hugh Williams went a step further to argue, "If we close every school and stop all this talk of fostering education and development of Natives, we would much sooner become an asset to the British Empire."[32]

One can see that from the time that Rhodes formulated his philosophy of education towards the education of the Africans to the end of the colonial rule of Zimbabwe in 1979, that the education of the Africans was controlled in order to sustain this basic objective. This is evinced by the statement that Andrew Skeen, a member and spokesman of the Rhodesia Front Party that ruled Zimbabwe from 1962 to 1979, made in the legislature when he said in 1969,

> We in the Rhodesia Front Government are determined to control the rate of African political advancement till time and education make it a safe possibility. Besides we wish to retain the power to retard the advancement of the Africans through education to make sure that the government remains in responsible (white) hands.[33]

In 1983, Ian Smith, the last RF colonial prime minister, defended the educational policy of his government as he told the author during an interview,

> We knew that there was a gap between white education and African education. This was not due to any thing that we did, this was part of our history. Before the Second World War, the Africans did not believe in education because they thought that it was something that belonged to the white man.[34]

What Smith was saying, in effect, is that although his government knew that there was need to innovate education to serve the needs of all students, it was not possible to do so because it would be going against the precedence of history. Cecil John Rhodes could not have been happier to hear one of his protegees express his own views so well.

---

[30]*The Rhodesia Herald,* June 28, 1812.

[31]Southern Rhodesia: *Legislative Debates,* 1927

[32]*Ibid.*

[33]Rhodesia: *Parliamentary Debates,* 1969.

[34]Ian Smith, RF prime minister of colonial Zimbabwe from 1964 to 1979, during an interview with the author in Harare, Zimbabwe, July 20, 1983. For the entire enterview, see Appendix 6 of this study.

Summary and Conclusion:
The Effect of Colonial Educational Policy for Africans

This chapter has attempted to discuss the purpose of education from the perspective of its universality as defined by Jean Piaget, Immanuel Kant and Theodore Roosevelt to show that the educational process in Southern African needs innovation because its purpose was defined from a narrow perspective to suit the interests of a colonial society. Therefore, the definitions expressed by these men seem to underscore two basic conclusions. The first is that all societies, regardless of whether or not they are considered developed, must accept the principle of change in order to ensure their own development. The second conclusion is that any social change that fails to take education as the principal instrument of bringing it about loses the purpose for which it is designed.

In this chapter it has been shown that because education in traditional African society was complete and comprehensive, the Africans could not abandon it in favor of accepting Western education without losing some important components of their culture. This is why Canaan Banana concludes,

> In traditional African society education was an integral part of the entire social, economic and cultural system. It was related to the individual, the human group and the environment. Each part was essential to the coherent operation and sustenance of the whole system.[35]

This is also why Aldon Southall argues in his essay, *The Illusion of Tribe*, that when a people has lost the essential components of its culture in an attempt to accept those of another, it not only loses its own sense of self, but also fails to grasp the essentials of the one it is trying to accept as a new *modus vivendi*. In this manner it hangs perilously on the cliff of confusion.[36] This is the plight that the Africans of the nineteenth century faced as they considered the limited number of options that were before them.

The discussion in this chapter leads to three conclusions. The first is that the relevance of education in traditional African society made it possible for all students to have access to it. This was because the purpose of education was well defined with functionalism as its major guiding principle. In this context, African society regarded education as a means to an end, not an end in itself. This explains why educational process was a life-long endeavor, fully integrating it into major institutional structures and making it applicable and relevant from one generation to the next. With reference to education in traditional society in Nigeria, Babs Fafunwa discusses this integration and goes on to add,

> The warrior, the hunter, the medicine man, the priest, the farmer, the nobleman, the man of character who combined and embraced features of knowledge in its

---

[35]Canaan Banana, *Theology of Promise: The Dynamics of Self-reliance,* p. 73.
[36]Aldon Southall, *The Illusion of Tribe.* The Netherlands, R. J. Brill, 1970.

comprehensive form with specific skills on a variety of whom society benefited was a properly educated person.[37]

One must conclude that the completeness of education in traditional African society and its relevance to human condition is what the colonial governments saw as the backbone of the African culture itself, and that in order to break the resistance of the Africans to the intrusion of their society, they designed a strategy to discredit it as a justification for colonization. This is why the white man constantly argued that African culture was primitive and that the Africans themselves were immersed in barbarism. In this kind of setting educational innovation, or the little of it that took place, was intended to improve the proficiency of the Africans as laborers. That this objective was not compatible with universal purpose of education helped set a stage for a major conflict between the Africans and the colonial governments when time was right.

The second conclusion is that one would have thought that having succeeded in discrediting education in traditional African society, the colonial governments would have provided a better system of education that would have had the effect of promoting the development of the Africans in a new political and socioeconomic setting. But what actually came out of the educational system of the colonial governments was a system that was not only based on race, but was also calculated to place the Africans at a political and socioeconomic disadvantage, This is what Hilda Bernstein sees as one of the most crippling features of education during the colonial period when she said in 1971 that the education of the Africans was being perverted to create bondage out of a racial setting. In ignoring the universality of the purpose of education, the colonial governments set in motion a spiraling process that ultimately led to confrontation with the Africans. This was the ultimate effect of colonial educational policy in Africa.

The third conclusion is that throughout its history, the colonial educational system demonstrated far more serious shortcomings than education in traditional African society. The attitudes of the colonial officials, such as Cecil John Rhodes, Paul Kruger, Earl Grey, Ethel Tawse Jollie, Hugh Williams and Ian Smith, demonstrate a purpose of education for Africans that was incompatible with basic human values. The need for cheap labor and the desire to limit political and socioeconomic development of the Africans placed them on a level of bare existence and suffering. This is what Methodist Bishop James Crane Hartzell[38] saw when he wrote in 1918:

> Africa has suffered many evils. Slave trade and exploitation by the white man have through many years preyed upon the life of the people and have left them uncertain about the future. To their dismay, the Natives of Africa have realized that the white

[37]Babs Fafunwa, *History of Education in Nigeria*. London: George Allen and Unwin, 1974, p. 16.

[38]Bishop of the Methodist Episcopal Church in Africa from 1896 to 1916. Hartzell Secondary School at Old Mutare Methodist Center outside Mutare in Zimbabwe, which the author attended, is named after him.

socioeconomic development of the Africans placed them on a level of bare existence and suffering. This is what Methodist Bishop James Crane Hartzell[38] saw when he wrote in 1918:

> Africa has suffered many evils. Slave trade and exploitation by the white man have through many years preyed upon the life of the people and have left them uncertain about the future. To their dismay, the Natives of Africa have realized that the white man has offered them his form of education only to enable them to function as laborers.[39]

Albert Schweitzer (1825-1965), the German missionary to nineteenth century Africa agrees when he wrote:

> Who can describe the misery, the injustice, and the cruelties that the Africans have suffered at the hands of Europeans? If a record could be compiled, it would make a book containing pages which the reader would have to turn unread because their contents would be too horrible.[40]

Therefore, from its inception colonial education needed innovation because it was inadequate. It was inadequate because it was unable to meet the needs of all people as defined by themselves in the context of a new socioeconomic and political system in which it was cast. When, from time to time, the colonial governments introduced what they considered change, they did so, not in accordance with universal principles of educational innovation, but to train the Africans to serve better as laborers. Such an educational system was destined to create a climate of major conflict in the future. The next chapter discusses some theoretical considerations of educational innovation in Southern Africa today.

---

[38] Bishop of the Methodist Episcopal Church in Africa from 1896 to 1916. Hartzell Secondary School at Old Mutare Methodist Center outside Mutare in Zimbabwe, which the author attended, is named after him.

[39] James C. Hartzell, "The Future of Africa", in *The African Advance*. Vol. 12, No. 1, July, 1918.

[40] *The Christian Century,* October 8, 1975.

3

THEORETICAL CONSIDERATIONS OF EDUCATIONAL INNOVATION

Post colonial Southern Africa must seek to strengthen social institutions by focusing on educational innovation to meet the developmental needs of the individual. President Samora Machel, 1981.

Educational innovation must afford all students the freedom to choose their own course of study. High School Principal in Zimbabwe,August, 1983.

Educational innovation is the crown jewel of national development because it ensures the development of the individual. The Catholic Bishops' Conference of Zimbabwe, 1987.

Introduction: The Imperative of Innovation

When, on August 14, 1941, President Franklin Roosevelt and Prime Minister Winston Churchill issued the Atlantic Charter stating:

> We respect the right of all people to choose the form of government under which they will live and wish to see sovereign rights and self-determination restored to those who have been denied them,[1]

they were actually recognizing the fact that the war , devastating as it was, had created an imperative for change. The two leaders were convinced that the conditions that had created an environment of the war in 1939 must be altered in order to avoid another conflict in the future. They therefore concluded that one of the major conditions for future security of all people in all nations was to change the manner in which governments were instituted.

If the Atlantic Charter were issued under the pressure of the war, the two leaders subsequently disagreed about to whom it was directed. On the one hand, Roosevelt thought that the charter was directed towards changing the systems of government all over the world to bring out the representative character so essential to national development through individual and popular participation. This is why, in 1943, while he was on his way to the Casablanca Conference, he stopped in the French colony of Gambia to lay the ground work for implementing the charter.

---

[1]*The Atlantic Charter*, August 14, 1941. by Courtesy of the British Embassy, Harare, 1989.

Roosevelt was so appalled to see the conditions of life of the Africans that he expressed his deep disappointment with France's colonial policy.

On the other hand, Churchill did not think that the concept of self-determination and the process of instituting governments on Western principles included responding affirmatively to the needs of the Africans. He therefore argued that " I have not become the King's[2] First Minister in order to preside over the liquidation of the British Empire. We mean to hold our own."[3] The difference of opinion between Roosevelt and Churchill about the meaning of change said something very important about what it was intended to do. As the leader of a colonial power, Churchill saw change from its narrow perspective; Roosevelt saw it from a broader perspective. But in the context of the Atlantic Charter, a call for a more representative form of government was, indeed, a call for innovation in its more inclusive terms as an imperative of national development.

A question now arises: How did the Atlantic Charter affect the concept of change in its universal meaning? Robert Manners seems to provide an answer when he suggests,

> If you introduce change in any part, contingent changes of varying intensity will make themselves felt throughout the venture. The very change which may be welcomed by the group in power as a desirable innovation may be resented by those who feel oppressed by society because they feel that such change has been introduced to strengthen the status quo.[4]

This seems to suggest that change that may be interpreted as innovation is relative. That is, it means different things to different people. If nations went by the relativity of innovation, and many have done just that, then it is not surprising that most of them have been in trouble. The fact of the matter is that this is a definition of innovation the nations of Southern Africa cannot afford to go by. Change becomes innovation when it is designed with the main objective of improving the system.

Innovation in the Colonial Setting:
The Relativity of Theory and the Colonization Process

A study of the activities in Europe leading to the colonization of Africa would support Manners' conclusion that change which may be interpreted as innovation by those in power may be regarded as designed to sustain the status quo by those who are powerless. That while Europeans regarded the Great Industrial Revolution as a technological innovation that meant the improvement of the standard of living, the Africans considered it an improvement in the machinery of oppression suggests

---

[2]King George VI (1895-1952) who was on the British throne from 1936 to 1952.
[3]Martin Meredith, *The First Dance of Freedom: Black Africa in the Post-War Era.* New York: Harper and Row, 1984,p.35.
[4]Robert Manners, "Functionalism, Reliability, and Athropology in Underdeveloped Areas" in Thomas Weaver [Ed.], *To See Ourselves: Athropology and Modern Social Issues.* Glenview, (ill.), Scott, Foreman and Company, 1973, p. 117.

the relativity of change as innovation. This phenomenon represents the first phase in the colonization of Africa.

A few examples that will substantiate the accuracy of this conclusion will now be discussed. The formation of the Dutch East India Company in 1602 was an event that gave the Dutch an advantage in the competition in which major nations in Europe were engaged in the spices trade with the East. When the Dutch East India Company dispatched Jan van Riebeeck to the Cape in South Africa in 1652, the white man thought that this was a great breakthrough in facilitating trade between Europe and the East. However, when Riebeeck began to formulate policies to govern the company's relationships with the Africans, it became evident that while company officials saw the white man's action as an improvement in relationships between the white man and the Africans, the Africans themselves saw those policies as a machinery of their oppression. Therefore from its inception in South Africa, the Dutch East India Company created an environment of conflict between itself and the Africans. This is the environment that the apartheid paradigm has not been able to resolve until the escalation of that conflict forced F.W. de Klerk to make a new thrust to find a solution before it was too late.

In 1785 James Watt's experiment with the steam engine and Samuel Crompton's study in combustion combined to usher in technological development. Thus, a new era in the spinning jenny began to give the *mule* a new industrial capacity. This enabled Europeans to see this technological innovation as changing the course of industrial development. These simple technological innovations turned out to be the basis of the beginning of the a new industrial era which had far-reaching implications for the colonization process in Africa. It is important to understand that the events that led to the colonization of Africa began with a series of simple technological innovations that was taking place in Europe during the later part of the eighteenth century. The excitement that characterized the response of Europeans over these forms of innovation was a nightmare for Africans.

While the effects of the Industrial Revolution of the nineteenth century were profoundly felt in industrial production, it was in the area of innovation in transport and communication which gave a new meaning to entrepreneurial adventure in Africa by Europeans.[5] The ability to transport a large number of people to distant places and the knowledge of the distribution of products on a larger scale than had been done in the past combined to play a critical role in the quest for colonies in Africa. The completion of the trans-Atlantic cable in 1866 made possible by the work of an American inventor, Samuel Morse, radically transformed the system of communication with profound implications for the colonization process in Africa.

The knowledge among Europeans that they had become masters of what they considered technological feats boosted their own sense of superiority over people in distant lands and began to associate their accomplishments with the rightness of their objectives and endeavors in a larger context of human interactions. In this context they regarded colonization of Africa as a blessing that only the white man was capable of extending to the Africans and in return the Africans must be grateful for

---

[5]Dickson A. Mungazi, *The Struggle for Social Change in Southern Africa: Visions of Liberty*, p. 23.

receiving the blessings of Western civilization. The question of what was right or wrong for the colonized people could only be determined by the colonizers themselves. Therefore, any resistance by the colonized, especially the Africans, was regarded as an act of rebellion against properly constituted authority and civilized behavior of the white man. The sad part of this is that technological innovation did not translate into innovation in interactions between people of vastly different cultures.

The knowledge that Africa contained large amounts of new materials motivated European nations to launch an entirely new entrepreneurial adventure there. This was the beginning of the second phase in the process of the colonization of Africa in form of what became known as the *scramble for Africa* beginning in 1875. By the time of the Berlin conference of 1884, European nations recognized that it was not in their national interests to go to war over resources and colonies in Africa. An innovative idea came from Otto von Bismarch (1815-1898), the charismatic chancellor of Germany beginning with the conclusion of the Franco-Prussian war in 1871. Bismarch convened the conference to enable European nations to resolve their differences over the procedure of claiming colonies in Africa. That Bismarch himself chaired the conference suggests the extent of the power and influence he had over the course of developments both in Europe and in Africa.

That the theoretical considerations that were behind the colonization of Africa played a major role in shaping colonial policies to suit the conditions of each colonial power suggests their relativity. This is shown by the fact that European nations operated by different policy structures suitable to the colonial conditions they stipulated. While the colonial governments considered the introduction of the policies of *Deutsche Kolonialbund, evalue, Estado Novo, apartheid,* an innovation to improve the system of colonial administration, the Africans themselves, recipients of these policies, regarded them as improvement in the instruments of their own oppression.

What is important to recognize here is that these policy structures were based on one theoretical consideration, and that is, European colonial governments believed that their application would result in the advancement of the Africans as they would begin to see the value of accepting Western culture. One can conclude that these policy structures were designed to serve the interests of the colonial governments from the administrative systems that emerged as a result. But in the course of implementing their policies, the colonial governments went much further than the Africans would tolerate. The introduction of the system of pass books, the practice of registration, the introduction of forced labor and strict segregation laws were conditions of the application of the colonial policies which forced the Africans to feel the weight of the colonial power in a way they could no longer bear.[6]

While the colonial governments felt secure as a result of implementing these policies, they had a false sense of security because when the conditions were right, the Africans set out to prove that the theoretical basis of colonization was wrong. In Chapter 2 the views of Albert Schweitzer and James Crane Hartzell were quoted to

---

[6]Dickson Mungazi, "The Change of Black Attitudes Towards Education in Rhodesia," a dissertation. The University of Nebraska: Lincoln, 1977, p. 52.

conclude that the colonization of Africa resulted in suffering by the Africans. Was this a deliberate outcome of the theories and practices of the colonial governments? Courtland Cox suggests an answer when he wrote in 1972:

> At the base of the colonial political assumptions was the absolute belief in the inferiority of the African people and the certainty of chaos if their subjection was eased in the slightest.[7]

Kenneth Knorr adds that while the formulation of colonial theory by the colonial governments was intended to improve the effectiveness of the colonial administrative systems to benefit the colonial governments themselves, the ultimate effect of its application was that it "converted the Africans into a commodity or raw materials to be employed in the service of the white man. The Africans were not allowed to decide for their own future because they were considered incapable of doing so. It had, therefore, to be decided for them to serve the white man as their master."[8]

The theories formulated by the colonial governments, especially that the African were incapable of making decisions relative to their own development and that a national chaos would result if their subjection was eased in any way, combined to create a need for change, not only in the attitudes of the colonial governments, but also in seeking ways of improving the effectiveness of the colonial administrative structures themselves. Arrest and imprisonments for political activity considered incompatible with colonial politics, denial of voting rights, discrimination in economic and educational opportunity, and the administrative systems themselves became demonstrated evidence of that theoretical belief. All the Africans could do was hope that the white man would treat them humanely. They hoped against hope!

While the Africans were at a loss to understand why colonial governments were so set against giving them any opportunity for development, the colonial establishments themselves were totally convinced of the correctness of some eighteenth century theoretical notions , among them that "The brain of the adult Africans looks very much like the brain of a European in its infant stage. At puberty all development in the brain of the African ceases as it becomes more ape-like as he grows older."[9] This is the kind of theory that would not accommodate the aspirations of the colonized Africans. This is also the kind of setting in which innovation was intended to do only one thing: to improve the power of the colonial governments themselves. Until the Africans began to demand equal rights, the colonial governments made no effort either to modify this theory to change their strategy to initiate the process of developing the Africans.

There are plenty of examples to substantiate this conclusion. In 1952, for example, Godfrey Huggins (1883-1971), the prime minister of colonial Zimbabwe from 1933 to 1952, argued during a political campaign speech, saying:

---

[7]Cortland Cox, *African Liberation*. New York: Black Education Press, 1972, p. 82.

[8]Kenneth Knorr, *British Colonial Theories*. Toronto: Toronto University Press, 1974, p. 378.

[9]Charles Lyons, "The Educability of the African: British Thought and Action, 1835-1965" in V. M. Battle and C. H. Lyons, *Essays in the History of African Education*. New York: Teachers College Press, 1970, p. 9.

> We must unhesitatingly accept the theory that our superiority over the Africans rests on the color of our skin, education, and cultural values, civilization, and heredity. We must be sufficiently realistic to appreciate the fact that we have a paramount monopoly of these qualities. It would be outrageous to give the Native a so-called equal opportunity when he is likely to ruin himself as a result.[10]

Huggins' own protegee, Ian Smith (1919 -), the last colonial prime minister who served from 1964 to 1979, added to this melodramatic theoretical perception when he attempted to explain in 1965 why his own government resorted to mass arrest and imprisonment of the Africans to control their political aspirations, saying,

> We have had to resort to certain forms of political restriction and arrest of the Africans because when you have a primitive people such as the Africans of this country are it would have been completely irresponsible of the government not to have done so.[11]

As one seeks to understand the theories used by the colonial governments as a basis of strengthening themselves in Africa, one needs to understand first some reliable theoretical considerations in order to understand and put them in their proper context. Two examples come to mind. First, in his theoretical study, *Education for Liberation,* Adam Curle concludes that the effect of an educational theory in societies in which education is controlled to sustain the interests of those in power, rather than to promote the advancement of those who need it, is to create conditions in which habits of thought and action make those who are subjected to an imposition are forced to feel less than human.[12] Curle concludes that this objective is accomplished in two ways. The first is the formulation of a set of quasi theories which, in effect, is a result of myth. The second is by repeatedly trying to psychologically condition the controlled into believing that they are primitive because they are members of a primitive culture and society. Repetition of this myth often diminishes the self-worth of the controlled to the extent that they lose their self-esteem. Curle also suggests that this strategy negates the real purpose of education, to create an environment of mutual respect between the people of different cultures who live in the same society. Instead, it creates self-doubt and a feeling of inadequacy.[13] The feeling of inadequacy and self-doubt leads to further strengthening of myth and control by those in positions of power.

Second, in his own study, *The Colonizer and the Colonized,* Albert Memmi of Tunisia, a professor of philosophy at the Sorbonne, concludes that the essential character of the relationship between the colonizer and the colonized is the effect that the extent of control exercised by the former has on the latter is by utilizing myth

---

[10]Godfrey Huggins, prime minister of colonial Zimbabwe from 1933 to 1952, "Partnership in Rhodesia," a political campaign speech, Ref. 12/03/51, March 13, 1951. By courtesy of the Zimbabwe National Archives.

[11]George Sparrow, *Rhodesian Rebellion.* London: Brighton, 1966, p. 25.

[12]Adam Curle, *Education for Liberation.* New York: Wiley and Sons, 1971, p. 58.

[13]*Ibid.* p. 60

about their culture and intellectual potential.[14] Memmi goes on to add that after conditioning the colonized to believe in the superiority of the colonizer, they lose their sense of self-pride and motivation so essential to their development. This is the environment in which the colonizer formulates and strengthens mythical theory about the inferiority of the colonized to strengthen their control because they are presumed to come from a primitive culture. Under this condition any change in programs purported to promote the development of the colonized is, in effect, designed to promote the interests of the colonizer himself.[15] Therefore, any effort, apparent or real, made to improve the position of the colonized, forces the colonized to see it in the context of a desire on the part of the colonizer to sustain his own interests.[16]

What has been discussed so far in this chapter leads one to accept Curle' and Memmi's theories about the character of the colonial governments in Africa. Therefore, what the colonial governments considered innovation, the Africans considered a strategy to enhance the colonial government's power to control them. It was therefore not possible for the Africans to believe the colonialists who having gone to Africa in search of fortune, trained the Africans to function as cheap labor that motivated the colonial governments with a desire to ensure their advancement. Once this element of suspicion on the part of the Africans became part of their *modus operandi* in their relationships with the colonial governments, there was nothing that could be done to salvage the rapidly deteriorating situation caused by mistrust and doubt. This is the situation that ultimately led to the conflict between the two sides when time was right. This is why educational innovation, or the appearance of it initiated during the colonial period had actually peripheral meaning.

The Purpose of Purported Educational Innovation During the Colonial Period

The strategy of the colonial governments to make it look like they were trying to promote the political and socioeconomic advancement of the Africans was not limited to that aspect of national life, it extended to the educational process as well. Four examples in Zimbabwe, the Portuguese colonies of Angola and Mozambique, Namibia, and South Africa will furnish evidence to substantiate this conclusion. In colonial Zimbabwe the government considered the enactment of Ordinance Number 18 of 1899: The Appointment of Inspector of School, commonly known as the Education Ordinance of 1899, a milestone in its efforts to control education to suit its own purpose. There is no doubt that the government was trying to eliminate the effects of the war of 1896 in order to give the whites a new sense of security and hope for the future. It is for this reason that Section A of the ordinance provided for an academic education for white students and Section B provided for practical training and manual labor as a form of education for Africans.[17] In exercising control of African education in a manner provided for by the ordinance different

---

[14]Albert Memmi, *The Colonizer and the Colonized*. Boston: Beacon Press, 1965, p. 9.
[15]*Ibid*. p. 11
[16]*Ibid*. p. 12
[17]Southern Rhodesia: Ordinance Number 18 of 1899: The Appointment of Inspector of Schools

from the way it exercised control of white education, the colonial government operated by the theoretical consideration that this would force the Africans to come into line with "civilized" behavior, meaning acceptance of the white man culture.

This belief was so strong that by 1903, the colonial government amended the Education Ordinance of 1899 by enacting Ordinance Number 1 of 1903, which specified that African education must be of a simple and practical nature in order to inculcate habits of cleanliness and discipline.[18] Without even waiting to measure the effectiveness of this ordinance, the colonial government amended it four years later by enacting Ordinance Number 133 of 1907. The theoretical rationale that the colonial government used in these amendments is that they represented innovation in the education of the Africans to help them accept the value of what government officials called work ethics. In short, the colonial government was trying to persuade the Africans to accept its argument that the amendments were intended to promote their educational advancement.

That government officials did not address the real purpose of these amendments, to make the African function more effectively as cheap laborers because their education was of a practical and simple nature further created a climate in which the Africans doubted the intentions of the colonial government. Therefore, while the colonial government considered these amendments as innovation designed to improve the skills of the Africans to function as cheap labor, the Africans themselves regarded them as an improvement in the effectiveness of the mechanics of limiting their real educational advancement.

Perhaps what the colonial government considered the best innovation in education was Ordinance Number 7 promulgated in July, 1912, Ordinance to Control Native Education. That this ordinance had far more serious implications than any previous ordinance is demonstrated by the restrictive nature of its provisions. While the colonial government considered this ordinance a means to promote the advancement of the Africans,[19] the effect that it had on the Africans is that it implied serious limitations that meant, in effect, their inability to make any real progress because the ordinance's principal objective was to direct "the director of education to order the closure of any school if he is not satisfied as to the manner in which it is being conducted."[20]

One can see that throughout the colonial period in Zimbabwe, the colonial government claimed that it was doing what it was doing because it was trying to improve education by changing it in order to improve the education of the Africans. If this were true post-colonial Zimbabwe would not have faced the enormous problems that it is facing now.[21] In 1939, Huggins admitted that the educational amendments were "essential if the white students are expected to keep their position of influence in society. Therefore, they will prevent the creation of a poor white

---

[18]Southern Rhodesia: Ordinance Number 1, 1903.

[19]Southern Rhodesia: Ordinance Number 7: Ordinance to Control Native Education, July 12, 1912.

[20]*Ibid.*

[21]Dickson A. Mungazi, "Educational Innovation in Zimbabwe: Possibilities and Problems", in *The Journal of Negro Education*. Vol. 54, No. 1, 1985, pp.196-212.

class."[22] Huggins's statement substantiates the accuracy of the conclusion that whatever the colonial governments claimed to be an innovative action, in African education was, indeed, designed to safeguard the socioeconomic and political interests of the whites or of the colonial governments themselves at the expense of the Africans. One can also see that the theoretical assumptions of the colonial government in Zimbabwe, as elsewhere in Southern Africa, were carefully formulated to conceal their actual intent.

In the Portuguese colonies of Angola and Mozambique what appeared to be a theory of innovation in education came in various ways. For example, the Colonial Act of 1930 was designed to ensure that the Africans received only the rudiments of education in order to ensure their acceptance of the Portuguese culture. The late president of Mozambique, Samora Machel (1933-1986), understood the harmful effect of this line of thinking and action as a result of theoretical assumptions when he wrote, "Claims of educational innovation during the colonial rule was a strategy to sustain the fossilized structure of the African culture."[23] But by relating the educational process to the labor code of 1928, the Portuguese colonial government theorized that the development of manual skills formed an essential component of the educational process for Africans and that this, more than any other forms of education, was essential to their training so as to help them have new perceptions of an emerging social order.[24] It is therefore not surprising that the Portuguese nationals resident in Angola and Mozambique saw this change as an innovation to benefit the Africans. The colonial governments were never without theory of innovation. After the war in 1945, the Portuguese colonial officials felt so secure that they now ventured into new areas of strengthening their own positions by claiming that whatever they did represented innovation.

This is why, in 1948, Antonio Salazar launched what he called the first six-year national developmental program in which he presumably established development priorities. Increased economic productivity, the building of national railways, ports and harbors and improved education for whites, were all high priorities in that so-called plan of national development. Salazar outlined his theoretical reasons for placing the education of the Africans low on his priority list, to emphasize to them his position that self-help was a critical element of their collective development. However, the main objective of Salazar's plan of national development was to make both Angola and Mozambique ideal for Portuguese settlers. Of course, he would not say that openly.

In 1933, to make it look like his government was genuinely trying to promote the advancement of the Africans, Salazar reactivated a colonial policy that had been in place in 1889 as a result of the action of the Berlin Conference of 1884. This was the policy of *Estado Novo* (New State), which divided the Africans into two socioeconomic groups, the *assimilados* and *indigenas*. The assimilados were those Africans who were considered to have adopted Portuguese culture and had sufficient

---

[22]Godfrey Huggins, "Education Policy in Rhodesia: Some Notes on Certain Features," 1939
[23]Samora Machel, *Sowing the Seeds of Revolution*, p. 34.
[24]Dickson A. Mungazi, *To Honor the Sacred Trust of Civilization: History, Politics and Education in Southern Africa*, p. 95.

education to speak the Portuguese language fluently. They were allowed to vote in the quasi elections that were held from time to time. They were allowed to live in exclusive neighborhoods along with Portuguese nationals. But they were expected to live a life-style similar to that of Portuguese nationals and were not allowed to have any relationships with any Africans who were not *assimilados*. This means that as a group assimilados were isolated from their own culture. Although they received preferential treatment in educational and employment opportunity, the *assimilados* became strangers to their own society and culture.

The *indigenas* were those Africans who were poorly educated and so formed the backbone of the labor force needed to sustain the economy. They had no rights of any kind and were not allowed to vote in elections. They were required to carry pass books on their person all the time. The theoretical assumption behind the formulation of the policy of *Estado Novo* was that every African had equal opportunity for development. But one can see that if the policy of *Estado Novo* shows that Salazar was a genius of social change in Angola and Mozambique, one can also conclude that he was at the same time a master-mind of colonial miscalculations and theoretical misconception about African self-consciousness.

When the war of liberation broke out in Angola and Mozambique in 1961, Salazar was shocked to learn that the leadership of the liberation movement came from the ranks of the *assimilados* whom the policy of *Estado Novo* he thought his government designed to isolate from the African masses. It was then that Salazar was forced to reassess his own theory when he acknowledged,

> A law recognizing citizenship takes minutes to draft and can be made right away. But a citizen that is a man fully and consciously integrated into civilized political society takes centuries to achieve.[25]

When Gulf Oil discovered substantial new oil deposits in Angola in 1966, Salazar immediately dispatched troops to protect the area. Hundreds of Africans were evicted with no provision made for their relocation.

When Salazar argued that the education of the Africans would be in the form of employment offered by the oil fields, he was actually stating a new educational policy that their education must be of a practical nature. He saw the involvement of his government limited to the investment of facilities to make practical training and manual labor viable. This was clearly a reversal of his theory. His disappointment with the policy of *Estado Novo*, evident in the ability of the *assimilados* to provide the leadership of the liberations movement, created an entirely new climate which forced him to restrict the education of the Africans to practical training and manual labor. These were the elements of the original policy formulated in 1898. By the time he suffered a massive stroke in 1968, Salazar had, in effect, invested more than a hundred million dollars in the education of Portuguese nationals and less than half

---

[25]*The New York Times,* May 31, 1961.

that amount for African education.[26] The promise of improved educational progress he had made at the beginning of the war in 1939 was never kept.

When, in 1967, Unesco expressed serious concern about the lack of meaningful educational reform in both Angola and Mozambique, the farce of educational innovation that Salazar had hailed as a blueprint of national development and as the envy of other colonial governments in Southern Africa became clearly known. When Salazar argued that his government had increased spending for education from 5.4% in 1964 to 9.5% in 1967, he neglected to mention that the bulk of this increase benefited the white students and the children of a few *assimilados*. The benefit to the average African student was quite negligible. It was only after both Angola and Mozambique had achieved full independence in 1975 that the full extent of the educational malaise became known. Therefore, the concept of educational innovation during the colonial period in Southern Africa was not compatible with the universal purpose of innovation because it was intended to benefit the political and socioeconomic status quo, not to serve the educational development of the Africans. This is quite consistent with the behavior of colonial establishments every where.

In South Africa the purported educational innovation began at the inception of independence in 1910 under the Afrikaners. Prior to that date education had been the responsibility of the church because the South African government had been quite indifferent to the educational development of the Africans other than promoting practical training and manual labor . Because the church wanted the Africans to be able to read and understand religious literature, it offered education to them based on different theoretical assumptions from those used by the government. For this reason the church-related schools became more popular than government schools among the Africans. This explains why, by 1945, there were 4,400 church-related schools compared to only 230 government schools.[27]

From 1910 to 1925 the government was formulating its own theory of African education consistent with its main objective of restricting the political advancement of the Africans. In 1925 it enacted the Native Taxation and Development Act for the presumed purpose of improving African education and general development. The basic theoretical assumption behind this legislation was that the Africans would appreciate their education more when they contributed to its financial outlay. But, by 1935, when the Africans saw no significant improvement in their education, they initiated some self-help projects of their own independent of government control in order to improve their educational endeavors. That the government did not allow the operation of independent organizations in education because it feared the political implications they carried suggests the farce of its theoretical claim that having the Africans play a part in the financial planning of their education would increase their appreciation of it.

Amidst the confusion that was characteristic of African education came charges that the government was failing to innovate African education. In response the

---

[26]Dickson A. Mungazi, *To Honor the Sacred Trust of Civilization: History, Politics and Education in Southern Africa*, p. 29.

[27]Trevor Huddleston, *Naught for Your Comfort*. New York: Oxford University Press, 1956, p. 24.

government named a commission to supposedly investigate the question of African education. When the commission submitted its report in 1936, it made no effort to hide its bias in supporting the policy of the government, saying,

> The education of the white child must prepare him for life in a dominant society and the education of the Native child for a subordinate society. The limits of Native education must form part of the social and economic structure of society.28

That the government was pleased with this report suggests its unwillingness to seek a genuine improvement in African education and advanced a theoretical reason for its policy, saying, "The South African Native does not have the learning ability to be able to compete on equal terms with the average white student, except in tasks of an extremely simple nature."29 It is therefore not surprising that by 1947 new theoretical perspectives were being expressed in an effort to uphold ideas of apartheid when a *National Educational Manifesto* , a private organization made of conservative Afrikaners who unreservedly supported the government of South Africa, issued a statement in that year arguing that, "Education for Natives should be based on the principles of trusteeship, non-equality and segregation. Its aim should be to inculcate the white man's view of life and society."30

Taking these views into consideration, the Nationalist government that was returned to power in the elections of 1948 began to formulate its own educational policy based upon the theoretical assumptions that were emerging among the Afrikaners. When, in 1953, it enacted the Bantu Education Act, it thought that it manifested the notion of innovation, hardly aware that it had placed the country on a deadly explosive device which actually engulfed the country when it exploded in the form of the Soweto uprising of June, 1976, sending political ashes and lava that altered the course of national development. South Africa would no longer be the same.

Peter Molotsi, an eminent South African scholar, concluded that the purported innovation that Bantu Education Act claimed to bring about was a farce, saying:

> Although the Bantu Education Act was hailed by the South African government as an improvement, it was persistently opposed by the African people because it was introduced in the name of reform and innovation. But it soon became apparent that it was actually guided by the bigotry of the Afrikaner Nationalists. The mission and sustained rejection of Bantu Education will render the whole diabolical scheme a self-deceiving exercise and futility, a misguided mission.31

28South Africa: *The Report of the Inter-Departmental Commission on Native Education*, 1936.
29T. A. Jansen van Rensburg, "The Learning Ability of the South African Native," in Nicholas Hans, *Comparative Education and Traditions*. London: Oxford University Press, 1958, p. 35.
30Dennis Herbstein, *White man,We Want to Talk to You*. London: Oxford University Press, 1979, p. 84.
31Peter Molotsi, "The Educational Policy and South African Bantustans," a paper presented at the Africa-Asia-The Americans Conference on Teaching and Research, Empire State Plaza, Albany, New York, October 29-30, 1981. This author attended this conference.

The character of colonial educational innovation in Southern Africa leads to the conclusion that while the colonial establishment based its claim of educational innovation on the theoretical assumptions that meant, in effect, an improvement of white education, it entailed elements of underdevelopment of African education. Therefore what appeared to be an improvement in the educational structure was, indeed, a curtailment of the educational opportunity for the Africans. This situation, therefore, demanded a new approach to the concept of innovation after independence was attained. But for South Africa the agony of underdevelopment through a lack of genuine effort to innovate education continues to take its toll on the development of human resources which it needs for the future. It is not likely that the Afrikaners will see things from an angle different from what they have seen in the past.

Theoretical Considerations of Educational Innovation after the Colonial Period: The Individual and National Development

The attainment of political independence by Namibia on March 21, 1990, meant that of all the countries of Southern Africa only South Africa[32] was still under conditions of colonial forces. The attainment of political independence in Southern Africa also means that a new hope can emerge among the Africans for real progress rooted in the dreams and aspirations that had been eluded by the unwillingness of the colonial governments to do something real in trying to innovate the educational systems to serve the needs of all people. Although the nations of Southern Africa soon recognized that it was relatively easier to fight to bring the colonial systems to an end than to initiate the much needed innovation in education, they also recognized the imperative of such innovation in order to ensure social change consistent with their aspirations. This recognition demanded the formulation of a new approach.

The victory that the Africans had scored in the struggle against the colonial forces now set the stage for a new and more challenging struggle for national development through educational innovation. One sees the evidence to suggest that new theory elements began to emerge as soon as each country in Southern Africa was poised for independence. For example, speaking before the World University Service Conference held in London in December, 1979, at the conclusion of the Lancaster House Conference on the independence of Zimbabwe, Dzingai Mutumbuka, who was soon to be Zimbabwe's minister of education and culture,[33] outlined elements of a new theory that was to guide Zimbabwe in its efforts to innovate its education. In suggesting that the struggle for political liberation entailed two basic components, the place of the individual in society and nature of the society to emerge, Mutumbuka went on to argue:

> It is against this background that a new alternative system of education had been developing along new theoretical considerations designed to produce a new man

---

[32]Azania, as the Africans prefer to call it.

[33]As discussed in Chapter 1 of this study, in 1989, Mutumbuka, along with several other senior government ministers, resigned from the government after the Sandura Commission of Inquiry had implicated him in a major scandal.

richer in consciousness of humanity. This is the only way a new nation can make life better and more meaningful for all.[34]

What Mutumbuka was, in effect, suggesting is that since human action originates from ideas, "human consciousness of humanity" is therefore a product of properly educated and genuinely liberated individual mind. This line of thinking raises a fundamental question regarding a new theory of education in the post-colonial Southern Africa.: What must be the basis and focus of educational innovation? The answer to the first part of the question entails theoretical considerations, and the answer to the second part involves objectives. This demands addressing two essentials of a new theory, the position of the individual in society and the character of society itself.

One sees that emerging nations of the Third World, especially Southern Africa, are increasingly becoming aware that without education to sharpen the individual's consciousness of himself in order to enable him to acquire the skills that he needs to fulfill his own ambitions and aspirations, society itself remains unfulfilled and so underdeveloped. The Education Commission on Botswana of 1977 took this line of thinking to conclude, "The principal aim of education is to ensure the development of the individual. The individual is of unique value to society, and it is only through developing his capacities that society changes, not for change's sake, but to serve the needs of all people and so improve the quality of human life."[35]

One major reason why emerging nations are placing emphasis on having education focus on the development of the individual as a prerequisite of national development is that it enables the individual to play an important role in a collective endeavor to promote the development of society itself. It also helps the individual in defining and understanding what he needs to fulfill himself. Therefore, the importance of the individual in a larger social context has become the focus of educational theory in developing nations because they believe that national development is possible only when individuals in them are fully developed. This perception represents a fundamental change from the theoretical perspective of the colonial governments.

The importance of the educational development of the individual in developing nations as a new theoretical consideration has been addressed in a broader context than Southern Africa. When Paulo Freire of Brazil concludes that all human beings, no matter how oppressed, and so presumed ignorant, are capable of engaging in constructive interaction with other people, he is actually suggesting that without education defined in accordance with the ability of the individual relative to his relationships with other people, society itself pays the ultimate price of underdevelopment.[36] What Freire also seems to suggest is that while the struggle for national liberation entails collective strategies and endeavors, its origin is an

---

[34]Dzingai Mutumbuka, "Zimbabwe: Educational Challenge", paper presented at the World University Services Conference, London, December, 1979. By courtesy of the Zimbabwe National Archives.
[35]Botswana: *Report of the Commission on Education,* 1977, p. 23.
[36]Paulo Freire, *Pedagogy of the Oppressed,* p. 39.

outcome of individual endeavor. Similarly, the outcome of the collective struggle must, by its very nature, afford the individual the opportunity to set individual goals. Therefore, Mutumbuka's concept of a new educational theory to enable the individual to have a "richer consciousness of humanity" corresponds to Freire's theory that any education that fails to respond to the needs of the individual cannot possibly respond to the needs of the nation. If the colonial governments had operated under the premises of this theoretical consideration, an environment would have been created for finding solutions to the problems that developing nations are now grappling with.

Freire is not the only thinker in the Third World to outline theoretical components relative to the educational development of the individual. In a pastoral statement on education, the Catholic Bishops' Conference of Zimbabwe stressed the theoretical perspective that the educational process that does not focus on the needs of the individual has no real meaning to national endeavors.[37] The Catholic Bishops added:

> It is important for Third World nations, especially those of Southern Africa, to recognize that the individual cannot find educational fulfillment without freedom to choose his own course of study. Where there is no clear orientation towards choice in education, educators are like the blind leading the blind. In this kind of setting society itself pays the ultimate price.[38]

What the Catholic Bishops' Conference seems to suggest is that the educational development of the individual is the best way to ensure national development.

The fundamental importance of the educational development of the individual as a new theoretical perspective was expressed to this author by the principal of a high school in Harare in August, 1983, saying:

> Every state stands to benefit more than anyone else from its educated citizens. All governments have therefore a stake in the education of their people as individuals. The more the people are educated, the more they help create a happy society. Progressive governments recognize that by educating their people as individuals, they are actually creating conditions for social and political stability.
>
> Therefore, educational innovation must afford all students freedom to choose their own course of study. This will mean freedom to earn a decent income, to own a home, in essence, self-sufficiency. These are the elements that constitute a foundation upon which a good political and socioeconomic system must be built.[39]

President Robert Mugabe himself took this same line of thinking of theoretical perception of education in the new era when he launched a national literacy campaign in July, 1983, saying:

---

[37]Zimbabwe: Catholic Bishops' Conference, *Our Mission to Teach: A Pastoral Statement on Education*. Gweru. Mambo Press, 1987, p. 6.
[38]*Ibid*. p. 7.
[39]A high school principal during an interview with the author in Harare, Zimbabwe, August 8, 1983

> To set the mind free, to make observation and analysis accurate, to make judgment informed, objective and fair, to make imagination creative, are as important a cause of struggle for individual educational development as the collective struggle for political emancipation. Individual mental emancipation through educational innovation is both the major instrument and modality of political and economic emancipation, and cannot be taken for granted.[40]

This is also the same line of theoretical perception that the late President Machel of Mozambique took into consideration when he argued in 1981 that a theory of educational innovation in post-colonial Southern Africa "must seek to strengthen social institutions by focusing on educational innovation to meet the developmental needs of the individual"[41] as a prerequisite of national development.

The reader must not have a misconception that a new theory of educational innovation in emerging nations of Southern Africa is designed to promote the individual as an end in itself because it is not. This chapter has advanced the argument that the best route to national development is through the development of the individual because only when the individual is able to meet his needs is he able to meet the needs of his society. The Conference of Catholic Bishops in Zimbabwe argued that a theory of educational innovation must seek to make it possible for emerging nations to educate the individual so that he can respond to the needs of his society:

> It is our belief that the individual should be educated to utilize his talents to meet the needs of his society. It is the role of the government to provide education to develop the competencies of each person compatible with the needs of the community as a whole. Conventional wisdom suggests that this cannot be done in the context of existing systems of education. Therefore, educational innovation is the crown jewel of national development because it ensures the development of the individual.[42]

What this perception of theory of educational innovation seems to imply is that the thrust for educational innovation must result from a carefully considered elements that must undergird its essential considerations in terms of both focus and expected outcome.

---

[40]Robert Mugabe, "Literacy for All in Five Years," a speech given in launching National Adult Literacy Campaign, July 18, 1983. Quoted by permission of the Zimbabwe Ministry of Information.

[41]Samora Machel, *Mozambique: Sowing the Seeds of Revolution*. Harare: Zimbabwe Publishing House, 1981, p. 35.

[42]Zimbabwe: The Catholic Bishops' Conference , *Our Mission to Teach: A Pastoral Statement on Education*, p. 7

Summary and Conclusion

The discussion in this chapter had made a clear distinction between the purpose of education during the colonial period and theory of educational innovation in Southern Africa in the post-colonial era. The former stressed the development of the Africans as a group to serve the needs of the colonial status quo. The latter stressed the importance of educational innovation to serve the needs of the individual as a prerequisite of national development. Three basic conclusions arise from differences in theoretical perceptions of the two. First, by emphasizing the importance of sustaining colonial status quo, the colonial governments created a society in which, in the words of Bernard Chidzero, now Zimbabwe's Minister of Finance and Economic Planning, "inequality was the very foundation of its structure underpined and sustained by an inadequate educational system."[43] In this setting education, especially for the Africans, became a mechanical exercise, void of any real meaning for the people whose needs it was intended to serve.

Second, the inadequacy of the educational system during the colonial period has created a critical demand for educational innovation as an imperative condition of national development in post-colonial Southern Africa. This reality has also demanded that nations of Southern Africa formulate new theoretical perspectives on educational innovation to place emphasis on the development of the individual. To approach this task with a faint heart or without a clear focus would harm the very purpose for which innovation must be initiated. The fact of the matter is that nations of Southern Africa cannot afford not to initiate educational innovation because preserving educational status quo would be tantamount to committing a national developmental suicide. Emerging nations which fail to realize the importance of educational innovation also fail to realize the importance of the educational development of the individual submerge their people, and thus, their nations, to perilous depths of underdevelopment.

Third, some Third World nations have yet to realize that educational innovation is meaningless without a corresponding freedom of choice. Freedom to choose is itself an important component of democracy. Because the colonial governments did not allow freedom to choose, they did not practice democracy, contrary to their claim. In emerging nations the recognition of the right of students to choose their course of study consistent with their needs and aspirations must translate into the practice of democracy in society itself. This is the context in which nations of Southern Africa must see the importance of theoretical consideration of initiating educational innovation. In this regard most emerging nations of Southern Africa have still a long way to go, although, however, some have made a good start. In Chapter 4 we discuss the purpose of educational innovation in contemporary Southern Africa and the problems that this critical region encounters in that endeavor.

---

[43]Bernard T. Chidzero, *Education and the Challenge of Independence,* IEUP, Geneva, 1977, p. 13.

educational system."[43] In this setting education, especially for the Africans, became a mechanical exercise, void of any real meaning for the people whose needs it was intended to serve.

Second, the inadequacy of the educational system during the colonial period has created a critical demand for educational innovation as an imperative condition of national development in post-colonial Southern Africa. This reality has also demanded that nations of Southern Africa formulate new theoretical perspectives on educational innovation to place emphasis on the development of the individual. To approach this task with a faint heart or without a clear focus would harm the very purpose for which innovation must be initiated. The fact of the matter is that nations of Southern Africa cannot afford not to initiate educational innovation because preserving educational status quo would be tantamount to committing a national developmental suicide. Emerging nations which fail to realize the importance of educational innovation also fail to realize the importance of the educational development of the individual submerge their people, and thus, their nations, to perilous depths of underdevelopment.

Third, some Third World nations have yet to realize that educational innovation is meaningless without a corresponding freedom of choice. Freedom to choose is itself an important component of democracy. Because the colonial governments did not allow freedom to choose, they did not practice democracy, contrary to their claim. In emerging nations the recognition of the right of students to choose their course of study consistent with their needs and aspirations must translate into the practice of democracy in society itself. This is the context in which nations of Southern Africa must see the importance of theoretical consideration of initiating educational innovation. In this regard most emerging nations of Southern Africa have still a long way to go, although, however, some have made a good start. In Chapter 4 we discuss the purpose of educational innovation in contemporary Southern Africa and the problems that this critical region encounters in that endeavor.

---

[43] Bernard T. Chidzero, *Education and the Challenge of Independence,* IEUP, Geneva, 1977, p. 13.

4
THE PURPOSE OF EDUCATIONAL INNOVATION IN CONTEMPORARY SOUTHERN AFRICA

The purpose of educational innovation in post-colonial Southern Africa must be to accentuate cultural diversity as a national enrichment. Samora Machel, 1970

Social change which is meant to improve the quality of human life is the main purpose of educational innovation. Botswana: Report of the Commission on Education, 1977.

Introduction: The Setting

Chapter 3 concluded that the purported purpose of formulating and implementing the colonial policies of *Estado Novo, evalue, Deutsche Kolonialbund*, and indirect rule was to fulfill the political and socioeconomic interests of the colonial governments themselves, and not to promote the development of the Africans. It has also concluded that the formulation and implementation of these colonial policies were quite compatible with the behavior of colonial establishments everywhere, and that there was nothing unusual in their application to the countries of Southern Africa except in their effect. The restrictive character of education in the colonial setting meant that the Africans were isolated from their own people when they made a concerted effort to secure it.[1] The psychological effects of that isolation were devastating. The Africans educated under these policies failed to identify themselves with either the white community or with the African community.

The Problems of Education in Contemporary Africa

Chapter 3 also concluded that this tragic situation was the outcome of seeking to fulfill the purposes of the colonial governments. This chapter discusses some fundamental purposes of educational innovation in contemporary Southern Africa. Before its does that, the chapter first discusses some educational problems left behind by the policies pursued by the colonial governments to underscore why educational innovation is a critical factor of national and regional development today. Because the colonial governments' educational policies were directed towards fulfilling purposes that were incompatible with the development of the Africans, the

---

[1]Canaan Banana, *Theology of Promise: The Dynamics of Self-Reliance*, p. 53.

educational process itself left a legacy of problems that African nations have not been able to solve.

In a special report on problems of education in Africa issued in October, 1981, *The Chicago Tribune* outlined the following problems as legacy left behind in Africa as a result of the action of the colonial governments in pursuing their purposes: Of every eight teachers in the primary school, six had completed only 9th grade. For every 360 children in the primary school, 200 dropped out before they reached 4th grade, wiping out any literacy they may have acquired. This means that of Africa's 430 million people in 1981, only 11% could read and write.[2]

The economic legacy of the policies pursued by the colonial governments in Africa can also be seen in the financial outlay for education. The average expenditure for education in 1981 was $149.00 per student per year compared with the average for the world of $612.00. With a population growth rate of 3.9% annually this means that in twenty years per pupil expenditure would decline sharply, putting Africa's developmental efforts perilously to the brink of disaster. The lack of financial resources also means that 56.4% of all primary age children actually attended school. But only 20% continued their education to the end of the primary school. An average of nearly 50% of all teachers in the primary school failed to meet the qualification criteria established by their governments. This also means that the teacher:student ratio of 1:45 was among the worst in the world. Because the colonial governments often emphasized practical training for African girls in order to have them serve as domestic servants, a practice emerged among African parents of preferring to send their sons to school, rather girls, in the hope that they would secure a better employment opportunity in industry. As a result girls constituted only 41% of the students in primary school, 37% in secondary school, and 31% in higher education.[3]

When the countries of Africa achieved political independence, they came face to face with the hard realities of these problems. No country has been immune to them. When Zimbabwe achieved independence in April, 1980, it was forced to recruit heavily teachers from other countries. At that time it had an enrollment of 790,000 students, but within one year that enrollment had jumped to 1.82 million students, and Zimbabwe could not produce teachers fast enough to meet the need.[4] In addition to finding a workable solution to this problem, Zimbabwe had to borrow $1.8 billion from the International Monetary Fund (IMF) to expand its educational facilities.[5]

It was soon evident that the $300 million that the government of Zimbabwe had allocated towards education during the first year of independence was insufficient to meet the need. That all countries of Southern Africa went through this experience shows how they were trying to off-set the adverse effect of the colonial legacy. This is why, when Namibia achieved independence in March, 1990, it encountered the same problems that resulted from seven decades of benign neglect

[2]*The Chicago Tribune*, October 1, 1981.
[3]*Ibid.*
[4]Government of Zimbabwe: *Parliamentary Debates,* August 3, 1983
[5]Dickson A. Mungazi, "Educational Innovation in Zimbabwe: Possibilities and Problems," in *The Journal of Negro Education*, Vol.54,No. 4, pp.196-212.

by the government of South Africa which administered it from 1920 to 1990. This chapter discusses five major purposes of educational innovation in Southern Africa. These are: socioeconomic, literary, political, cultural and technological. A discussion of each and how its influence is felt on the need for educational innovation follows.

Economic Development as a Purpose of Educational Innovation

The importance of economic development in developing countries must be discussed in the context of its relation to the purpose of educational innovation. The reality that the colonial governments used the education of the Africans to strengthen their own socioeconomic and political positions indicates why independent countries of Southern Africa must state their own purposes of educational innovation to guide their developmental efforts. The fact of the matter is that stating new purposes can only be done when educational innovation is initiated. Developed nations have wrestled with the question of what to develop first, the economy or education. For Third World nations this is a question of what came first, the chicken or the egg because conditions compel them to recognize that without the one the other cannot take place.

During the colonial period, the Africans who received some form of Western education regarded it as a way of escaping the scourge of deprivation and poverty. They came to realize that success in life, whatever definition it implied, came only by achieving success in education as defined by the colonial governments themselves. For Africans to function as teachers, preachers, messengers, domestic servants was, in essence, an escape from poverty because they were considered to have achieved success in education. Therefore, economic success and educational success could not be separated. The obsession of the colonial governments with the notion of practical training and manual labor as the only viable form of education for Africans, translated into a policy of economic deprivation. This is the context in which George Stark, director of native education in colonial Zimbabwe from 1934 to 1954, argued in 1940, "A Native who has completed a course of study in practical training is not as efficient as a European[6] artisan."[7]

In contemporary Southern Africa, the economic purpose of educational innovation must entail considerations that are critical to developing a viable economic system. The introduction of a less restrictive, and, thus, a more productive economy, would demand a skilled manpower. This will create difficulties in calculating the effect of a better educational preparation, but it is an endeavor African nations must undertake in the context of educational innovation in order to have parallel development of the economy and education itself. It is not in the best interest of the African nations to rank-order the two. Each is vitally critical to the

---

[6]As it was used in colonial Africa, the term *European* meant any one of European origin.

[7]George Stark, Director of Native Education in colonial Zimbabwe, 1934-1954, in *Southern Rhodesia: The Annual Report of the Director of Native Education,* 1940. p.15 For detailed discussion of Stark's philosophy of education for Africans, see Dickson A. Mungazi, "To B ind Ties Between the School and Tribal Life: Educational Policy for Africans under George Stark in Zimbabwe, in *The Journal of Negro Education.* Vol.58,No. 4 Fall, 1989.

development of the other. Experience in developed countries seems to suggest that educational innovation is best achieved in the context of increase in economic production, which is only possible with better trained people who run it.

Another fundamental economic consideration of educational innovation must, by necessity be diversifying the economy so that it can be sustained should its mainstay be disrupted, such as the production of copper in Zambia and Zaire, agriculture in Mozambique, chromium ore in Zimbabwe, natural gas as in Angola. Because agriculture is critical to sustaining the economy in general, African nations must guard its development carefully because it determines both the pace and direction of national development.[8] In this respect SADDC can play a crucial role in the development of a regional economy so that there is a regional approach to a critical problem. This strategy would ensure that prices are stable, inflation controlled, competition from more developed nations has a promotional effect, and that currency devaluation is more effectively controlled. The present system of international trade in which Third World nations owe billions of dollars in interests to loans reduces the ability of African nations to set new economic goals and to establish national developmental programs. The combination of educational innovation and regional economic planning would enable the Africans to accept the challenges of national development in a more manageable fashion.

Among the essential components of the economic purpose of educational innovation is to build an economy that creates new employment opportunity. George Psacharopoulos concludes that the higher the rate of unemployment a country experiences, the less its rate of economic development.[9] To reduce the chances of that happening, nations of Southern Africa must broaden the base of their economic development so that as many people as possible are employed. Unemployment undercuts a national effort to initiate effective planning for the future. It also reduces the best national resources, people, to the level of mere existence. It also destroys national morale and weakens a national resolve to build infrastructure that are essential to national development. This is what George Psacharopoulos means when he argues, "When unemployment occurs between graduation from school and the first attempt to secure a employment, it is often misinterpreted as inefficiency of the school system itself to produce graduates needed to sustain the needs of the national economy."[10] This misinterpretation of the role of the school in strengthening the national economy arises from an effort to rank-order the two.

Therefore, under the error of rank-ordering economic development and educational innovation both education and the economy are hurt. Central to this reality is that Third World nations must observe the concept of free enterprise, the rush to nationalize the economy hurts the purpose for which educational innovation must be initiated. The fact of the matter is that a country is far more secure when its citizens are economically secure. This should become one of the major objectives of

---

[8]George Psacharopoulos, *Higher Education in Developing Countries. A Cost benefit Analysis.* Washington, D.C. World Bank, 1980, p. 19
[9]*Ibid.* p, 46.
[10]*Ibid.* p. 48.

governments every where. Corruption by government officials must be regarded as a cancer that destroys the vital parts of nation's life and must never be allowed.

An important consideration of the economic purpose of educational innovation all developing nations must take into account in relating it to efforts towards national economic development is that all citizens must be allowed the human dignity of earning a decent income in order to allow them a reasonably good standard of living. This allows them to own their own homes and enables them to provide their families a decent standard of living. This is a prerequisite of self-pride or self-actualization so critical to national development and stability. Any government that is based on stratified socioeconomic structures is bound to lose something important in its endeavor to anchor the country on a sound economic and political foundation. This is how a fragile economy threatens the very basis of the government's own survival. Decent income, decent conditions of living, and freedom of choice combine to produce ideal conditions of a happy society. These in turn constitute elements required to make educational innovation relevant to national effort to ensure socioeconomic development.

Another critical consideration of the economic purpose of educational innovation is the importance of sustaining public health. The health of the citizens is a critical factor of national development. The increase in the slums or, as they are called in Africa, *shanty towns,* the increasing number of the unemployed and the homeless, the increase in differences in the standard of living between people in the rural areas and those in the urban areas, must form a major national objective to resolve if economic development and educational innovation are to combine to give the nation a distinctive purposeful direction. It is in the best interest of the governments themselves to ensure that national resources are directed towards improving the health of the people.

Malnutrition, malaria, measles, and other diseases that are common in places where sanitation, water supply and preservation of food are inadequate, rob nations of Africa of the best national resources they need for development, the people. Among the things that governments must do to ensure good health of the people are: to provide health education, to teach people proper nutrition, to create recreational facilities, to teach people how to preserve food,to provide child care and to establish educational clinics where information on food and health are readily available. This creates a national climate in which educational innovation takes on powerful and more meaningful dimensions. This climate also helps generate a national feeling among citizens that their government is interested in cooperating with them in their effort to secure an education that is pertinent to their needs.

Literacy as a Purpose of Educational Innovation

Experience in developed countries shows that the success of education lies in what is known as the basics: reading, writing, and arithmetic. There is no reason to think that developing nations do not wish to see the same for their own people. These universal elements of education have been recognized world-wide as fundamental tenets of national development. If anything at all, they are far more critical to Third World nations today than to developed nations because they are struggling for development. Therefore, concern for educational innovation in Southern Africa must, by the nature of its form, extend far beyond school enrollment. In a much larger context, all countries of Southern Africa are encountering serious problems in their national developmental efforts because illiteracy is also rising at a disturbing rate.[11]

Literacy is also important to national endeavors in that it must come first in any national educational programs. Literacy is the touchstone that opens the door to an opportunity to other areas of human enterprise. Without literacy there is no escape for both the individual and the nation itself from the oppression of the tentacles of an old and vicious octopus, ignorance. President Mugabe recognized this fact when he launched a national literacy campaign in July, 1983, and acknowledged the critical nature of literacy as a means to self-fulfillment by both the individual and the nation. Paulo Freire suggests that self-consciousness itself invokes in the individual an ability to think critically and "the ability to communicate ideas consistent with the essence of being human."[12] In this context educational innovation acquires a compelling influence to place the individual on the level of human effort that every person in society is entitled to.

Unlike political liberation, literacy makes possible the liberation of the human mind as an absolute necessity for the creation of a socioeconomic environment for the educational process itself to serve its intended purpose. This is the setting that makes self-determination, that indispensable human quality needed to distinguish man from other living species. It enables one to set goals, to establish priorities and to design strategies to fulfill them. Ndabaningi Sithole,veteran nationalist thinker and political activist, recognized the importance of literacy and equated it with the universal definition of education and what it does for the individual.

> Education provides the individual who has certain feelings and thoughts with a mechanism of articulation and self-expression. Before one acquires basic literacy it is impossible for one to articulate sufficiently what one wants to communicate. Literacy translates into education which gives one a wide scope, a depth to one's thinking. It provides one a comprehensive grasp of who one really is, and the problems that one faces. Adjustment to a new social environment is virtually impossible without literacy. Innovation in the educational system must seek to accomplish literacy as a basic component of its purpose.[13]

There are two basic elements that must be understood as forming the core of the importance of literacy as an outcome of educational innovation in Southern Africa to ensure self-determination. The first is that an enlightened and genuinely liberated nation can only emerge from enlightened individuals. Many nations of Africa have yet to come to grips with this reality. Without enlightened citizens a nation will always be oppressed by a combination of forces such as social ills, racial or ethnic bigotry, tribal conflict, political dissension. In short, illiterate individuals cannot

---

[11]*World Almanac and Book of Facts,* 1990.
[12]Paulo Freire, *Pedagogy of the Oppressed,* p. 62.
[13]Ndabaningi Sithole, during an interview with the author in Harare, Zimbabwe, July 22, 1983.

build an enlightened nation. Illiteracy is a harmful colonial legacy that all countries of Southern Africa have not yet been able to eliminate, suggesting that educational innovation is an imperative for it. The fact that the colonial governments were interested in literacy among the Africans only as a means of improving their labor capacity suggests the reason why nations of Southern African must make a greater effort to provide basic literacy to their people.The table on the following page illustrates the accuracy of this confusion:

The second element is that all governments of Southern Africa must recognize that basic literacy is a right that belongs to all citizens and must therefore endeavor to direct their energies and national resources to the full development of the human potential that is so critical to national development. This must be undertaken in the full knowledge that ultimately it is the nation that will benefit from the development of the people. To emphasize this line of thinking, Mugabe rhetorically asked, "How can a farmer improve his farming if he cannot read instructions on the use of fertilizers?

The Question is: How can the people themselves run their own factories and shops if they cannot count their money and write their budgets?"[14] What Mugabe was implying is that citizens who provide sufficient food and run their own affairs will provide the essential elements of a happy, thus, stable society. Experience in other countries show that governments are secure only when their people are secure. This means that unlike the colonial governments the independent governments of Southern Africa become the major beneficiaries to the life insurance policy that the people, through literacy, can guarantee by a favorable response to government policy designed to ensure their own advancement.

In launching a literacy campaign Mugabe was aware that the inability of the citizens to develop their mental capacity perpetuates oppression of the nation itself because ignorance of the ideas expressed by others and inability to communicate create a condition of exploitation. This was a situation created by the colonial educational policy, which the governments of Southern Africa must now seek to eliminate. This is why Mugabe concluded,"It was therefore not by accident that the white settler regimes of our colonial past denied the majority of the African people the opportunity of going to school."[15] It is for this reason that Mugabe acknowledged the fact that the campaign for literacy was not aimed merely at some illiterate people, but at all adults outside the formal educational process.

Therefore, nations of Southern Africa must recognize that basic literacy is a major objective of educational innovation, and that it has benefit to the nation because it has benefit to individuals. The reality of this situation must translate into an imperative of a realization that universal basic education must become a new reality in all of Southern Africa and that there should be no reason why all children should not receive it. Achieving this fundamental objective must become a major commitment and a national challenge understood by those who are charged with

---

[14]Robert Mugabe, "Literacy for All in Five Years." July 18, 1983.
[15]*Ibid.*

the responsibility of planning and implementing educational programs to ensure its innovation.

Literacy Rate in Southern Africa: 1983 and 1990 Compared

	1983		1990	
Country	% of 5-19 pop.in school	Literacy % in school	% of pop	Literacy %
Angola	28	12	30	30
Botswana	56	30	35	61
Mozambique	20	20	14	25
Namibia	-	15	13	40
South Africa	55	98 white	99 white	
		55 black	50 black	71
Tanzania	60	60	85	89
Zaire	40	40	55	62
Zambia	50	50	54	75
Zimbabwe	37	30	50	78

Source: *World Almanac and Book of Facts*, 1983 and 1990

Political Integration and National Unity as Purposes of Educational Innovation

The fact that the colonial governments did not practice democracy in Africa because they argued that the Africans were not educated sufficiently enough to understand its complex process must dictate a fundamental change in both the political process and the educational system. Central to this reality is the fact that if the colonial governments believed that the lack of educational opportunity inhibited the political ability of the Africans, then why did they not do something to change the situation? Realizing that this line of thinking was not in the scheme of things of the colonial governments is precisely why African nations must initiate an educational innovation to realize the importance of political integration and national unity as critical factors of national development.

A conclusion was drawn earlier in this chapter that economic development and literacy must benefit the individual before they can benefit society itself. In the same way, educational innovation intended to realize some political objectives must first be directed at improving the position of the individual in society as a supreme political being. But the process of becoming supreme political being demands an education that is comprehensive to enable the students to grasp the essential components of a political society.

A. R. Thompson argues that in order to serve the needs of the people in a way it was intended to do, education must not be removed from focusing on political interests of the individual first and then of society as a whole.[16] When he goes on to argue that national governments "must recognize that the growing scale and complexity of educational planning must be met largely from the public purse and must therefore be subject to political accountability,"[17] Thompson is actually suggesting that educational innovation must be directed towards political integration and national unity. One must therefore ask the question: What do political integration and national unity mean?

Thompson argues that it has been recognized that in Southern Africa education and politics have remained as distant apart as they were during the colonial period because of an inherent unwillingness to acknowledge their interdependence. The proper thing to do for developing nations is to formulate national policies which seek to bring education and politics together in a productive manner. To that fundamental objective change in the educational system is essential. It would enable all people to view the political process from a perspective of a healthy activity intended to ensure national development. This kind of setting creates a new social environment that enables citizens to develop a collective political identity which suggests that although they hold different political views and belong to different political parties, as they must to sustain democratic principles, they would still subscribe to a common national endeavor to sustain a national pasture and political goals compatible with commonly held national values. In essence these are the elements that constitutes a definition of political integration and national unity.

The important thing to remember is that once these elements are in place, they would provide all citizens an opportunity to appreciate the fact that political diversity and freedom of expression are sacred principles that must be preserved at all times, and that this cannot be done through maintaining status quo in education. This is why Thompson suggests that the pursuit of national goals in terms of political integration and national unity can best be done through innovation in education because, he goes on to conclude, "Schools are the principal instrument through which individuals take up positions of leadership within their society."[18]

One must therefore conclude that African nations have a solemn duty, not only to preserve democracy, but also to ensure that it is never threatened. The system of one-party rule or president for life that some African nations have adopted is a sure recipe for national disaster. It is important for government leaders to recognize that no citizen, from the president to the average citizen, is above the law. Educational innovation intended to offer basic courses in civics or political studies would underscore the importance of respecting the law among all people. But when law is dictated from a president who holds office for life, it serves as an instrument of

---

[16]A. R. Thompson, *Education and Development in Africa*. New York: St. Martin Press, 1981, p. 47.
[17]*Ibid*. p. 48
[18]*Ibid*. p. 49.

oppression and the citizens have a right to demand a fundamental change in the government itself.

The recognition that law must result from a democratic process is the reason why it is important to initiate educational innovation along similar lines to ensure compatibility of the two. This is how basic human and political values are sustained. The inclusion of civics and political studies into the educational system will remind all the people the calling of a president for life or the one-party rule by any name does not really conceal its true dictatorial character.

In normal practice educational systems tend to seek the sustenance of socioeconomic and political systems because they are designed to operate as instruments of distributing rewards to individuals, But, because developing nations cannot afford to maintain outdated systems, an endeavor for educational innovation must inculcate in all students the principle of equal opportunity as a basic component of political integration and national unity and enables them to rise up to the top rung of the political ladder and make a viable contribution to the development of their country.

A disturbing practice has been emerging in Southern Africa in recent years. Those leaders who were in the forefront of the struggle for political independence assume that they only have the right to form exclusive political clubs which become intolerant of change or a more inclusive political structure once they are in the seat of government. They therefore regard their experience in the independence movement as a badge of honor and consider any one who has not been directly involved in the struggle less patriotic and so less qualified to run for political office. In this way some African governments oppress their own people far more severely than the colonial governments which they replaced.

The reality of the fact is that flexibility in educational innovation will mean a corresponding flexibility in the political process. It is important for the nations of Southern Africa to recognize that a more inclusive political system based on diverse political ideology is the cornerstone of a truly democratic state. The system of political patronage and conditions of offering political benefits only to party members or their admission to the party on the assumption that the governing party enjoys an exclusive support of all the people is an illusion that robs nations of Southern Africa of a vital element of their developmental efforts. The conclusion that educational innovation must parallel political inclusiveness and diversity must become an operative principle or an article of faith in all national endeavors.

It can be seen that if educational innovation is designed to ensure political integration and national unity, then those who design it must first define the kind of society that a political system must seek to create. In the same way the educational system that emerges as a result of innovation must endeavor to define the kind of political skills the students need to acquire in order to play a role in effecting political integration and national unity. In no way must the school teach students the notion that definition of political values and formulating plans for change to envisage a future different from the past is the exclusive power or right of the government. Rather, they must be taught to recognize the importance of collective action and responsibility. This is one viable definition of political integration and national unity.

Unlike the political thought process of the colonial period, in contemporary Southern Africa, political integration and national unity must make it possible for all to understand the essential nature of sustaining distinct two-party political structure.

It is also important to recognize political integration and national unity as objects of educational innovation do not demand a blind acceptance of the existing political system or loyalty to the ruling party. Rather, they encourage the concept of political diversity to allow all citizens to examine all possible political options before they cast their ballots in elections, both local and national. This process is so important that it must not be left to chance, but should form a major component of the educational system itself. It is for this reason that educational innovation that takes this into account becomes a critical factor of national development.

Therefore, participation in the political process as a product of the educational process ensures the stability of society because it extends to the individual a sense of belonging. The elections held in Namibia in November, 1989 stand out as an example of the applicability of this critical concept. Nations of Southern Africa must also realize that participation in the political process cannot be isolated from participation in the educational process. The principle of participatory democracy must operate in both the educational process and the political process to ensure political integration and national unity. While education may not enable the nation to find solutions to all its problems, it helps create an environment in which solutions can be found.

It is quite clear that if education is expected to equip citizens with political skills so that they can function effectively in their society, it cannot do so in its existing form. This suggests that it must be broad enough to enable students to make a thrust to determine precisely the nature and the extent of their involvement in political decisions that have to be made for the benefit of all. Educational innovation, therefore, must seek to broaden the range of human talent and potential in order to inculcate in all students, not passive or conforming frame of mind or social norms, but to adopt creative and imaginative attitudes that are essential to making continuous effort to improve the conditions under which people live. Julius Nyerere of Tanzania took this line of thinking when he said in 1974, "Africa needs change to ensure its development. Innovation in education must be the starting point towards meaningful social change, not for change's sake, but in order to improve the quality of human life."[19]

Samora Machel, arguing that because both political leadership and national responsibility must, by their very nature, be collective, it is the responsibility of those in government to ensure that all citizens receive an education that enables them to participate in both. Machel then goes on to add:

> We must never think of man as a form of automation who must receive and carry out orders irrespective of whether he understands them or has assimilated them. Leaders must fight against the harmful tendency of seeking solutions to political problems through administrative decisions arbitrarily imposed on the people. This tendency leads to a bureaucratic dictatorship and creates sharp contradictions with

[19]Julius Nyerere, during a speech to the Dag Hammerskjold conference, in Dar es Salaam, May 20, 1974.

the rank and file. To avoid this tendency, national educational system must embrace the concept of change to allow a greater degree of participation in the political process.[20]

There is no doubt that Machel was suggesting that participation in the political process must be regarded as one of the best ways of increasing political integration and national unity and that educational innovation could help facilitate the process. This is why he called for a new form of education, saying:

> In our children 's future we as a struggling people have three decisive tasks. The first is to educate the new generation and to instill a new way of thinking which will make true champions of the revolution. The second is to teach students so that they master science and become agents of the transformation of society. The third is to educate all people to accept women as equal partners in the struggle for national advancement.[21]

Conventional wisdom suggests that these three goals constitute an important dimension of the political purpose of educational innovation.

Cultural Diversity as a Purpose of Educational Innovation

If there is a part of the world that must recognize the importance of cultural diversity as a national enrichment, it is Africa. Some leaders of African nations fail to realize that existence of many ethnic groups creates a national variety than can only act as a spice of national life. Many of them, instead, regard cultural diversity as a threat to their own definition of national unity and their own political power. It is true that members of a cultural or ethnic minority group create an inner circle whose ideas may be considered incompatible with national policies. It is also true that the preponderance of ethnic groups in Southern Africa creates a situation in which members of an ethnic group consider themselves loyal to it before they consider themselves members of the country in which they live. This often creates a conflict situation between the group and the government.

For better understanding one must discuss this serious problem of national development in Southern Africa in the context of the policies adopted by the colonial governments. In practicing the policy of *divide and rule*, the colonial governments devised a strategy which they used to conclude that some ethnic groups were better than others. For example, in South Africa, the government portrayed the Zulus as better than the Xhosas. In colonial Zimbabwe, the government told the Shonas that they were better than the Ndebeles. In Zambia the Bembas were considered better than the Lozi. It was this cultural and colonial setting that allowed the colonial governments to provide some education to different ethnic groups in different ways.

This colonial practice of the policy of *divide and rule* was so pervasive in Southern Africa that some ethnic groups were set against others, Violent clashes

---

[20]Samora Machel, "Leadership is Collective, Responsibility is Collective", a speech given to the Joint Meeting of Frelimo Instructors, February 2, 1972. Courtesy of Mozambique Ministry of Information.
[21]*Ibid.*

between different ethnic groups, such as those that took place in the mining compounds in South Africa beginning in 1936, would play into the hands of the colonial officials as they exploited cultural and ethnic differences to conclude that the Africans were uncivilized. The competition and the climate of conflict that the South African government often created between different ethnic groups did not help the Africans in resolving the problems created by the colonial governments. In South Africa the government's secret involvement in promoting violence between different ethnic groups has created a situation that is close to a major national disaster.

Indeed, it is not by coincidence that since the release of Nelson Mandela from prison on February 11, 1990, Inkatha, a Zulu political and cultural group led by Chief Mangosuthu Buthelezi, intensified its fighting against the supporters of the United Democratic Front (UDF), which supported African National Congress (ANC) which Mandela, who is Xhosa, leads. That Buthelezi and the South African government hold periodic consultations indicates the extent of its involvement in the renewed fighting, which, by the end of March, 1990, had cost 2,500 lives.[22] That on April 1, 1990, Buthelezi blamed ANC for the violence, instead of the continuation of apartheid, and the fact that he and Adrian Vlok, the South African Minister of Law and Order, held secret talks on the situation, suggests the tragic outcome of the South African government's strategy to apply the old principle of *divide and rule* to new settings. The fact that the fighting was mainly between rivalry members of the same Zulu group did not mean anything to both Buthelezi and the government of South Africa. One must therefore conclude that although, by 1990, the government of South Africa did not openly accuse ANC of the violence, it had not abandoned its secret involvement in promoting violence between different ethnic groups and the application of the colonial principle of *divide and rule.*

What came out of the application of the colonial educational policy is what Canaan Banana of Zimbabwe calls *culture of poverty.*[23] This means that the colonial governments repeatedly belittled and discredited African culture to the extent that the Africans' self-image was reduced to the level where it had no meaning in their life. This was done in order to serve the purposes of the colonial governments themselves. Translated into the kind of relationships that emerged between the Africans and the colonial government as a result of this strategy and between the educational process and the concept of cultural diversity, the colonial purpose of putting ethnic differences into the educational system created socioeconomic and psychological conditions which inhibited the ability of the Africans to function in a larger social order.

Therefore, one can see that this resulting situation was, in reality, a colonial cultural imposition. It was by clear intention that the problems of education in the colonial setting were, in themselves, a mirror of cultural domination and alienation so effectively put in place for the sole purpose of controlling the Africans and reducing the influence of their culture in their endeavors towards development so that they were educated to fulfill the larger purpose of the colonial culture. It was

---

[22]*The New York Times,* April 1, 1990, p. 4.

[23]Canaan Banana, *Theology of Promise: The Dynamics of Self-reliance,* p. 34.

therefore the intent of the colonial governments to utilize its system of education as the principal instrument of ensuring their cultural supremacy. Dzingai Mutumbuka has argued that "The colonial condition of cultural domination and alienation as a consequence of colonial domination was also a consequence of economic, political, and educational domination."[24]

What Mutumbuka said must not be regarded as flogging a dead horse, but a critical appraisal of all relevant aspects of the past in order to chart a new course to the future. Therefore, when Mutumbuka calls on all nations of Southern Africa to re-direct their efforts towards educational innovation to restore their cultural heritage and pride,[25] he is, in effect, suggesting the emergence of an entirely new dimension of cultural diversity as a purpose of educational innovation.

One must search for a wider perspective from which to understand the concept of cultural diversity as a purpose of educational innovation in Southern Africa. When Paul Freire concludes that efforts of the oppressed to restore their belittled culture constitute an essential step towards self-rediscovery,[26] he is suggesting that the educational process must be divorced from the culture of the oppressor. For nations of Southern Africa this suggests establishing a new purpose of cultural enrichment as an outcome of a new educational process in a new socioeconomic and political order. Samora Machel suggests about the importance of this line of thinking when he says that cultural rediscovery creates a new social ideology formulated in the context of new conditions and promoted by a new system of education in order to strengthen it.[27]

The recognition of the importance of cultural rediscovery suggests that for Southern Africa as a region redefining cultural values as a purpose of educational innovation has an importance that cannot be taken for granted. It entails the transformation of values to students at the primary school level that are of rudimentary nature but are critical to the wider application of life-style in a multi-ethnic society. It is here where education plays an important role in teaching students early in life the spirit of cultural tolerance and acceptance, not of division and conflict, as was the case during the colonial period. Once students are taught early to eliminate cultural prejudice, they will see all human beings, not as members of distinct ethnic groups with stereotypes so characteristics of the colonial period, but as members of an embracing human family. Once this objective has been accomplished, tribal or ethnic conflicts that paralyze national efforts towards advancement will also be eliminated.

Beyond solving the problems of human conflict, placing cultural acceptance and diversity extends to all the people a sense of confidence in themselves and the national leaders as they are made to believe that the notion of superior-inferior complex had no place in the new social system. When education emphasizes the national character of a plural cultural enrichment, no ethnic group is threatened, and

[24]Dzingai Mutumbuka, "Zimbabwe's Educational Challenge," December, 1979.
[25]*Ibid.*
[26]Paulo Freire, *Pedagogy of the Oppressed*, p. 33.
[27]Samora Machel, The Liberation of Women as a Fundamental Necessity for Revolution, an opening address to the First Conference of Mozambique Women, March 4, 1973.

5

CONDITIONS OF EDUCATIONAL INNOVATION

The introduction of free and universal primary education must form a basic condition which must direct our efforts to improve the educational system. Kenneth Kaunda, 1979

Introduction: Conditions of Educational Innovation

In an address to the nation on December 31, 1980, President Robert Mugabe of Zimbabwe outlined some conditions under which his government would undertake to improve education, saying:

> The envisaged educational program will be designed to absorb every child completing his primary education into secondary school. Because of the shortage of secondary school teachers, a recruitment drive for this category of teachers is being carried out by the Ministry of Education overseas and elsewhere in Africa.[1]

Two critical conditions are important to making efforts to bring about innovation in education in Southern Africa. These are: the right to every student to schooling, and the availability of facilities, including teachers. Mugabe must have been aware that educational innovation does not necessarily occur when these two conditions are met because there are other important conditions that must be fulfilled as well before a country can have innovation.

In this chapter six important conditions that must be fulfilled in order to have educational innovation consistent with national goals and objectives are presented. These are: the influence of history, theoretical assumptions, educational objectives, population projection, economic development and the need to eliminate inadequacies in the existing system of education. A discussion of these conditions must not lead to the conclusion that they are the only ones essential to educational innovation, but should suggest that they are among the most important.

---

[1]Zimbabwe, *President's End of the Year Message to the Nation: Policy Statement Number 2,* December 31, 1980. By courtesy of the Zimbabwe Ministry of Information.

The Influence of History as a Condition of Educational Innovation

Among the conditions that nations of Southern Africa must observe as essential to educational innovation is the influence of history. It has been noted that the idea of universal primary education has a national appeal to the Africans because they see it as basic to all forms of national development. When Ian Smith, the last colonial leader of Zimbabwe, told this author during an interview in 1983, "We knew that there was a gap between African education and white education. This was not due to anything that we did, this was part of our history,"[2] it was clear that he was trying to place blame on history for the inadequacy of the educational policy of his own government.

That Smith's government, by the outbreak of the war of independence in April, 1966,[3] was spending $206.00 per white student compared to $18.00 per African student,[4] suggests the strength of historical influence. This was one tragic outcome of the educational policies of the colonial governments in Southern Africa, they were designed not to reflect the need of change in the conditions of the existing systems of education, but to provide a continuum that was in effect, incompatible with the needs of all the people. Needless to say, the educational policy of the Smith government became a major contributing cause of the war of independence.

What Smith said about the influence of history on educational policy was not an isolated example, but an established practice among colonial officials. For example, after establishing an administrative system at the Cape in 1652, the Dutch East India Company ordered Jan van Riebeeck to open schools for both white children and children of slaves imported from the Indian sub-continent. By 1658 Riebeeck had formulated a policy which provided for segregation, not only in the educational process, but also in the curriculum itself.[5] Therefore, the policy of apartheid had its origins in these developments.

That the education of slaves was designed to make them more efficient laborers indicates its oppressive character. This is why many of them ran away forcing many schools for Africans to close down.[6] The fact that slaves were oppressed created an awareness, a knowledge of the necessity to reject a system of education that was oppressive. By the nineteenth century, however, when the imposition of educational conditions destroyed African cultural traditional socioeconomic system, the Africans were forced to seek low paying employment opportunity in order to escape from economic deprivation.

Therefore, a new start was made to provide the kind of education that would enable them to function as slaves. The end of slavery did not bring an end to segregated education. In other words, there was a significant improvement in the

---

[2]Ian Smith, during an interview with the author, in Harare, Zimbabwe, July 22, 1983.
[3]Smith himself told the author that the war actually started in 1962. But recorded evidence seems to point to April , 1966, as the actual time it started.
[4]Dickson A. Mungazi, "Educational Innovation in Zimbabwe: Possibilities and Problems," in *The Journal of Negro Education*, Vol. 54, No. 2, 1985, p. 198.
[5]Kathy Bond-Stewart, *Education in Southern Africa*. Gweru: Mambo Press, 1986, p. 15.
[6]*Ibid.* p. 16.

kind of education the Africans received. This is why from time to time African students protested and boycotted schools. Its character was essentially the same as it was during slavery, it stressed manual labor as a viable form of education. But the Africans wanted something substantially more. This is how the seeds of conflict between the Africans and the colonial systems were sown.

That the Bantu Education Act of 1953 entrenched the oppressive elements that were in place since 1658 created a new situation that did not permit either a new reappraisal or a new approach to the educational process. Indeed, the Bantu Education Act of 1953 was, in itself, a product of the influence of history. This means that it would be amended or reformed only in the context of the influence of history. This is why Hendrik Verwoerd (1901-1966), then Administrator of Bantu Affairs Administration, argued in 1957, "I will reform the Bantu Education Act so that Natives will be taught from childhood that equality with whites is not for them."[7] This is the same line of thinking that Riebeeck had used in 1658 to introduce segregation in education. Verwoerd's argument is precisely the same line of thinking that his successor, John Vorster, used to amend the Bantu Education Act in 1975. This amendment led to the uprising in Soweto in 1976 and violent demonstrations in Cape Town in 1990. There is no question that one of F. W. de Klerk's major tasks is to find a formula for educational innovation to create a new system that will avert further disaster in South Africa. In order to do that de Klerk must overcome the influence of history.

The colonization of Namibia by Germany in 1885 led to fears that if Africans were educated in the same way as whites they would demand equal rights in society. The end of the German colonial rule in 1915 transferred the responsibility for education to South Africa. The meeting between government officials of South Africa and church leaders in 1926 resulted in a partnership between the two institutions so that the church would operate the schools and the governments would provide both financial support and curricular requirements. The introduction of the provisions of Bantu Education Act in Namibia in 1955 altered the character of education and the development of the Africans was now in accordance with the requirements of apartheid itself. It is not surprising that by the time that Namibia achieved political independence on March 21, 1990, it needed a crash educational program to bring about much needed improvement, not only in education, but also the character of society itself.

In the Portuguese colonies of Angola and Mozambique, the reactivation and implementation of the policy of *Estado Novo* created a historical condition that, by 1961, bonded Portugal to its past and left a legacy for the future that made it hard for Africans at the time of independence in 1975 to have a clear sense of a new direction to take. As a result, both Angola and Mozambique have endured the scourge of underdevelopment more than any other countries in Southern Africa. In 1967 Samora Machel concluded that because for three hundred years Portugal had a system of education that was designed to preserve the colonial status quo, independent Mozambique must make a new thrust to change its educational system

---

[7]*Ibid.*

so that national development can take place. He went on further to argue that any strategy that any country in Southern Africa may adopt to ensure educational innovation must first seek to eliminate the influence of history.[8] The attempt by Portugal to use *Estado Novo* to integrate some Africans into Portuguese culture, rather than to create a new society in an African cultural setting, furnishes clear evidence to show that Portugal utilized the influence of history in designing its policy for the future. How would educational innovation occur if it was initiated under the weight of this negative influence of history?

The failure of the Portuguese colonial government to alter the influence of history as a factor of education so that it would have universal meaning for the future is why, by 1950, it became a major topic of discussion among members of the international community. In that year Unesco estimated that less than 40,000 Africans in Angola had attained the status of *assimilados*, yet less than 3% of the entire population had acquired basic literacy.[9] Samora Machel recognized the harmful effect of this influence of history when he argued in 1970 during the height of the struggle for independence, saying, "A study of history enables us to understand that the main battle is against illiteracy. Without the active participation of the masses in the battle against illiteracy it will not be possible to wipe it out because we are victims of history."[10]

What Machel seems to suggest is that the influence of history often has two possible effects. First, it retards the course of change and so fails to promote it. The reality that society is never constant was not a hallmark of vision and foresight of colonial establishments. Instead, it was a factor that the colonial governments seemed to struggle against. Second, in the context of the colonial conditions, the only possible outcome of the influence of history was to strengthen the colonial status quo. Therefore, change in those conditions to accommodate the aspirations of the Africans was also not possible because the influence of history was so strong that it would not permit the colonial society to see things in any other way. But as time went on, it slowly became evident to the colonial governments that it was not possible to sustain the status quo.

The most important result that came from the influence of history is that contemporary Southern Africa has been forced to accept the concept of change in order to ensure national development. Since the national character is a product of history, it is man's duty to change the course of history so that it has a positive influence on his thought process and action to shape the kind of the future of society that is compatible with the aspirations of its members. This is why nations of Southern Africa must recognize the influence of history as an important condition of educational innovation. It is not possible to initiate innovation without taking this influence into account.

---

[8]Michael Samuels, "The New Look in Angolan Education," in *Africa Report,* November 1967, p. 63.

[9]*Ibid.*

[10]Samora Machel, "Educate man to win the war, create a new society, and develop our country.", Sept. 1970.

Theoretical Assumptions

One of the major conditions of educational innovation is the formulation of theory. Theory helps to determine educational goals and objectives. It assists in defining the purpose of education. Without theory there is no good education. In the same way, without theory, there cannot be educational innovation. When President Julius Nyerere of Tanzania said in 1967, "The purpose of education is liberation through the development of the person as a member of society. Therefore,the education that serves the needs of the individual has to be transformed to enable him to serve the needs of society,"[11] he was, in effect, discussing a new theoretical perspective as a condition of Tanzania's effort to design a new educational system to suit the demands of the times. For Nyerere to urge his country people to think in terms of the liberation of the individual in a larger social context was to urge them to formulate a new theoretical component which had not been taken into consideration before as a condition of educational innovation.

The promotion of education to serve the needs of the individual must be recognized as a condition of meeting those of society. This perspective demanded fundamental change in the way Africans viewed themselves and the future of their society. This meant that the role of education in shaping new social structures must also be recognized. This thinking demanded that education itself be reformed to enable it to do that. The importance of the individual in society was itself a condition that was created by the end of the colonial condition that had inhabited it. This new way of looking at education was explained to this author by a 13-year old girl in a remote rural school in Zimbabwe in 1983.

Having observed the enthusiasm and the determination with which she approached her schooling, the author could not resist the temptation to ask what he had always regarded as a question unbecoming a well informed person, asking school children what they plan to do after their education was completed, because if college students are not often sure of what they plan to do, how does one expect school children to know that much in advance? However, the girl, with a sense of self-assurance and confidence in her future, never hesitated as she responded,

> "You really want to know that I will do after my education is completed? I have absolutely no doubt about that. After completing my primary school here I will go to St. Augustine's Secondary School.[12] Then, with a first class pass, I will go to the University of Zimbabwe to study to be doctor. I will then get married and have two children, one boy and one girl. You see, without the educational development of the individual, there is no development of society."[13]

One sees that while political independence is an essential manifestation of collective liberation and a new national identity, it is the educational development of the individual that evinces the ultimate liberation of society itself. The essential nature

---

[11]Tanzania, *Education for self-reliance*. Dar es Salaam: Government Printer, 1967

[12]St. Augustine's Secondary School was the first secondary school for Africans in Zimbabwe. It was opened in 1939 by the Anglican Church.

[13]A thirteen-year old girl during an interview with the author in eastern Zimbabwe, July 15, 1983.

of the relationship between the individual and society is that their development is a product of a new form of education. It is equally true that while collective action comes only from individual commitment to it, it is the action of the individual that originates it. Therefore, the educational development of the individual is essential to the development of society itself.

Placing emphasis on the educational development of the individual as a condition of the development of society in emerging nations of Southern Africa seems to underscore two critical factors of theoretical assumptions of educational innovation. The first is that without reforming the educational process, the individual is handicapped in discharging his responsibility first to himself, then to his society. The second factor is that the thinking that the individual comes before society is a reversal of traditional African philosophy of the proper relationships between the individual and society. It is true that traditional African society, by the elements of its culture, was a collective one. That is, it placed the interests of society above those of the individual. Any person who tried to place his own interests above those of his society was considered to be mis-educated.[14] Indeed, emerging nations of Southern Africa are struggling to set their own developmental priorities by trying to resolve the conflict that exists in this setting. This is why Robert Mugabe observed in 1982:

> We feel that there is a link between the Marxist-Leninist thinking and our traditional collective ideas, and we are linking these together. On the basis of this we are evolving a philosophy which we hope will be acceptable to our people. There is individuality in a collective society. But we want to emphasize the collective aspect of our society and still allow individuality as a principal factor of a new society.[15]

Indeed this is one of the major challenges the emerging nations of Southern Africa are facing in their endeavor for national development.

In order to initiate innovation in education emerging nations of Southern Africa now recognize that change in the relationship between the individual and society is essential because, unlike traditional society, their perception of the role of the individual in shaping the character of society is largely determined by the kind and level of education that the individual receives which can only be done on individual basis. This is not to suggest that the Africans reject their own cultural traditions and values, but to conclude that they need to recognize the importance of change in the character of society as a condition of national development. One must therefore conclude that the perception of the individual in relation to his society in emerging nations of Southern Africa constitutes an important component of a new theory as a condition of educational innovation.

Another critical component of theory as a condition of educational innovation is the concept of equality in educational opportunity and in society. In 1979, President Kenneth Kaunda of Zambia equated equality in both education and society with what

---

[14]Dickson A. Mungazi, *The Struggle for Social Change in Southern Africa: Visions of Liberty*, p. 51.
[15]Robert Mugabe, "Not in a Thousand Years: From Rhodesia to Zimbabwe," a documentary film, PBS, 1982

he called *humanism*.[16] The philosophy of humanism, as a basic principle of equality in society, takes the position that *man* and society- in their universal definition - are quite capable of attaining perfection through education. Kaunda went further to argue:

> For us as a nation to embrace humanism as a social ideology and as a condition of educational change is a futile exercise unless it is done with a full appreciation and knowledge that equality of educational opportunity combines with the practice of democracy to allow power in the hands of the humblest citizens of our country. Equality of educational opportunity cannot become a reality unless it becomes a condition of educational innovation.[17]

The reality of acknowledging this factor would help emerging nations of Africans to set educational goals and programs that are consistent with the purpose of the individual. One can see that the nations of Southern Africa now recognize that equality in both education and society has become a principal factor of national development.

Therefore, in concluding, "There will be no genuine or lasting peace until man has developed society to such an extent that it is based on the theory that all people are entitled to equal educational opportunity as a condition of national development,"[18] Kaunda was suggesting that a new thrust must be initiated in efforts to transform the educational process so that it helps in sustaining the principle of equality in order to create a new society. Therefore, Kaunda concluded that the concept of equality is an important condition of educational innovation. There is no question that he was trying to base a new approach to education on the accomplishment of Zambia since it attained independence in October, 1964.

Since that time the Zambian Ministry of Education has carried out an ambitious innovative program in education, " a complete transformation of the educational scene."[19] Indeed, enrollment in primary school had increased from 378,400 in 1964 to 810,739 in 1973.[20] At the same time the number of students starting primary school in 1974 had increased considerably. This increase could not have occurred if the educational process had not changed enough to accommodate it. When properly defined and applied, the philosophy of humanism has meaning to Southern Africa in important dimensions. It becomes a guiding principle of the relationships between the individual and society. It helps initiate purposeful change based on the belief that each person has value to society because he sees value in himself. It helps transmit a new conviction that men and women must liberate themselves before they can liberate their society. It helps create a new education that brings out the best in each

---

[16]Kenneth Kaunda," Zambia: Blueprint for and Economic Development," an address to an economic conference, Mulunguishi Hall, Lusaka, October 8, 1979.
[17]*Ibid.*
[18]*Ibid.*
[19]Zambia: Ministry of Information, *Zambia in Brief.* Lusaka: Government Printer, 1980, p. 15.
[20]*Ibid.*

person. It helps guide individual growth and development in a way that offers mutual benefit to himself and his society.[21]

A fundamental tenet of theory as a condition of educational innovation is that it must protect the concept of the freedom of the human mind. Julius Nyerere agrees with Paulo Freire when he concludes that this liberating theme must reverse the process of domination of the mind of the universal human being as it was practiced by the colonial systems. Nyerere goes on to add:

> The ideas imparted by education or released in the human mind through education, should be liberating ideas. The skills acquired by an individual through education should be liberating skills. Nothing else can properly be called human mind if the individual is not free to exercise his freedom of his thought process. We cannot call it innovated education if it fails to uphold this basic tenet of human endeavor.[22]

Ngagiwa Thiongo, the Kenyan educational thinker, suggests that freedom of the human mind is an indispensable condition of being human and that education must take account of it if it is to be meaningful to national development:

> Education for the liberation of the human mind must also aim at producing a fully developed individual who understands the forces at work in society, an individual who uses Reason to understand reasons of his role in society. This cannot happen by maintaining status quo in education, but by initiating reform. Therefore, freedom of the human mind must stand out as a principal condition of educational reform.[23]

A central question that must be asked in considering components of theory as condition of educational innovation is: What is education intended to accomplish? The answer determines some important principles which would guide its development. Without keeping the answer to this question in mind, educational innovation loses its meaning. As a result, the emerging educational process becomes an exercise in futility. Keeping this question in mind also helps put all relevant aspects of the process of innovation in perspective. But the formation of theory is in itself undertaken in the context of the environment in which it is cast. It cannot be done haphazardly. The challenge before the emerging nations of Southern Africa is to formulate theoretical assumptions in order to direct the course of educational innovation.

Educational Objectives

Conventional wisdom suggests that objectives constitute a critical condition of educational innovation and that without establishing objectives, the entire educational process has no meaning. In 1974, Kenneth Kaunda seemed to understand this truth when he argued that Zambia needed a set of objectives to guide its endeavor to initiate educational innovation, and added that free and universal primary education was an important condition of the change that the ministry of education was

---

[21]Zambia, *Educational Reform,* 1979, p. 5.
[22]C. William Smith, *Nyerere of Tanzania.* Harare: Zimbabwe Publishing House, 1981, p. 15.
[23]Kathy Bond-Stewart, *Education with Production,* p. 5.

proposing. Kaunda went on to outline a set of objectives which he said must influence the development of education, saying:

> The introduction of free and universal primary education must form a basic condition which must direct our efforts to improve the educational system. We must look at the expanded educational facilities in every district. More teachers, colleges, technical colleges, more secondary schools, more primary schools, and more trade institutions. We must expand university facilities rapidly in terms of student enrollment, the curriculum, and the acquisition of skills so that the nation benefits from the contribution of the student population.[24]

This was, indeed, a challenging endeavor. Did Zambia have national resources in sufficient amounts to realize these objectives so as to realize educational innovation envisaged in their fulfillment? The fact that Zambian literacy rate had increased from 50% in 1983 to 54% in 1990 suggests how difficult it was to realize these important objectives. The challenge is, therefore, still to be met.

That universal and free primary education has become a major objective among emerging nations of Southern Africa is evinced by their efforts to accomplish it. This is precisely what Robert Mugabe had in mind when, on July 18, 1983, he launched a national campaign to raise the literacy rate from 30% to 100% in 1988.[25] But that Zimbabwe's literacy rate increased from 30% in 1983 to 50% in 1990 also suggests that this objective has remained elusive. In a similar manner President Samora Machel of Mozambique promised in 1970 that by 1980 the country must achieve a universal primary education to achieve a 100% literacy rate. That the literacy rate of Mozambique actually declined from 20% in 1983 to 14% in 1990[26] also indicates that Mozambique was having great difficulties in trying to reach this objective.

There is a common thread that runs through all the countries of Southern Africa, except South Africa, and this is: efforts to introduce free and universal primary education were made in the belief that reaching a 100% literacy rate would produce a more functional population able to contribute to national development. A troubling question must therefore be asked. Why has the objective of universal literacy not been reached? There are three possible answers. First, the emerging nations of Southern Africa do not have sufficient resources to meet them. Second, the educational innovation itself may not have been designed to fulfill objectives consistent with national development. Third, the implementation plan might have been flawed. Meeting the objectives of universal and free primary education cannot be done in this kind of environment. However, the knowledge that setting objectives was an important condition of educational innovation helped the nations of Southern Africa find solutions to the problem.

The struggle for literacy as a principal educational objective in Southern Africa must be seen in the context of other national objectives. The concept of national unity and identity has eluded many nations of Africa simply because the leaders themselves have failed to convince their people that the governments are there to

---

[24]Kenneth Kaunda, *Zambia: Blueprint for Economic Development,* 1979.
[25]Robert Mugabe, "Literacy for All in Five Years," July 18, 1988
[26]*World Almanac and Book of Facts,* 1990

serve them. Rather, the people see government operations as a means of enriching the bureaucrats and themselves. While the leaders are increasingly aware of this serious problem, they have done little to change the situation in order to create an environment of trust and public support through participation. This is the message that Kenneth Kaunda attempted to convey to his people when he said 1979:

> The government belongs to no one person, not even to the most active members of it. The government belongs to all the people. Therefore every Zambian is a shareholder in this institution. No one owns the government and no one can take it away from you.[27]

But in all his efforts and attempts to convince his fellow Zambians that the government belongs to all the people, Kaunda must have ignored an important consideration, and that is, the action of turning the country into a one-party state is hardly an environment in which the government can have the full trust and support of the people. As long as nations of Southern Africa impose a one-party system of government, they should not expect their people to have full confidence in them. Therefore, the introduction of a multi-party democracy is an important condition of educational innovation. The introduction of a one-party system suggests the conclusion that the government really belongs only to those who run it and that the services it offers are exclusively their prerogative. This is hardly the kind of social climate that a nation may need to initiate educational innovation.

Indeed, this author does not share the reasons that many national leaders of Southern Africa repeatedly advance to argue in favor of a one-party system of government. Among these reasons are: first, a one-party system brings about national unity; second, that multi-party democracy is a Western imposition; third, one party-system is consistent with African cultural and social practices; fourth, multi-party system is too costly; fifth, multi-party system distracts from making efforts to solve the problems of national development as politicians oppose the government for opposition's sake; and sixth, multi-party system creates an environment of conflict as the simple and unsophisticated citizens get confused and begin to focus on the negative features of the government, rather than on its policies and accomplishments.

This author totally disputes and rejects all these reasons. On the contrary multi-party system of government ensures that all relevant points of view are taken into consideration in formulating national policy and implementing it. No matter how much the leaders try to argue, the existence of a one-party system is nothing less than a form of dictatorship. The sad part of this situation is that the leaders fail to see things this way. Instead, they begin to blame other conditions for their own failure or inadequacy. Educational innovation is meaningless under political conditions that are less than absolute in affording the people freedom of choice in the political activity of the country. It is equally sad that leaders of one-party governments mislead their people by claiming that they are democracies. The reality of the situation is that they do not know that a multi-party system is in their own interest. In

---

[27]Kenneth Kaunda, "Zambia: Blueprint for Economic Development, "1979,

this kind of national environment, establishing objectives as a condition of educational innovation becomes a peripheral exercise.

Population Projection

If there is a major national problem that African nations are unable to solve and so handicap their ability to solve other national problems, it is the rapidly rising population rate. Worse still, the inability of African nations to make accurate population projections paralyze their efforts to provide adequate services to their people. The rapidly rising population, declining economy and unfavorable trade balance combine to create a frustrating situation for African nations.

That the average population growth rate of Southern Africa increased from 2.3% per year in 1960 to 3.1% per year in 1984[28] has placed heavy demands on national resources. In 1984 children under the age of 15 years accounted for 45% of the population compared with 37% in Asia and 40% in Latin America.[29] This problem of keeping accurate population projection records translates into serious problems of making effective educational plans. That "Education is critical to slowing down population growth rate"[30] suggests a critical change in a fundamental aspect of African culture, the desire among Africans, especially those in the rural areas, to have a large number of children.

Somewhere within the scheme of things among African nations a basic change must take place in shifting the emphasis from dependence on children in old age to economic self-sufficiency. This requires a radical restructuring of the socioeconomic system so that during their years of production, the people build a sound financial base to live comfortably in retirement. This will reduce dependence on children for support and so reduce the need for large numbers of children. While this requires a considerable financial outlay by the government at the initial stage, the results in the long term can be beneficial. But to do this two essential ingredients are necessary. The first is for the government to build a solid economic base that makes it possible to initiate such as program. The second is to create confidence in the people so that they do not fear that they will lose the money they have taken years to save. The advantage of this program is that it enables the government to make plans for the future based on accurate population projection. This is important because educational innovation must take into account projected number of students. This in turn will determine facilities to be built, the number of teachers to be trained and employed, and the operational budget , as well as teacher-student ratio.

In 1877, the Report of the National Commission on Education in Botswana recognized the imperative of this reality when it concluded,

The rapid population growth rate of 3.00% per year puts considerable strain on both the economy and the educational system. It results in large numbers of

---

28The World Bank, *Toward Sustained Development in sub-Sahara Africa*. Washington, D.C., 1984, p. 26.
29*Ibid*. p. 27.
30*Ibid*. p. 28.

students in school without sufficient financial resources. A unbalanced population structure creates its own peculiar problems in terms of reforming the educational system itself.[31]

It is, indeed, ironic that Botswana, with an area of 582,000 Square kilometers and a population of 712,000 in 1977, was considered sparsely populated. But when population had increased to 1.2 million with a literacy rate of 35% in 1990, the situation had been transformed in magnitude. The mass migration from rural areas to urban areas increased the urban population by 12% per year.

This situation has created socioeconomic and educational problems that, in spite of government efforts to plan educational development of the country, it was not possible to have accurate population projection in order to adopt educational innovation to this critical consideration. Even the Education Commission itself concluded that its projection of an increase in urban population of 45% by 1990[32] was nothing more than a guess. However, the commission concluded that without accurate population projection it would be hard for Botswana to make adequate educational plans for the future because " social infrastructures, including new schools, are more expensive to provide."[33]

The World Bank has suggested that it is very important for developing nations to keep accurate census and population projection figures in order to make accurate budget allocations to various national items and that if this is not done those countries will always endure the adverse effects of underdevelopment because it is always difficult to make plans for national development without a full grasp of the essential facts.[34] Therefore population projection is an important condition of educational innovation.

Economic Development

National and regional economic development is another important condition of educational innovation is a reality that all national leaders in Southern Africa must take into consideration as they attempt to place their nations on the road to development. With tremendous national resources that nations of Southern Africa possess, one would like to think that the task of developing them is made much lighter than in other regions. But the truth of the matter is that it is not the case for a number of reasons.

Among these reasons are the following: In South Africa international boycott has reduced the production of minerals considerably. During the Smith government in colonial Zimbabwe sanctions imposed by the U.N. had a devastating effect on the economy. In Angola and Mozambique the civil wars have hurt the economy badly. In Namibia, the conflict between the U.N. and South Africa over its future eroded

---

[31] Botswana: The Report of the National Commission on Education. Gaberone: Government Printer, 1977, p. 10.
[32] *Ibid.*
[33] *Ibid.*
[34] The World Bank, *Toward Sustained Development in Sub-Sahara Africa,* p. 28.

away the confidence of investors to the extent that a national economic system has not been developed until the attainment of independence in March, 1990. In Zambia and Zaire competition on the world market has hurt the production of copper.

Therefore, in general, the economic development of Southern Africa has been experiencing considerable difficulties due to a combination of these factors. That the gross national product grew at an average rate of 3.6% per year from 1970 to 3.8 in 1980 was a heathy sign. But with a population increase rate of 3.2 per year, per capita income dropped from 4.00% in 1970 to 3.4 in 1980.[35]

Because the mainstay of the economy is agriculture, the combination of extended drought, population increase, and the policies of the multi-corporations have combined to hurt agricultural productivity. Massive starvation in Mozambique has played into the hands of South Africa as much as it has put economic strain on Zimbabwe due to its decision to take care of refugees from this country. Industrial production has declined considerably to the extent that basic essentials are hard to secure. "Poor investment choices, failure to develop export opportunity, falling domestic income, inadequate foreign exchange for materials and spare parts"[36] and the distabilizing activity of South Africa have all created a situation in which the economy of Southern Africa has become vulnerable.[37]

Following independence many countries of Southern Africa made an impressive show in building the economy . This made it possible to invest in education and building supporting infrastructures. But as national leaders remained in office longer than they should, the confidence and excitement of the people about the future transformed into a general state of depression. When corruption and unwillingness of government officials forced the economy into spinning decline, depression among the people translated into apathy in the political process. The socioeconomic transformation of Southern Africa, once envisaged as the basis of educational development, was not only steadily being halted but was also being reversed. This created a situation in which government leaders found it easier to place blame elsewhere than at their own doorsteps.

When, in April, 1980, the black-ruled countries of Southern Africa formed an organization known as Southern Africa Development Coordination Conference (SADCC), it was anticipated that at last they had found a solution to the economic problems of regional development. With its main objective of reducing economic dependence on South Africa, SADCC felt that black-ruled countries in the region would no longer be vulnerable to South Africa's distabilizing tactics. But because SADCC's success depended on the ability of its members to mobilize national resources and cooperate in developing them in the first place, the technology needed to make it possible was not readily available. Therefore, the economic salvation that SADCC was expected to be to the countries of Southern Africa actually turned out to be a mirage as a combination of factors derailed the expected economic growth needed to invest in education.

---

[35]World Bank, *Sustained Development in Sub-Sahara Africa*, p. 2.
[36]*Ibid.*
[37]The author saw evidence of the rapidly declining economy while he was a study trip to Southern Africa in 1989.

In case the reader misunderstands, the author neither disputes the basic objectives of the development of Southern Africa nor questions the national economic policy. The point he is making is that economic problems must be resolved as an important condition of educational innovation. He is also arguing that economic development is so important to educational development that it has to be achieved and maintained at a healthy level to make that innovation possible. If this is not done, then educational innovation cannot take place at the desired level to make it viable. This is one of the challenges that nations of Southern Africa face. Neither the formation of SADCC nor the objectives established by the Lagos Plan of Economic Action in 1980 has yielded the desired results. It is not possible to envisage educational innovation under conditions that have serious implication for doubt about the economy.

The question now arises: What must nations of Southern Africa do to ensure economic development so that they can invest in educational development? Among other things, they need to control the price of goods. They must play a role in shaping international trade. They must diversify the economy. They must provide opportunity for free enterprise and resist the temptation to nationalize major industries. They must provide production incentives to both the workers and the management. They must provide tax breaks to business and wage earners so that they can invest in expansion. They must reduce both national spending and taxes. They must design uniform domestic production and trade policies. They must resist the temptation to overtax the people so that they can spend less and save more. This is good for the economy.

An important dimension of economic development which national leaders of Southern Africa do not seem to understand as an important condition of educational innovation is political stability. Without political stability, it is very hard to develop plans, for the short term and the long term, for economic development. The conditions of political stability are as important to educational innovation as the economic growth and development. An important factor that many nations of Africa seem to ignore is that political stability must result from free participation by the people in the political process. determined by popular action, not dictated by the government. The notion that one-party rule or one-man government provides political stability is a farce that many national leaders have yet to recognize. United Methodist Bishop Ralph Dodge, who served in Zimbabwe from 1956 to 1964, argued on this point in 1964:

> The strength of a political system and stability depends upon the full and free participation of its citizens. The citizens of every country should have access to all essential information regarding the policies of their government. National security must not be imposed to justify illegal activities directed against any person. When law and order are imposed under these conditions, the confidence of the people is eroded away. With it the economy suffers and educational development is hurt.[38]

---

[38]Ralph Dodge, "A Political Community," an unpublished essay, May, 1964. By courtesy of the Old Mutare Methodist Archives.

This is a reality that nations of Southern Africa must recognize to improve the economy so that educational innovation can be initiated.

The Inadequacy of the Existing System of Education

Another important condition of educational innovation that nations of Southern Africa must take into account is the recognition that the existing system of education is inadequate. Low literacy rate, wide differences between rural and urban schools, shrinking budget allocation, imbalances in teacher-student ratio, rigid examination systems, irrelevant curriculum, shortage of trained personnel, poor working conditions for teachers, excessive government regulations, are among the problems that nations of Southern Africa must recognize as needing immediate change in order to create a climate for educational innovation.

While nations of Southern Africa have made commendable efforts to provide universal primary education, failure to make fundamental change in important areas of education has hurt their developmental strategies. In many respects the continuation of these problems leads one to the conclusion that some nations have hurt the educational system more than the colonial governments they replaced. It is true that some nations of Southern Africa, such as Zambia, Botswana, and Zimbabwe, have inadvertently maintained inadequacies in the educational process by arguing that they are trying to maintain educational standards. For example, maintaining the distinction between the "O" level and "A"[39] level leads not only to fewer numbers of students going on to college, but is also wasteful in terms of finances and students who are frustrated because they cannot continue their education beyond high school.

The examinations conducted at the end of the year at various levels of the educational process place serious strains that are detrimental to the educational advancement of the students. In a similar manner continuing to require certain courses for one sex only, such as home economics for girls and shop for boys, is an educational practice that can no longer be justified under contemporary conditions. Therefore, the recognition that the existing system of education carries some serious inadequacies constitutes another important condition of educational innovation.

There is another situation which tends to perpetuate inadequacies in the existing educational systems in Southern Africa and which must be eliminated as a condition of educational innovation. This is the fact that the system of education in most countries of the region is based upon models which have been imported from developed countries and have not been adopted to suit local conditions. For example, emphasis on Western history has the effect of alienating students from their own cultural history. At the same time emphasis placed on passing government - controlled examinations as a measure of educational achievement is done at the detriment of the actual learning itself. The belief that passing public examinations as proof of educational achievement is a myth that is still alive in all countries of

---

[39]The "O" level and the "A" level are systems used in the British system of education to to indicate a difference in edcuational attainment. The "A" level is for those students who seek to qualify for entrance into college.

Southern Africa. The thinking that when one fails to pass public examinations one has failed in education has damaging and retarding psychological effect on students.

The main task of the school in contemporary Southern Africa is to teach the students that learning is far more important than passing public examinations. Placing emphasis on passing these examinations forces students to memorize facts. In this situation their ability to engage in critical thinking is severely impaired. Public examinations have also a negative effect on teaching itself. They deny teachers the flexibility and freedom which they must have to expose their students to a wide range of learning activity that is needed to produce well-rounded educated citizens.

Public examinations also tend to develop in students a dependence complex as they begin to rely on the lectures given by their teachers with little or no opportunity to examine critically the wider implications of what they are learning.[40] The practice of a national curriculum undercuts the very essence of the philosophy of education as an outcome of the concept of academic freedom and forces all the schools in the country to approach the teaching and the learning processes in a mechanical manner. For educational innovation to be meaningful it has to remove these serious inadequacies. The nations of Southern Africa must also realize that there is no single strategy that can be used to do so, but that conditions of the economy and political conditions can combine to create a national climate in which the need to remove inadequacies can be understood in its proper perspective.

Summary and Conclusion

The discussion in this chapter leads to three basic conclusions. The first is that while economic, social and political conditions have a profound impact upon the development of education, nations of Southern Africa must avoid the temptation to rank-order them because in its own way each has a considerable impact on educational development. In their formative stage, and most nations of Africa are in their formative stage, many nations of the Third World find it hard to determine policies for national development because they do not establish a clear agenda for corrective action. It is for this reason that this author warns against putting educational development and economic development in a rank order. In a similar manner, political stability and economic development depend on each other. The best that developing nations can do is try their best to improve all these conditions so that they combine to influence the development of education so critical to endeavors for national development.

The second conclusion is that there is no question that an essential outcome of the thinking about ways of improving education in Southern Africa has been the emergence of the concept of how conditions outside the educational process affect education itself. Among these conditions are socioeconomic and political factors. While nations of Southern Africa strive towards their own definition of national unity and progress, they seem to neglect the fact , as Unesco put it in 1976, that

---

[40]Botswana, The Report of the National Commission on Education, p.19

"Education in Africa is a maze of innovative activity. Innovation may be defined as a deliberate effort to improve a particular component of the educational system."[41]

This suggests that African nations must recognize that change is not necessarily an innovation unless it is designed to ensure improvement. When, on April 5, 1990, de Klerk announced that segregated state schools for whites would be able to admit black students if 90% of the white parents in any school so voted, there was a feeling that he was not quite sincere in claiming that his government wanted to have dialogue with ANC to resolve the problems of the the country. Mandela himself responded, "This is inadequate because the parents voting requirement would paralyze the whole initiative."[42] To have change become innovation the conditions discussed in this chapter, as well as others, must be be met.

The third conclusion is that the nature and extent of the applicability of the conditions of educational innovation have implications on management or strategies for seeking improvement. While human factors and political considerations have inhibited educational innovation in the past, they can become national assets when the spirit of urgency prevails at all levels of authority from the people to the government. Mutuality of understanding and respect will enable nations of Southern Africa to approach the task of educational innovation from a perspective of an endeavor to improve the system so as to serve the developmental needs of all the people in order to serve the developmental needs of the nation. Any other course of action is likely to yield limited results.

---

[41] Unesco, *Educational Studies and Documents, Number 25: Education in Africa in Light of the Lagos Conference*. Paris, 1976, p. 16.

[42] Anthony Lewis, "The Harsh Reality is that Apartheid is Still in Place," *The New York Times*, April 6, 1990.

6

STRATEGIES FOR EDUCATIONAL INNOVATION

The nature and character of practical experience that the individuals acquire in the course of their daily economic activities form a critical component of a strategy for improvement. Zimbabwe: Transitional National development Plan, 1982.

Introduction: The Concept of Change as Innovation

In discussing the thrust for educational innovation in Southern Africa one must remember that the concept of change has always been an operative principle of human experience and endeavor. From the age of Nero through the religious reformation movement of Martin Luther, to the struggle for political independence in Africa in the twentieth century, human society has always embraced the concept of change, not for change's sake, but in order to improve the condition of human life. Change is meaningless unless it is directed towards improvement or efforts to correct a situation that is less than adequate in serving human needs.

The relationship between the concept of change and innovation is the line of thinking that Samora Machel took into consideration when he urged his fellow Mozambiquans to approach what he regarded as the enormously important question of basic literacy as an important strategy for educational innovation, saying in 1970:

> The main battle in the field of education is against illiteracy. If we are to succeed in our efforts to change and so improve our educational system, we must mobilize the masses in this battle, making them aware of the need to gain literacy and showing them the catastrophic consequences of illiteracy. This basic concept of change represents a powerful strategy for educational innovation, and we must approach it with all the urgency and the importance it requires. Without the active participation of the masses as part of the strategy for change in the battle against illiteracy, it will not be possible to wipe it out.[1]

The purpose of this chapter is to discuss some strategies which nations of Southern Africa can employ in initiating innovation in their systems of education.

---

[1]Samora Machel, "Educate Man to Win the War, Create a New Society, and Develop a Country, September, 1970.

Principles of Strategies for Innovation

There are two essential elements of the strategies for educational innovation that Machel discussed in his address in 1970. The first is that recognition of the problems constitutes an important strategy of change. That recognition enables the nation to make an accurate assessment of all the relevant problem areas of the existing system of education. This diagnostic exercise makes it possible to pin-point the areas that need attention . This enables the nation to design strategies of finding solutions.

The second critical element is the involvement of the people in seeking improvement through change. Without popular support and participation in any national endeavor, success cannot be assured. George Watson goes further to ague that success in seeking improvement in any national endeavor must entail the ability of national leaders to arouse a popular passion for meaningful change.[2] Therefore, the success of educational innovation as a major national endeavor, depends upon the demonstrated commitment of the national leaders to inspire their people with confidence for the future and the enthusiasm that they are an important part in the national effort to bring about change for the good of all. The national leaders must never underestimate the ability of the citizens to rise up and and accept a challenge in a national cause, provided that this is done within the spirit of democracy and free expression of ideas.

As one examines the challenge of educational innovation in Southern Africa, one sees seven basic principles that underlie any strategies to initiate it successfully. A brief discussion of each principle and its contribution to strategies for successful educational innovation is provided. The first is that once innovation has been initiated, it must be continued until positive or desired results begin to show. This suggests that educational innovation must be a continuous process because conditions of human life continue to change. The continuous nature of educational innovation must also take into account two principal aspects of it. The first is that it must be initiated with specific objectives in order to determine success or failure. The second is that it must entail graduated stages to ensure success of one stage before the next is attempted.

The second principle is that educational innovation must originate from within, rather than from without. This means that educational innovation must not be initiated by duplicating educational programs in other countries because conditions are fundamentally different. Outside considerations, such as demands by developed nations that nations which receive aid to abide by certain requirements as a condition of the aid, have the effect of minimizing the proper purpose of educational innovation. In this kind of setting, educational innovation is undertaken with the express purpose of receiving the needed financial aid. For this reason the fundamental goal of innovation itself is lost in the conflict that emerges between the purpose of outside pressure group , such as the World Bank and International Monetary Fund (IMF) and the intentions of the nation itself. Therefore, educational

---

[2]George Watson, *Change in School Systems*. Washington, D.C. National Training Laboratories, NEA, 1967.

innovation initiated as a response to outside pressure or demands loses its value and direction. Nations which offer assistance to developing nations in their effort to improve their systems of education must respect their national goals and objectives in order to retain their relevance.

The third principle is that innovation must be initiated from a perspective of considering the best educational interests of the students as prerequisite of promoting national development. This means that expediency and political benefit must never come into the picture. Along with this approach those who initiate innovation must operate under conditions of absolute honesty and conviction that what is being initiated reflects the express will of the people and the needs of the students. Once consideration of expediency and political benefit have been removed from the process of innovation , the people and their government join hands in mutual trust and confidence because a collective effort has gone into the decisions surrounding the thrust for innovation and that the people do not feel exploited politically. This approach ensures that the best educational interests of the students have been taken into account.

The fourth principle is that a strategy for innovation is more effective and may yield tangible results if it is a product of integrated approach. This ensures that cumulative effects are measured more accurately than those of a disintegrated approach. The integrated approach to innovation eliminates a haphazard strategy so that one form of success may be recorded in one aspect of innovation, while limited success may be recorded in another aspect. For example, an effort made to attain a universal primary education leading to improved literacy rate may disrupt the development of technical or secondary education . An integrated approach would ensure that no aspect of innovation is accomplished at the expense of another. Educational innovation as a whole would suffer a setback if it is directed at some aspects and neglects others. An integrated approach would help take all relevant aspects into consideration.

The fifth principle is that innovation demands leaders who are well informed about the issues surrounding it . They must also know the environment in which it is cast. The system initiated by the colonial governments of appointing members of commissions to study ways of improving education from overseas[3] was a practice initiated under the assumption that the local people did not know the educational needs of their country as much as people in Europe did. Some nations of Southern Africa have perpetuated this practice to the detriment of their efforts. The author does not take the position that outsiders have nothing positive to contribute toward meaningful change in education, but that emerging countries aught to exercise more care than did the colonial governments in resorting to people outside the country to carry major tasks because, no matter how good they may be, their knowledge of all important conditions of the country is limited. This is likely to undercut the effect of their task.

---

[3]For a detailed discussion of this practice and the problems it created in the educational process in Africa, see, for example, Dickson A. Mungazi, *Education and Government Control in Zimbabwe: A Study of the Commissions of Inquiry, 1908-1974*. New York: Praeger Publishers, 1990.

The sixth principle is that innovation must be undertaken at a basic or fundamental level. That is, to have the desired effect in critical aspects of it, educational innovation must begin at the beginning, If innovation is sought at the college level, for example, it becomes a futile exercise to ignore the primary and the secondary levels because it would entail a fractured approach that negates the integrated approach. Similarly, if innovation is sought at the secondary level, it becomes meaningless if it ignores innovation at the technical or college levels. The concept of basic or fundamental level also has two added advantages: it makes it necessary to examine all facts of innovation from the integrated perspective. It also makes it possible to measure its results. In this manner superficial considerations are eliminated.

The seventh and final principle under consideration is that the primary concern of innovation must be to improve the system, rather than to see the promotion of individuals in one way or another. It is quite common in human nature to have an ulterior motive behind a national program. The programs initiated by the colonial governments in Southern Africa often carried a hidden agenda in order to promote the political fortunes of those who were involved in them. This is why the Africans in Angola and Mozambique and of South Africa today reacted negatively to national policies thrust under this environment. In Mozambique and Angola national policy was designed to promote the political fortunes of Antonio Salazar, Marcello Caetano and other colonial officials. In South Africa the Bantu Education Act of 1953 had the effect of promoting the political star of Hendrik Verwoerd, Daniel Malan, and John Vorster instead of ensuring the development of the African population.

Therefore, nations of Southern Africa must remember that innovation undertaken from the perspective of seeking to meet the needs of students, rather than to promote the political interests of certain individuals, is best designed to meet the developmental interests of the nation. Once this perspective becomes a *modus operandi*, it makes it possible to design a set of goals and objectives that are compatible with national goals. Therefore gearing the thrust for educational innovation to goals and objectives creates a national climate in which the formulation of purpose in the educational process itself carries a much more meaningful intent than otherwise. The relationship between seeking improvement in the educational system and providing an opportunity for students to realize their own ambitions must remain the balancing rod of educational innovation.

Strategies of Educational Innovation

The observance of these seven principles does not, in itself constitute educational innovation, but when considered properly, they combine to form a set of strategies that would enable nations to undertake that task with a clear direction of its intended outcomes. However, the nations of Southern Africa must not assume that there is only one strategy for educational innovation because there is a variety of them that can be adopted to suit different conditions and to meet specified objectives. The adoption of any strategy is determined by a combination of factors put together in order to accomplish those objectives.

However, the initial stage of designing a strategy must involve a thorough assessment of needs before it is undertaken. It is not feasible to undertake innovation without conducting an assessment of needs. This exercise constitutes an important strategy for innovation. In doing so, it is necessary to determine exactly why innovation must be initiated, the objectives to be accomplished, the time and resources needed to complete it, the expected outcomes, and the problems to be encountered. Unless all these factors are taken into consideration, the innovation exercise has a potential for failure, and failure leads to frustration, and frustration poses serious national political implications. Therefore, an assessment of needs is an exercise that must be undertaken with absolute care. Once innovation is undertaken as a result of conducting an assessment of needs, it must not be allowed to fail.

An assessment of needs must also indicate the magnitude, the complexity and, indeed, the risk of having national interests subordinated to those of the individual. On the one hand in succeeding to protect the educational interests of the individual, the educational process will protect national interests. On the other hand, seeking to protect national interests as the first priority does not necessarily protect those of the individual. Assessment of needs must take this reality into account if successful innovation is to be initiated. In 1977, the Educational Reform Report of Zambia cautioned against the consequences of ignoring this fact when it warned:

> It is against this background that there have been many examples in the world of educational innovation which did not succeed even though the idea behind it seemed valid and promised many benefits. Educational innovation must aim first at sustaining the educational interests of the individual in order to promote national development. If educational innovation aims at national development first, it fractures the wheel on which it must run, the importance of the individual.[4]

A fundamental principle of undertaking an assessment of needs must focus on the theory that behind every example of successful educational innovation is an understanding that quite often without taking all aspects of assessment of needs into consideration, efforts aimed at innovation itself becomes a narrative of a comedy of errors. This does not ensure success. The Lagos Conference of 1976 urged African nations to ensure that the needs assessment exercise was carried out with specific objectives in mind, saying:

> In its content structures, operations, methods, costs, as indeed in its alternative aims , the educational system must remain close to the needs of the students before it can meet the needs of the nation. The assessment of needs must not seek to maintain the educational status quo, but to improve it in the way that the resulting education meets the needs of the students."[5]

[4]Zambia: *Educational Reform: Proposals and Recommendations,* October, 1977.
[5]Unesco: *Education in Africa in the Light of the Lagos Conference,* 1976.

Evaluation of Existing System of Education

It must also be remembered that assessment of needs as part of a strategy for educational innovation entails evaluation of the existing system of education. In all countries of Southern Africa the emphasis placed on universal education has yielded limited results for a number of reasons. The increase in population has translated into an unprecedented increase in enrollment at the primary level. This has not produced a corresponding increase in financial resources and facilities to accommodate the increase. While the cost of producing primary education is less than that of producing secondary and higher education, the enrollment figures themselves place heavier demands on financial resources at the primary level than at the other two levels. Therefore, an evaluation of the existing system would help facilitate planning financial resources to be allocated to different levels of education in order to undertake successful innovation. Failure to make an accurate evaluation of the existing system is acting in a manner similar to "the farmer who eats his seed corn; he may be fed today, but he will be hungry tomorrow."[6]

An essential component of conducting evaluation of the existing system as a part of a strategy for educational innovation is considering the educational needs of students in terms of manpower approach. This demands directing attention from the need for developing national resources to directing the educational system in response to basic consideration of educational development of the students. This approach is often based on the assumption that it provides useful guidelines to the country in its initial stage of innovation and stresses the importance of focusing on the fundamental importance of placing control of the process under collective responsibility.

Manpower approach also requires making projections about the number of trained teachers required by a given time. For example, the number of medical people, level of competency required to operate various institutional infrastructures, would have to be taken into consideration in order to initiate innovation. This can be done on the basis of improving existing facilities while new ones are being created so that inadequacies which currently handicap development are eliminated without creating a break in the flow of the educational process. This has the advantage of not confusing students about the direction that their education is taking. In 1977 the Botswana Commission on Education saw this approach as offering advantages to the educational system when it observed, "Areas of employment, political decision, teaching and medical services afford manpower planers an opportunity to estimate the future demand for staff with different types of specialized training."[7]

Another important feature of evaluating the existing system of education in order to initiate effective educational innovation is to practice openness and candor in this exercise of national self-examination in order to allow full participation of the people and to encourage interaction by both politicians and professionals and ordinary people in the community. This consultation process has advantages that are

---

[6]Botswana: *The Report of the National Commission on Education*, 1977, p. 38.
[7]*Ibid.*

not fully understood. It creates a climate of mutual trust and acceptance of new ideas. It implies the decision to observe democratic principles. It makes it possible for citizens to understand and appreciate the national efforts to improve education. It creates an environment of trust between the people and the government. It enables the people to have a sense of belonging so crucial to the success of national endeavors and programs. The painful exercise in self-criticism, which evaluation of existing system entails, must be shared by all to have its desired effects recognized.

Evaluation of the existing system must also include an examination of the impact of the problems that national development might have on innovation. Among these problems is resistance to change by some people, especially for political reasons. Therefore, taking political considerations into account is an important strategy for educational innovation. One way of resolving this problem is creating a constitutional provision that makes political accountability part of the duties those who hold public office have to discharge to their constituencies. It also makes it possible for "all parties to discuss key issues, whether or not there is an immediate requirement for legislative action and assures that politicians are exposed to the analysis of professionals and members of the public, and that the constraints and opportunities the nation faces are fully discussed."[8] This strategy ensures politicians do not exercise veto power or undue controlling influence over the process of innovation.

Any evaluation that does not take the projected rate of economic growth in relation to projected population growth rate can give a false picture of critical factors surrounding educational innovation. The rate of economic growth enables the nation to make appropriate budgetary allocation to the various items related to economic growth. Important factors related to the rate of economic growth include the rate of inflation, foreign trade to facilitate foreign currency flow, and the rate of unemployment. All nations in Southern Africa must remember that they simply cannot afford a haphazard approach to educational innovation because it is crucial to efforts directed at national development.

Taking the rate of economic growth as a factor of educational innovation demands demonstrated fiscal responsibility in two critical areas of national development. The first is exercising expenditure control so that the citizens are not overtaxed. This implies that as soon as funds have been released as a result of budgetary allocation, an efficient and properly structured process of spending must be initiated in an economical manner. A national finance unit must be instituted to assist the accounting officials in discharging their fiscal responsibility and to ensure proper collection of revenue in the first place. This would make sure that accurate financial records are kept to reflect correct expenditure vote designated by the legislature itself.

The system of checks and balances that this process provides also acts as a deterrent to corruption, a serious problem among Third World nations. It should be a standard procedure in all countries of Southern Africa that, by the constitutional

---

[8]World Bank, *Public Sector Management in Botswana. Washington,* D.C., 1984,p. 20.

nature of his duties and responsibilities, the auditor-general be required to ensure that the financial books are audited regularly. The responsibility of overseeing finances of implementing strategies must be shared among several high-level government departments. The introduction of this system would ensure that actual payments are made and records kept in more than one department.

Any liabilities for services rendered or goods delivered must be entered in the ledger books of each department and receipts must be kept by each department involved in the transaction. When auditing is carried out careful check of all records must be made to see if they match exactly. If they do not, it becomes relatively easy to trace where the error is. The net result of this process is that if the system is stalled at the time plans are being formulated it provides clear knowledge of expectation and the temptation for corruption is reduced when those who hold large sums of money are charged with the responsibility of discharging them. Therefore, the process of innovation can have much more reasonable chance of success.

The second area relates to monitoring expenditure, not only in the cost of educational innovation, but also in all areas of national fiscal responsibility. With reference to how economic growth determines whether or not educational innovation succeeds, the World Bank concludes that the efficiency of national system of management of finances as a measure of the rate of economic growth gives a clear picture of the overall financial situation that must be carefully watched to ensure that cost overrun does not occur.[9]

Another critical consideration in the process of financial management is the nature of relationship that exists between two components of the national budget. These are the reoccurring budget and the development budget. In many Third World nations deficit occurs when expenditure exceeds revenue. This often arises from unexpected increase in expenditure on new projects or expenditure caused by extended drought, refugees, or major civil strife, all of which most nations of Southern African have experienced. Therefore these nations need to be conscious of the fact that to sustain the rate of economic growth so that a steady flow of finances is sustained for national developmental projects, reoccurring budgetary items pose financial implications that must be assessed accurately right at the time they become noticed.

It is equally important for nations of Southern Africa to be aware of the fact that "While the critical constraint upon national development is the lack of trained manpower,"[10] the lack of manpower itself is a consequence of failing to make an accurate projection of the rate of economic growth. This failure inhibits the ability of nations to ensure adequate fiscal management. If the thrust of educational innovation is to be a successful national endeavor, it must take all these financial implications into consideration.

---

[9]*Ibid.* p. 31.
[10]*Ibid.* p. 35

Human Resources Development as a Strategy for Innovation

A major strategy for educational innovation in Southern Africa is embracing the concept of human resources development. All governments need to recognize that an important component of the educational process is the acceptance of the importance of developing technical and scientific skills. This must be done under the assumption that nations need trained people to run institutions. In essence this represents a different approach to innovation from what is intended by the formal educational process. Zimbabwe appears to recognize the essential character of this strategy when it concluded,

> The nature and character of practical experience that the individuals acquire in the course of their daily economic activities are an important factor of human resources development and form a critical component of a strategy for improvement.[11]

One must add, however, that the various dimensions in which people gain such experience depends, to a very large extent, on the level of their involvement in the formulation and implementation of development plans. This suggests the conclusion that at the initial phase of the formulating developmental plans, the knowledge of, and proper attitude towards, institutional operational process constitute an ideal environment that helps emerging nations appreciate that the change that is being initiated is intended for their own benefit. This level of understanding makes education far more meaningful than placing emphasis on formal educational innovation alone.

It is true that all levels of formal education transmit experiences and knowledge of the real world and so enhance the ability of citizens to understand human condition from a proper perspective. But it is the concept of human resources development that enables students to accept change as a imperative of national development. It molds their attitudes towards the world of work and so helps them accept the concept of change in a manner that translates into a realization of larger social conditions that must not be taken for granted. The development of adequate health conditions, proper nutrition, proper housing, agriculture, sanitation, and healthy work environment must all be understood as essential components of human resources development.[12] Their acceptance also means acceptance of important features of a strategy for innovation.

Eliminating Rural-Urban Contradiction

In Southern Africa, as in most Third World nations, differences in educational facilities and economic opportunity form the basis of socioeconomic components that translate into differences between rural areas and urban areas. What many nations do not seem to understand is that neglecting the development of rural areas is

---

[11]Zimbabwe: *Transitional National Development Plan,* Vol. 1, November, 1982. By the Zimbabwe Ministry of Information.
[12]*Ibid.*

tantamount to neglecting the development of 80% of the population. The question is: What strategies can the nations of Southern Africa adopt to solve the problems of rural-urban contradiction? To find the answer to the question it is necessary to discuss the problem of land holding during the colonial period. Throughout Southern Africa the best land forming conditions of human settlement was reserved for white farmers who employed Africans as cheap labor. A network of urban centers, such as Bulawayo and Harare in Zimbabwe, Johannesburg and Cape Town in South Africa, Maputo and Beira in Mozambique, Lusaka and Ndola in Zambia, was developed to facilitate transport and distribution of agricultural products in markets that the colonial entrepreneurs controlled.

In order to have this land the colonial legislatures passed laws that made Africans in both urban areas and rural areas foreigners and had to depend on the white man for economic survival. In the urban areas they were employed in factories, and in the rural areas they were employed as laborers. Such laws as the Land Act of South Africa of 1913, the Land Apportionment Act in Zimbabwe of 1929, effectively deprived the Africans of any land rights. They were therefore forced into crowded patches of desolate land which "consisted of poor land with a generally less favorable natural environment, inferior possibilities for development of productive infrastructures, demographic densities, and a suboptimal settlement pattern. This inferior socioeconomic space was forced upon the Africans by the colonial governments."[13]

Because the colonial farmers were interested only in the profit that came from their agricultural enterprise, they did not endeavor to develop the land or the Africans in any way. Therefore, they neglected education, health services, and socioeconomic aspects of their life. It was not surprising, for example, that during the rain season all family members, including children, were forced to work on tobacco farms. Any educational activity was suspended and the teacher became a supervisor of students working on the farm. The colonial governments enacted laws to protect the farmers who became managers of schools on their property. The establishment of schools on farms owned by the farmers was itself a strategy for enhancing the supply of cheap labor. This is how tobacco farmers became wealthy land owners. In Zimbabwe names like B. D. Goldberg, A.M. Tredgold, Ian D. Smith, Winston Field, and Godfrey Huggins, became synonymous with the political power which that wealth accrued to the white farmers.

In urban areas tobacco auction sales floors captured the imagination of business enthusiasts who made a fortune by taking risks. Investment in building industry boosted the romance and the adventure of many whites to the extent that laws were soon passed to make Africans also foreigners in urban areas.[14] Godfrey Huggins, the prime minister of colonial Zimbabwe from 1933 to 1953, explained in 1937 why such a law was necessary, saying:

---

[13]*Ibid.*

[14]Dickson A. Mungazi, "The Educational Policy of the British South Africa Company Towards Rural and Urban Africans in Zimbabwe: A Dilemma of Choice, 1899-1923" in *African Urban Quarterly*, Vol. 2, No. 1, February, 1987,

Our municipal areas must not be polyglotted with a mixture of black and white. We must proceed with the policy of segregation to keep our urban areas as white as possible. The Native is a visitor to our cities for the purpose of serving the whites who live there.[15]

One unfortunate outcome of the rural-urban contradiction that emanated from the policies of the colonial governments in all of Southern Africa is that in neglecting the development of both the rural areas and the urban areas, the rural Africans suffered from a systematic stagnation in their advancement efforts and the urban Africans suffered from an array of social dysfunctions that the colonial governments failed to foresee. Beginning with the influenza of 1917, the problems of sanitation, food supply, transport, housing and deterioration in health care all combined to create a socioeconomic environment that made urban areas unpleasant and unsafe places for Africans to live and work in.

By 1923 conditions all over Southern Africa had deteriorated so badly that church leaders took it upon themselves to warn:

The whole life is a scourge of disease. Every epidemic flourishes and until there is a meeting of the minds between the officials and the Natives about what must be done to improve the situation and solve the handicapping differences between the rural areas and urban areas hope cannot be held for an improvement . This situation threatens the entire population.[16]

The rural Africans were fairing no better. A. J. Wills aptly described the problem, the dilemma of choice that the educational policies of the colonial governments forced the Africans to encounter in being denied the opportunity for adequate education and rural training programs:

By assuming that African agricultural produce was inferior to white produce the colonial officials created a bias against rural development. At the same time it expressed displeasure for an academic education because the qualified Africans would be knocking at the doors of society which would not find suitable employment opportunity for them.[17]

Due to years of neglect, the rural -urban contradiction that the policies of the colonial governments created became an accepted socioeconomic system. When new independent nations were born their leaders found the problems so complex that they decided not to try to do any thing to solve them. "They felt that this was better than trying to do so and create an impression among the people that their governments were incompetent because they would not be able to solve problems of national development."[18] But by failing to grapple with a major national problem, the independent nations of Southern Africa compounded it. They preferred to blame

---

[15]Southern Rhodesia: *Legislative Assembly Debates*, April 2, 1937.

[16]Ralph Diffendorfer [Ed.], *The World Service of Methodist Episcopal Church*. Chicago: Methodist Council on Benevolences, 1923, p. 115.

[17]A. J. Wills, *An Introduction to the History of Central Africa*. London: Oxford University Press, 1964. p. 285.

[18]An interview with a rural African leader, in Mutare, Zimbabwe, July 15, 1989.

the colonial governments rather than to accept the reality that the responsibility had to be placed squarely on their shoulders.

The strategy for resolving rural-urban contradiction to ensure educational innovation evolves around the application of simple principles. These include a thorough assessment of needs, especially those of the rural areas because they have been neglected for many years. They also involve formulating objectives, not only to ensure their educational development, but also to restructure the entire socioeconomic system itself. This will enable them to become viable. The fact of the matter is that the problems of rural-urban contradiction are so severe that nothing less than a radical approach will do. But radical approach does not in any way mean a pre-dawn revolution. Rather, it means a steady process of the complete transformation of the system because it has inhibited the ability of the nations of Southern Africa to initiate meaningful reform.

The application of these principles also means that the nations of Southern Africa must recognize the importance of regional cooperation as a strategy for solving rural-urban contradiction in order to initiate innovation. Regional cooperation would generate sufficient resources, both human and financial, needed to initiate innovation. This also makes it possible to consult each other on investment and development policies because the problems of development are quite similar. It would also offer incentives to the local people for participation. In this process three considerations are critical. These are: ensuring that the need and all aspects of innovation are fully understood and accepted by the local people, the necessity of national assistance to rural areas to enable them to reach a functional level of eventual autonomy would be assessed, and developing sufficient technological manpower and know-how to tape resources needed for development.[19]

There is no question that educational opportunity, health services, and community development are at the center of the rural-urban contradiction. It is equally true that these pose one of the most serious challenges to efforts directed at national development. As long as African nations bend under the weight of these problems, the entire thrust for educational innovation and national development itself lose both the purpose and the direction they must take. For nations of Southern Africa, therefore, this is a call they must answer, a challenge they must accept. The result of evading that challenge will inevitably perpetuate the scourge of underdevelopment that has been inherited from the colonial period.

Among the areas of national focus in an effort to resolve problems of rural-urban contradiction as party of a strategy for educational innovation are land resettlement programs, reform and expansion of structures of supplementary services including research, and extension of agricultural development. This would create local markets, create a new credit system, and facilitate the flow of capital,[20] all of which are essential to local development. Educational innovation that is initiated under these conditions stands a much more improved chance of success than in other settings of rural life. Other areas of focus in the rural-urban contradiction

---

[19]Zimbabwe: *Transitional National Development Plan*, Vol. 1, November, 1982.
[20]*Ibid.*

include improving the production of free cooperative enterprise, the development of water resources, local industries to generate internal capitol flow, and building investment that would be needed in education. One must conclude that the ability of nations of Southern Africa to solve problems of rural-urban contradiction constitute an important component of a strategy for educational innovation.

Principles of Innovation of the Curriculum

That educational innovation is meaningless unless it takes some critical factors into account is now apparent. Now, an additional consideration is that educational innovation is also meaningless unless one of its major purposes is to transform the curriculum so that it is in accord with the demands of the times. This is one of the major tasks of innovation that nations of Southern Africa have either failed to accomplish or have simply not attempted to initiate because they are afraid to fail. This is why they have found it easier to maintain the curriculum designed by the colonial governments with only cosmetic alterations than to initiate fundamental innovation. But nations of Southern Africa fail to realize that however difficult the task may be, it is one that must be undertaken.

There are six basic principles that must guide efforts towards innovation of the curriculum. The first is that a new curriculum must reflect an environment structured to facilitate the emergence of a set of dynamic ideas intended to ensure progressive education suited to the needs of the students and of a new era. This means that an educational system designed to meet the needs of students also meets the needs of the country. The two objectives become compatible only when the educational interests of the students come first. In this kind of setting the educational process makes it possible for its recipients to express "the values and aspirations of all the people based on the principle of total equality."[21]

The second principle is that the fundamental objective of education is to enable the individual to function fully in his environment, to be secure in his personhood, to see himself as an important contributing member of society and to help shape the direction of its development. Only the individual who is secure in his personhood is able to see the problems of his society from a broader perspective than is otherwise possible. Only a curriculum that provides an education to the individual to ensure his security will eliminate the elements of national conflict. Therefore, in order to adequately prepare the individual to play this important role, innovation must be initiated based on this principle.

The third principle is that the new curriculum must entail essential elements of innovation that would mean, *inter alia*, ability of all students to comprehend the diversity of human interests and aspirations. Without taking this diversity into consideration, society loses the emergence of new ideas and a variety perceptions necessary for its own development. This demands that the curriculum become flexible enough to accommodate this important diversity of interests. Once the opportunity is there it offers different people an opportunity to pursue different

---

[21]ZAPU, *Zimbabwe Primary Syllabus*, August, 1978.

professional goals. This is how society benefits from the education of its members. To enable it to accomplish this objective, the curriculum must be innovated.

The fourth principle is that because education in the colonial period was designed to sustain the colonial status quo, a fundamental change must now occur in order to redirect its development along the lines that lead to a new era of human endeavor and interaction. This means that the elitist character of the colonial educational policy must be replaced by the application of the principle of equality of educational opportunity. This is essential to the development of the talent that manifests in every student and which the nation needs as a critical resource needed to ensure its development. Maintaining a curricular status quo hurts the purpose for which education exists.

The fifth principle of curriculum innovation is that because the colonial educational system had the effect of *divide and rule*, the aim of the new educational system must be to enable all students to realize the concept of unity of *purpose*. This means that the educational objectives of the individual students and those of the nation must be compatible. The only way in which this essential balance can be achieved is by designing a curriculum that is different from that of the colonial period. It is important for nations of Southern Africa to remember that an effective implementation of this kind of curriculum demands deliberately careful collective action. It must never be imposed. The excuse that many national leaders in Africa give for imposing new programs is that the people are not sufficiently educated to understand the process of change merely hides their real intent, paternalistic behavior. This behavior undercuts the very purpose of the endeavor for meaningful change and must be avoided at all costs.

The sixth principle of innovation in the curriculum is that because the capacities of students to learn and muster concepts in general develop at different rates,[22] the new curriculum must be reorientated towards suiting this reality. The application of this principle can be done by individualized instruction, selecting classes, counseling methods, group or cooperative learning activity, informal instruction and placing less emphasis on teaching in order to pass public examinations. The challenge of the nations of Southern Africa is to accept these principles as essential components of educational innovation or to inflict harm to the educational process by failing to recognize the imperative of innovation.

The acceptance of these principles would assist in designing a new curriculum that has components of the objectives of a new era. Instead of teaching such misconception as "Cecil John Rhodes was the founder of Rhodesia," "David Livingstone was the first man to discover the Victoria Falls," "The Africans were uncivilized until the white man came," the new curriculum would help students reach such conclusions as "Although the colonial governments invaded the African society on the assumption that it was primitive and uncivilized, the Africans themselves refused to be what the white man said they were, primitive and uncivilized."

This simple strategy has wider implications for a strategy for educational innovation than appears on the surface. It revives the essence of a new sense of pride

---

[22]Roger Riddell, *From Rhodesia to Zimbabwe: Education for Employment*, p. 52.

and positive self-image that are distinct characteristics of the Africans before colonization. Even the age of slavery could not destroy these two human qualities. Once these qualities are instilled in students, a new breed of people will emerge to help chart a new course in the struggle for national development. This new thinking about the curriculum would seek to solve three serious problems that the colonial condition created. The first is that it would transform the educational system from seeking to produce a new elite to provide a broadly based education that makes realization of the concept of equality possible. The second is that it would help students in relating the educational process to real life situation. The third is that it would help strengthen a new cultural and national identity.[23]

Establishing Priorities

Important features of any strategy for educational innovation must of necessity involve the establishment of priorities. This is very difficult task in light of the fact that there are great educational needs that must all be met in Southern Africa. However, with priorities any efforts directed towards meaningful change may be futile because the implementation of innovation plans may lose direction if they are spread too thin. Nations of Southern Africa need to consider the following questions in determining their priorities: What is the greatest educational need right now? Is it primary education, secondary education, adult education, higher education, or vocational and technical education? What are the consequences of failing to establish priorities in the first place? What is the best method of financing innovation, and how much would it cost? What agents can be used in implementing innovation plans? What other national resources are needed for successful innovation? How long will it take to implement these plans? What objectives must direct the course of innovation? What are the outcomes of innovation?

Finding answers to these questions suggests two critical aspects of educational innovation itself. The first is that detailed plans must be made before innovation is attempted. The second aspect is that the formulation of such plans demands a collective action. This means that plans cannot be worked out over night, but must take considerable amount of time and energy to complete. The danger is that if too much time elapses, people will lose their enthusiasm and the whole plan may go down the drain. It is therefore important that leadership of tested ability and integrity be part of the planning exercise of the strategy for innovation.

Because the establishment of priorities varies from one country to another, this aspect of educational innovation may be harder to coordinate at the regional level than other aspects. The needs are so divergent that trying to coordinate programs may yield only marginal results. But with a comparatively low rate of literacy, it seems that all nations may need to place both adult education and universal primary education at the top. This is why the National Commission on Education in Botswana stated in 1977:

---

[23]Unesco, *Education in Africa in the Light of the Lagos Conference,* 1976, p. 17.

> Of all the levels and types of education it has been asked to consider, this commission feels bound to accord the highest priority to the improvement and reform of the primary level. Despite the expansion achieved, the sizable resources allocated to it, and the untiring efforts of many devoted teachers and administrators, this sector of the educational process is in disarray.[24]

In reaching this finding the Botswana commission on education deliberately examined the evidence that suggested the conclusion that primary education, considered from any perspective, was the most important level of education because "it is the foundation on which further learning is based, and opens up to the young person a range of opportunities for further study and work which are closed to the uneducated."[25] Indeed, under proper influence, the students' character, their study and work habits, attitudes and potential begin to form at the primary school.

In addition to this, the concept of nation-building so important to all nations, begins to take shape at the primary level as the school process helps implant in the students a sense of belonging to a wider social order and so they come to understand and appreciate the full meaning of what it means to be part of a national endeavor to sustain national development. But this is not to suggest that primary education must be placed at the top of the priorities, but only advance an argument in favor of doing so. One can make a similar case for adult literacy or vocational and technical education. Priorities must be established also by considering all possible options and through a collective process, they must not be imposed.

Cooperation Between Agents

Educational innovation can be costly in terms of resources, both financial and personnel. Therefore every effort must be made to resolve duplication and wastage. Before innovation is initiated, nations of Southern Africa must ensure that there is full cooperation between agents. The ministries of education, home affairs, economic development and finance must have a shared responsibility in formulating and implementing innovation programs with full cooperation of the people. It must be decided exactly what each ministry must do and how much money and other resources it will contribute.

Cooperation between implementation agents has advantages over a single agent. It facilitates the implementation plan. It helps in coordinating the innovation programs. It makes sure that the resources of one agent are not depleted. It makes it possible for all the parties to sustain their level of energy. It makes it possible to control spending and avoid cost overrun. It helps in ensuring that innovation plans are implemented within a reasonable time frame.

---

[24]Botswana: The Report of the National Commission on Education, 1977, p. 53.
[25]*Ibid.*

Summary and Conclusion

The discussion in this chapter leads to two basic conclusions. The first is that there is a variety of strategies for educational innovations. This chapter did not exhaust them all, it discussed only some specific examples as options that can be used to suit the specific needs of different nations. The fact that has been stressed in this chapter is that educational innovation cannot be initiated without careful planning. That planning constitutes strategies. Because innovation is so crucial to national development, it must be a product of careful consideration of all the relevant factors.

The second conclusion is that whatever strategy, or a combination of a number of them, is adopted, it is essential to take all factors into consideration in planning educational innovation. No matter how adequate a strategy is, it is ineffective if inadequate consideration is given to these determining factors. Designing strategies for successful educational innovation takes two critical elements into consideration. The first is a collective approach to ensure that it has the support of all people. Without that support success in implementing innovation plans cannot be assured. The second element is that innovation must be accomplished within a reasonable amount of time. These two elements must supplement each other to make sure that implementation is not hurriedly put in place. Once these two elements become an operative component of innovation, they help reduce the possibility of failure because every other aspect will have been accommodated. This is what it takes to initiate strategies of successful educational innovation.

7

OUTCOMES OF EDUCATIONAL INNOVATION

Any change in the educational system that does not envisage the emergence of a new concept of self cannot be regarded as innovation. A fifteen-year old high school girl, Harare, August, 1989

Introduction: Educational Innovation and Social Change

Writing on the effect of educational innovation in Botswana in 1977, the National Commission on Education observed:

Education is close to the center of life of any society because it is intimately involved with its culture and values, its political system and its economic situation. For this reason a fundamental outcome of any educational reform does not only concern itself with the overall change in the operation and benefits of the school system, but also with the basic improvement of the conditions of life in important areas of national life.[1]

The Transitional National Development Plan of Zimbabwe of November, 1982, seemed to reiterate the importance of this outcome of the educational innovation when it stated:

The underlying outcome of the educational reform movement is to improve the structure of relationships between citizens and their society in order to create a new social order. This means achieving the correct relationship between the people and the level of economic production, not as an end in itself, but in order to provide qualitative dimensions to enhance the transformation of our society.[2]

What these two reports are suggesting is that educational innovation cannot be undertaken for its own sake, but to focus on its structure and content as a major factor of socioeconomic change to serve the needs of an emerging nation. In this context, therefore, nations of Southern Africa need to examine broader implications as an outcome of educational innovation before it is initiated in order to assess its

---

[1]Botswana: *The Report of the National Commission on Education,* April, 1977,p.9.
[2]Zimbabwe: *Transitional National Development Plan,* Vol. 1, November, 1982,p.17.

direction and contribution to the development of the individual in order to ensure the development of the nation.

The purpose of this chapter is to discuss some outcomes of educational innovation in light of what it is intended to accomplish. The fundamental considerations that will become its focus is the question: How does educational innovation benefit the individual in order to benefit the nation? It will be seen that educational innovation cannot be initiated for its own sake, but to improve conditions of human life in a larger social order. Also critical considerations of how educational innovation benefits the individual as a prerequisite of benefiting society will be presented. These are: the concept of self and freedom to choose.

Outcomes of Educational Innovation

Indeed, nations of Southern Africa will undergo a much faster rate of social change than they have experienced in the past if they direct their efforts towards meaningful change. It is certain that conditions of both regional and national life quite different from the past will emerge in form of dramatic political developments, urban and industrial transformation as a result of meaningful educational reform. This leads to the conclusion that when innovation becomes a factor of social change, national institutions are profoundly affected in such a way that nations of Southern Africa, as nations everywhere, cannot cling to traditions of the past and hope to ensure their development.

Social change will therefore mean, *inter alia*, the emergence of new cultural practices adopted to new conditions in order to enable the people and their society to respond to a new social order. Against this background, linkages must be created between the innovated educational process and the character of social change. If linkages are broken, or if they dot not function in terms of seeking an improvement of society, then one must conclude that those responsible for educational innovation have failed to fulfill their assigned task and that a new start must be initiated.

It is a known factor that all nations of Southern Africa must realize that initiating educational innovation can be expensive. But a more important outcome of it is that unless educational innovation enables the nation to do self-examination to initiate creative planning, to develop new skills, to initiate efficient management of national resources, to redesign competent administrative structures and effective delivery systems so that persons responsible for their operations become more sensitive to human needs than was the case in the past. Educational innovation also creates a new environment of motivation and improved level of performance in the educational process. It also provides people an opportunity to discover new levels of potential as a reservoir of national service.

An important outcome of educational innovation must be a realization by national leaders and the people alike that, in the age of self-consciousness, human development is precious to the sustenance of national character and that providing a good education must be a fundamental national objective.[3] Unless educational

---

[3]Zambia: *Educational Reform: Proposals and Recommendations*, 1977, p. 15.

innovation is initiated with this objective in mind, its effects are likely to be more negative than positive, more detrimental than progressive, more inhibiting than promotional.

The Effects of Educational Innovation on the Individual

An important conclusion in this study is that unless educational innovation serves the developmental interests of the individual and elevates him to a new level of self-actualization, it cannot possibly serve the interests of the nation, and therefore, must be considered a failure. The question now is: How does educational innovation serve the developmental interests of the individual as a prerequisite of serving the developmental interests of the nation? To furnish an answer to the question two complimentary aspects pertaining to educational development of the individual must be discussed. The first is the concept of self. The second is freedom of choice.

The Concept of Self

The thinking that the individual has value and worth to his society demonstrates his importance to himself first as an outcome of the supreme act of creation. This suggests the very essence of the human being. Although the colonial society failed to build human institutions on the importance of this fundamental principle, this belief had its origin in the African heritage itself. In designing strategies to give meaning to the concept of self, the African traditional society was wise enough to help its members understand the truth that utilizing it in its original form would yield limited results, but that seeking to improve it through education, the human person was quite capable of attaining a higher level of performance than a limited environment would allow him to. Therefore, the Africans rejected the Western notion that perfection could not be reached. Aiming at reaching perfection through education was evident in the ability of the individual to base his life on moral and spiritual values as a basis and manifestation of the positive attributes which distinguish man from other living species. The philosophy of humanism in Zambia is based upon this fundamental tenet.[4]

In recognizing the emergence of a new concept of self as an outcome of educational innovation, emerging nations of Southern Africa must build into the new educational system a strategy that enables students to appreciate that their individuality grows out of an environment that enables them to eliminate the negative features of human existence. Individuality cannot come out of a narrow curriculum, nor does it result from a narrow definition of education or the rigidity of instructional methods. The teaching of the importance of individuality as a critical component of self, must begin simultaneously with the beginning of the educational process itself. That is, it must start as soon as the learner is aware of his environment. This

---

[4]*Ibid.* p. 6.

environment, by its very nature, must include providing the student the tools that he needs to develop his unique talents and to realize his interests and needs.

One sees six critical principles that are essential to the realization of the concept of self as an outcome of educational innovation. The first is that both the curriculum and the educational process must be broad and flexible enough to enable the student to choose his course of study carefully and to design his own unique strategies to develop abilities that are essential to serve his needs and interests. Out of this environment the student learns to attain a level of intellectual excellence that gives him a set of new experiences needed for success in both his educational endeavors and in life. The second principle is that the student inculcates in himself the discipline that he needs to carry out learning tasks that elevate the spirit of human endeavor to new heights. The third principle is that the student learns techniques of problem-solving in his unique way.

The fourth principle is that the student will learn to apply logic and human reasoning to show that he is not controlled by emotion. This is the setting from which moral and spiritual values have a new meaning to the individual. This is how these values benefit society. The fifth principle is that the student must learn to appreciate his cultural values as he demonstrates his aesthetic appreciation of its content. This gives him a new sense of his identity and individuality. The sixth principle is that the student learns to develop the spirit of self-reliance, not only to learn what he must learn, but also in developing a sense of independence, both in thought process and in integrating his action consistent with his individuality.

The application of these principles leads to an important conclusion regarding strategies of seeking to accomplish the concept of self as an outcome of educational innovation in Southern Africa. It enables the student to ask the question: Who am I? The answer defines the concept of self. This approach was explained to this author by a fifteen-year old high school girl in Harare, Zimbabwe, in August, 1989, saying:

> The advent of political independence to Zimbabwe in April, 1980, meant a tremendous opportunity for the rapid transformation of the system of education to enable all students to realize their unique individuality. The essential element of this transformation is the realization that before the student learns about the characters of William Shakespeare, or the principles of Archimedes, or the theorem of Pythogoras, or Edward Gibbon's interpretation of history, or the theories of John Dewey, or the political philosophy of Godfrey Huggins, *she* must learn to understand *herself* in relationship to *her* needs and interests. This entails *her* understanding of the concept of self.

> This, then, means that the student must have a thorough grasp of the concept of self in order to set goals, to determine priorities,to design learning strategies, and to motivate *herself*. These are essential elements of success and they demonstrate the concept of self at its best. Unless the student has a clear understanding of the concept of self, her educational endeavor is meaningless. Therefore, any change in the educational system that does not envisage the emergence of a new concept of self cannot be regarded as innovation, and has therefore failed.[5]

---

[5]A fifteen-year old high school girl, during an interview with the author, in Harare, Zimbabwe, August 6, 1989. The principal of the school told the author, "This girl is one of the brightest students i have ever had in my twenty-four years as a teacher."

Indeed, in addition to enabling the student "to set goals, to determine priorities, to design learning strategies, and to motivate *herself*," the concept of self, as an outcome of educational innovation, entrenches the basic principle that differences between people constitute manifestations of the importance of their individuality. In Southern Africa, where differences between men and women and between boys and girls determine the kind of opportunity one gets, both in school and in society, educational innovation to realize the concept of self acquires an added importance. It becomes a guiding light to young women's search for self in more meaningful ways than they did in the past. This is why this fifteen-year old high school girl went on to add:

> As an African girl struggling to carve a new concept of self in a set of changed circumstances, I find myself caught between cultural traditions that force me to accept an inferior position in society and the need to raise myself above the level of mediocrity to assert my own definition of self in order to realize my individuality. I am caught between the need to strive to attain academic excellence as a measure of my own understanding of the concept of self and strengthen that male mystique that my culture says a woman must always try to preserve by allowing boys to do better in school.

> I hope that change in the educational system will allow me to strive towards excellence without threatening that male mystique. I hope it will mean change in the attitudes of our society towards the education of women so that the curriculum will no longer compel girls to take home economics and reserve mathematics and science for boys. Any educational system that enables all students to realize their own goals as a distinct feature of individuality and self, is a manifestation of the outcome of its innovation.[6]

This suggests the conclusion that the concept of self goes far beyond the school activity as an outcome of educational innovation. It elevates one's image of self to the extent that one refuses to be controlled by the weaker side of human existence. It enables a girl to refuse to become pregnant. It enables a boy to see himself as someone who has value to himself and his society beyond the present. It enables the school and the community to see students as their prime reason for being. It enables the government to reevaluate educational programs and policies in order to respond adequately to conditions that demand new approaches to national problems. It demands that students become the center of the educational activity because their needs and interests supersede any other consideration. In short, the concept of self is of paramount importance to the entire educational process.It also becomes an instrument of eliminating negative features of the African culture, especially the practice of placing group interests above those of the individual.

The concept of self, when fully comprehended and embraced as a product of educational innovation, becomes a major motivating instrument of preserving personal growth . It helps to provide a potent incentive to determination and perseverance in efforts to overcome learning problems. It generates resourceful energy in seeking to master concepts that are essential to further learning. It

---

[6]*Ibid.*

provides continuity and the unity of purpose in endeavors that are related to the learning process. Its arouses curiosity and strengthens the pursuit of goals that are critical to successful human enterprise. It makes it possible for students to pose new and relevant questions in the process of learning. It influences the formation of new attitudes needed to engage in purposeful activity. Therefore, the concept of self, as an outcome of educational innovation, stands out larger as a social entity and gives the student something far more important than the educational process itself. This is why the colonial governments could not possibly conceive educational innovation from this perspective.

In 1989, the principal of a high school in Mutare, Zimbabwe, explained to the author what he considered to be the concept of self as an outcome of educational innovation, saying:

> The change of educational system from what it was during the colonial period to what it must be following independence demands a corresponding change in both content and purpose. A fundamental product of education in the post-colonial period must be to promote the concept of individuality. Individuality means self-concept. Self-concept means independence of thought process. This means freedom to grow, to set goals, to ask searching questions, to pursue the fulfillment of goals consistent with the spirit of inquiry, to formulate appropriate attitudes that put the student in the frame of mind that enables man to be himself.
>
> Unless these are outcomes of reform in education, unless new education accomplishes these results, it cannot be regarded as innovation The colonial governments never thought of education from the perspective of its inclusive quality. This is the challenge that many nations of Africa face. Can they rise to meet it?[7]

Freedom to grow suggests two critical elements as a product of education directed towards fulfilling the concept of individuality and the student's own definition of self. The first is that it cultivates an environment of intellectual growth, that potent force in human existence, that distinguishes the individual with motivation and purpose from an individual who does not possess them

The second element is that it provides an individual with the ability to comprehend the world of reality so that he can function in it without having to make major adjustment or relearn essential factors in order to function in society. John Dewey, the American educator, takes this line of thinking in discussing the importance of individuality as an outcome of education, saying, "He is lucky who does not find that in order to make progress, in order to go ahead intellectually, he does not have to relearn much of what he learned in school."[8]

What all this seems to suggest is that the concept of self is central to the pursuit of a career, whether or not one sees oneself as possessing abilities that lead to success in life. Success in life includes a decent standard of living, a decent income, ability to provide for one's family, security in one's person, good medical care and

---

[7]The principal of a high school during an interview with the author, in Mutare, Zimbabwe, August 7, 1989.

[8]John Dewey, *Experience and Education*. New York: Collier Books, 1938, p. 47.

good educational opportunity for one's children. Because, by their very nature, these outcomes of self are individual, the educational process has meaning only if it is so designed that each student gets from it the opportunity to fulfill his own definition of its purpose. This is a critical dimension of the challenge of educational innovation in Southern Africa.

Paul Hirst, a British writer, concludes that a good educational program creates an environment from which the concept of self and the search for individual fulfillment combine to generate a knowledge of reality about how one seeks to relate it in order to attain a higher level of achievement than would otherwise be the case.[9] In the concept of the struggle for individuality in Southern Africa, it is not so much the fault of the student that the educational process becomes a flaw, but the failure of those in positions of responsibility to structure it in such a way that it elevates the individual to the utmost level of performance, to which he is entitled. This is the line of thinking that *The Educational Reform Commission* of Zambia took into consideration when it concluded:

> Educational reform, therefore, must involve change in direction, in depth, and in breadth. It should include a substantial change to mean acceptance of the intrinsic value of individual enterprise, not only in education, but also in society itself. It must take into account the various factors which are the basis of the interplay between the educational system and the individual student's search for fulfillment.[10]

It is for these reasons that educational innovation must reflect the "components and the structure intended as a framework of the vehicle which will carry the essential elements of developing individual character so important to the dynamics of building a nation."[11] A guiding principle in this endeavor should be the knowledge that every student possesses a potential to be his best and in his own way.

For this human endeavor to yield tangible results, there must be two ingredients. The first is the support that comes from the school without which the student cannot succeed. Support is crucial in the student's efforts to set goals, to design strategies to fulfill them and to identify those areas of both potential and interest which the student may not be fully aware of on his own. The second ingredient is cooperation among all levels of the school system, from the principal to the teacher, and the parents and the community. This demands a close study of the student's environment, both home and community, to see if there are detracting influences that must be eliminated. Any student's deprived environment or background, which is a common feature among many nations of Southern Africa, must not be regarded as a sentence of his educational death. Rather it must be viewed as challenge to be overcome, a factor of motivation that can be utilized to attain new heights of personal achievement. Once these ingredients are in place, the student can place himself in a position that he understands he must be in to envisage himself as

---

[9]Paul Hirst, *Knowledge and the Curriculum: A Collection of Philosophical Papers*. London: Routledge and Kegan Paul, 1974, p. 30
[10]Zambia: *Educational Reform: Proposals and Recommendations*, 1977, p. 7.
[11]*Ibid.*

an individual human being with a unique potential for making a contribution to the development of his society. This is what the concept of self, as a product of educational innovation, means.

Freedom of Choice

One major reason why United Methodist Church Bishop Ralph E. Dodge[12] was deported from colonial Zimbabwe by the Rhodesia Front government in July, 1964, was his persistent call for the recognition of the concept of the freedom of choice in education and in the national political arena. In 1963, convinced that freedom of choice was a fundamental human right, Dodge argued:

> We hold governments responsible for the promotion and protection of the rights of all people as part of the fundamental freedoms of speech, choice in education and in society itself. The elimination of political mistreatment of persons for any reason is the first step towards granting all people freedom of choice.
>
> Freedom of choice in the educational process cannot be exercised in situations in which the educational system is controlled to suit the political purpose of those in power. Reform of the system of education is needed to ensure that freedom of choice combines with innovation in the curriculum to form a major factor of the advancement of the individual.[13]

For Dodge to expect the colonial government to respect the principle of freedom of choice was to expect the colonial government to accept the the concept of self. This was a tenet that any colonial government rejected because accepting it would undercut the basis of its own survival. But it was the concept that Dodge and the Africans felt must be expressed in order to shape the direction of their development. The refusal of the colonial government to accept this principle did not invalidate it.

This suggests that the principle of freedom of choice is an aspect of education that most nations of Africa have found difficult to implement because the influence of the colonial period is stronger in this regard than many nations would like to admit. The problem of freedom of choice in Southern Africa is compounded by three basic factors. The first is that with a rapid population increase, it is more difficult to cater to the educational needs of all the students. The second factor is that many children who are ready to begin primary schooling do not have the opportunity to actually enroll because there is simply not enough space.

Although the children in rural areas experience more educational problems than those in urban areas, the problem of enrollment has created serious national concern in all nations of Southern Africa. The third factor is that many parents try to enroll their children in school at a younger age than they did in the past because they want to introduce them into the school environment early in order to protect them from detracting influences around them. Parents also believe that the earlier the students

---

[12]Bishop Ralph Dodge first went to Angola as a missionary in 1936. He was then elected Bishop in 1956, and was assigned to Southern Africa with his administrative office in Harare, Zimbabwe.
[13]Ralph E. Dodge, "The Church and Political Community," an unpublished essay, July, 1963. By courtesy of the Old Mutare Methodist Archives.

are introduced to the educational environment, the better their chances of remaining in school.

Indeed, in these three factors lies the fabric of the challenge of educational innovation in Southern Africa. In 1977, the Educational Reform Commission of Zambia recognized this challenge when it observed:

> The shortage of space in the lower primary school is greater in urban areas than in rural areas. In some urban areas the shortage is so serious that one-third of the number of children cannot go to school. This is because the urban child population has increased faster than new classrooms have been built.
>
> The rapid rise in population, the desire of parents to send their children to school earlier than usual have come to cause problems that demand a corresponding rapid reform of the school system to enable all children to receive the education they need.[14]

An important factor for nations of Southern Africa to remember in these difficulties relative to the freedom of choice, as the Report of National Commission on Education of Botswana noted, is that "Students need help in identifying their own talents and abilities. They also require exposure to different opportunities in the adult world. Much better information on career options should be provided to students so that they exercise their freedom of choice."[15] But for the students to exercise this freedom of choice the school authority must recognize that the educational system itself has to be reformed because the educational process, as it existed during the colonial period, was out of place with the needs of the students. The fear that change represents some risks of failure which may damage the credibility of the government must be substituted for by the knowledge that it is better to risk failure through change than trying to maintain a system that is out of date.

This is a situation that demands the exercise of freedom of choice in education by all students. In order for this to happen, two considerations must be central to its application. The first is a broad and diverse curriculum that eliminates the narrow perception of education. Broadening the curriculum would allow students an opportunity to exercise all their options. The second is the availability of adequate educational opportunity so that students carry out an educational activity that is consistent with their own objectives and interests. Unless these two considerations are present, the concept of freedom of choice may have a shallow meaning.

A serious problem that may arise relative to the concept of the freedom of choice in Southern Africa is the disparity that still exists between opportunity to exercise it between boys and girls. Clearly, this is one of the negative legacies of the colonial period, and nations of Southern Africa should recognize that to resolve this disparity is to meet the challenge to their efforts towards educational innovation. In July, 1989, Faye Chung, Zimbabwe's minister of primary and secondary

---

[14]Zambia: *Educational Reform: Proposals and Recommendations,* 1977, p. 13.
[15]Botswana: *The Report of the National Commission on Education,* April, 1977.

education, acknowledged this disparity. Speaking during the opening of a seminar on rural women's access to education held at Kadoma, Chung noted:

> Enrollment in schools and other educational institutions indicate that there is a higher percentage of boys than girls despite the fact that women constitute 51% of the population. This disparity increases with increasing levels of education. The inadequacy of proper facilities and financial resources coupled with negative aspects of out dated traditions and culture militate against women's access to education.[16]

The fact that this kind of educational disparity impinges heavily upon the students' freedom of choice is shown in the disability that women suffer in both education and in society itself.

However, like many African politicians in the post-colonial nations of Southern Africa, Chung elected to blame other factors, such as cultural traditions and limited financial resources, for her inability to resolve a serious national problem. She was not likely to recognize the reality that government policy itself is essentially responsible for many of the problems that these emerging nations are facing. The fact of the matter is that educational innovation has not been carried out in bold and decisive fashion because many governments fear that failure may reflect negatively on the government itself. The fear that initiating change is risky inhibits the ability of nations of Southern Africa to initiate the much needed change that would serve the interests of all students. Until these nations face this reality and become resolved to do something to improve the situation, they will always experience the scourge of underdevelopment.

While Chung went to considerable lengths to argue that, "My government introduced free and universal primary education on attaining independence,"[17] she did not address the real cause of the problem, failure to initiate innovation. She may not have been aware that the Africans are quite capable of understanding the need for change if there is clear leadership, clearly stated objectives and strategies to fulfill them, and if they are directly involved in the process of formulating and implementing change. Chung's recognition that "For many decades women have been left out in most development plans and activities,"[18] is precisely the reason why innovation must be initiated to ensure that the problem is fully resolved. What good does it do the people to acknowledge the existence of a problem and then do little to resolve it?

Most nations of Southern Africa seem to recognize the importance of freedom of choice in the educational process as a critical outcome of innovation. In 1988, for example, Dzingai Mutumbuka, then minister of education and culture in Zimbabwe, addressed this aspect when he argued that emerging nations of Africa must recognize

---

[16]Faye Chung, "Women Are Less Educated Than Men," a speech delivered during the opening of rural women's access to education in Zimbabwe. Ref. 230/89/CB/SM/SK, July 25, 1989. By courtesy of the Zimbabwe Ministry of Information.

[17]*Ibid.*

[18]*Ibid.*

that it is in their own best interest to give the students an opportunity to select their own course of study with the assistance of the school. Allow students :

> to develop as skilled persons who can adopt to changing technological development. This applies to the types of courses, the levels of the courses, and their depth and breadth. It is important to realize that the training the students receive is only a basis on which to develop further knowledge and skills to enable the learner to develop as a good craftsman and good technician, to substitute self-doubt with self-confidence, to balance the concept of collective identity with that of the individuality. This allows freedom of choice as a distinct outcome of reform of the educational system.[19]

But in all his enthusiasm to put the concept of freedom of choice in education into practice, Mutumbuka, like other national leaders in Southern Africa, may have missed an important consideration, and that is, before it can be put into practice, the concept of the freedom of choice must be realized only as a result of educational innovation. The reason why it has up to now not been realized is that educational innovation itself has not been established. In 1979, the ruling ZANU of Zimbabwe issued an election manifesto in which it outlined thirteen freedoms which it said every citizen was entitled to. Among these freedoms was the freedom of choice in the educational process.[20] But, in 1990, eleven years later, this form of freedom looked as distant as it had in 1979. National leaders of Southern Africa, like Faye Chung did in July, 1989, argue that limited financial resources are the cause of many of the problems their nations experience in education. It would be erroneous to place blame on limited financial resources without taking other important considerations, such as the inability of national leaders to initiate innovation, into account. In any event, limited financial resources are often a result of a faulty fiscal policy or mismanagement.

There is a dimension of freedom of choice that only a few nations of Africa fully understand, and this has to do with special education, that kind of education that must be provided students with special needs because they are mentally or physically impaired. Before the educational process can attempt to meet the needs of these students, it is necessary first to clearly identify the causes of their impairment and then determine the interests and goals of the individual students. Once this is done, full attention must be given to the physical, emotional, social and mental development of each student as an individual. The fact that some students are handicapped must not be the reason to deny them any opportunity to exercise their freedom of choice.

The Educational Reform Commission of Zambia took this line of thinking into account when it went on to add:

---

[19]Dzingai Mutumbuka, "Training Institutions Play a Vital Role in Educational Reform," a speech delivered at the Harare (Zimbabwe) Polytechnic College. Ref. 447/88/CC/SM/GS. October 7, 1988. By courtesy of the Zimbabwe Ministry of Information.

[20]ZANU-PF, Election Manifesto, 1980 (For details see, for example, Dickson A. Mungazi, *The Struggle for Social Change in Southern Africa: Visions of Liberty*, p.128.

All handicapped students are entitled to adequate education in the same way that other students are. They should receive basic and further education as any other students. Since the handicapped students are a special case, there should even be *positive discrimination* (affirmative action) in the provision of facilities and amenities for purposes of ensuring their educational development.[21]

The commission warned that realizing the educational needs of students with special difficulties requires basic reform as its prerequisite. In recognizing the fact that "Special education is not yet fully developed for a long time because it has not been properly organized,"[22] the Educational Reform Commission of Zambia was warning against the consequences of further delay in facing the challenge that this problem presents in the thrust for educational innovation.

This is the line of argument that this author has been advocating, that the nations of Southern Africa must overcome their fear of failure in initiating educational innovation because the consequences of maintaining the educational status quo are more devastating than those of failure to initiate change for both the student and society itself. Freedom of choice, as a critical outcome of educational innovation, must be accepted as such if the educational process must have meaning to national development.

The Effect of Educational Innovation on Society

This study has argued that for education to serve its real purpose, it has to be innovated to suit the conditions of the time. It has also argued that before educational innovation benefits society, it must demonstrate tangible benefits to the individual. This chapter has discussed two critical elements of the individual that educational innovation must focus on: the concept of self and freedom of choice. Once the individual secures educational benefits as a result of realizing these two elements, then society itself stands to benefit from properly educated individuals in it.

This study has also argued that because national leaders in Southern Africa focus on their own definition of national development, they tend to neglect the educational development of the individual as a foundation upon which any concept of national development must be built. The leaders of nations of Southern Africa must be reminded that any definition of national development is virtually meaningless if it is not based upon the educational development of the individual. The question now arises: How does educational innovation designed to benefit the individual also benefit society? This section provides some answers to the question.

When leaders of nations of Africa speak of the need for national development, they are thinking essentially in terms of political unity. In their enthusiasm to achieve this objective, some leaders adopt methods that entail dictatorial action. In doing so, they become intolerant of political views of those who hold different views from their own. Thus, they institute one-party systems that rob the citizens of their right and freedom of political dissent. They advance four reasons for turning the country

---

[21]Zambia: *Educational Reform: Proposals and Recommendations*, October, 1977, p.23.
[22]*Ibid.*

into a one-party system of government. The first is that the people are not sufficiently educated to understand the complexities of a democratic system. The second reason is that democracy is too expensive, it takes too much money and time. The third reason is that because attempts to practice democracy are related to tribal or ethnic affiliation, they become divisive and national unity is substituted for by national conflict. The fourth reason is that democracy is Western imposition and so it is alien to African culture. The author rejects all these reasons as totally invalid for a very simple reason: democracy is universal, and its application is not in any way the prerogative of any particular culture. The fact that the colonial governments did not practice democracy is no reason why nations of Southern Africa should not practice it.

The truth of the matter is that what the leaders of African nations who take this line of argument seem to neglect is that with proper education these problems need not exist in the first place. The character of educational innovation that this study has discussed would help create an entirely new political environment that would eliminate doubts and suspicion of any one group of citizens against another. The freedom that citizens have as students to choose their course of study must translate into freedom of expression of ideas in the national political arena. Nations of Southern Africa regard freedom of expression as forum of criticizing the government, and so they are not aware that it is an essential component of national political stability. The government is best served by advancing logical arguments to defend itself through the use of logical argument, rather than by silencing opposition because, once the government resorts to this method of eliminating opposition or criticism, the political stability it hopes for is seriously threatened. When people are properly educated, they fully understand the importance of exercising political responsibility in a way that does not threaten the government. This is how educational innovation designed to serve the needs of the individual serves society.

Another important outcome of educational innovation relative to national political development is that it negates the creation of one-party systems because the citizens come to understand the importance of true democracy and will contribute to its development in a way that eliminates the fear that dominates the thinking and the behavior of leaders, the fear of military coups and of one form of political violence or another, and of political disintegration. When citizens understand the need for political stability based upon genuine practice of democracy, they help create a national climate from which emerges a realization that one-party systems rob nations of the vitality that manifests itself in the people. They destroy the creativity, the emergence of new ideas and the resources that all nations need to sustain the momentum for national development.

Indeed, one-party systems strengthen the notion that political wisdom is a prerogative of the party in power and the individuals who are in government know more about national issues than any one else in the country. Nothing is more dangerous to efforts directed towards national development. When citizens are educated as a result of educational innovation, they help to eliminate the myth that one-party system represents national unity. They endeavor to create a multi-party system as the only form of true democracy. Under these conditions how can one-party systems be justified?

There is yet another important outcome of educational innovation that the leaders of nations of Southern Africa must understand as playing an important part in the national political arena and development. This is, citizens will help create open government operations through participation. This gives people a sense of belonging. It also creates an atmosphere of mutual trust. It protects the government from the temptation of engaging in corruption. It helps to eliminate the vail of secrecy so common when corruption becomes part of government operations. Open government operations afford nations the courage to face their problems in an honest manner. This is how confidence, mutual trust, and cooperation between the government and the people develop in the interest of national development.

Perhaps one example of efforts to create a national climate of open government operations is evident in what Zimbabwe has tried to do during the past few years. Not only is Zimbabwe the first country in Southern Africa to enact legislation making corruption a criminal offence, but the government has also enforced it. Whenever there are reports of impropriety by any government official, the President is required to name a commission of inquiry which carries out its investigation in public and its proceedings are reported fully by the media. In 1988, after receiving reports that a number of government officials were engaging in corruption, President Mugabe used appropriate clauses of the legislation to appoint a high level commission of inquiry under the chairmanship of Justice Sandura to investigate the charges.

When, in April, 1989, the Sandura Commission reported that, indeed, six senior government officials were implicated in corruption, President Mugabe immediately released the report to the public and ordered that the officials stand trial in accordance with the law.[23] Subsequently one senior government minister, Maurice Nyagumbo, died under suspicion that the scandal had so tarnished his political career and his family reputation that he had come to the end of the road. The other five ministers were found guilty and sentenced to heavy fines in addition to losing their position in the government. One senior official , Dzingai Mutumbuka, and his wife were fined a total of $105,000 in August, 1989.[24] President Mugabe told his fellow Zimbabweans that his government would not tolerate corruption and he would enforce the law. While the efforts by Zimbabwe to have open government operations will by no means lead to the end of corruption, they demonstrate that it is important to stamp it out.

The outcome of this effort towards open government operations must be understood in the context of the reaction of the people. In May, 1989, when reports of this corruption first surfaced, Edgar Tekere, an inner member of the ruling ZANU and a senior government official, resigned to form the Zimbabwe Unity Movement (ZUM) and charged the government with corruption, saying:

---

[23]*The Herald,* April 13, 1989,
[24]*The Herald,* August 18, 1989.

Zimbabwe's national leadership is already so thoroughly decayed by corruption that we are very close to the point of collapse of the executive. The ruling party is vigorously advocating the conversion of Zimbabwe into a one-party state and is seeking to entrench its undemocratic self as a dictatorship.[25]

Because President Mugabe had not tried to conceal the fact that some of his colleagues in government had, indeed, engaged in corruption , and because he often said that he would not tolerate it, Tekere's charges even helped him to "take a good deal of air out of his balloon by dealing with the corruption issue head-on."[26] But one must remember that Tekere's remarks underscores the importance of preserving a multi-party democracy. It is quite possible that the extent of the corruption would not have been fully exposed to the citizens if there was a one-party system of government. Openness in government is therefore a critical component of the democratic system and cannot be practiced under a one - party system, no matter how much the government tries.

While the citizens were still displeased with the corruption by government officials,[27] they came to appreciate the efforts that Mugabe was making to have open government operations remain part of the system of government itself. It is for this reason that President Mugabe continued to enjoy a reasonable degree of popular support.

The important thing to remember about political events in Zimbabwe is that because the openness with which Mugabe has handled them, the citizens were pleased with the knowledge that his government had nothing to hide. This view was expressed to the author by the principal of a high school who said in August, 1989:

> While we were quite displeased with this Zimbabwean Watergate because it robbed the people of their trust in their government, the fact that the President himself was was quite candid in acknowledging that some of his colleagues had engaged in corruption and allowing the media to cover the investigation on it suggests that he was concerned about the need to preserve the interests of the nation.

> I must say also that if there were a one-party system of government, there would never have been an Edgar Tekere to raise charges of corruption in the first place. This means also that Zimbabwe needs to educate its people so well that they can understand the process of government so that there is no reason to turn the country into a one-party state. This demands a basic reform of the educational system.[28]

This is precisely what this study has argued, and there is no question that the government of Zimbabwe has recognized the importance of respecting the democratic values for the good of the country. Allowing ZUM a political platform underscores this conclusion. Indeed, while this African form of *glasnost* is rare, it can provide a model that other nations of Southern Africa can follow. The violent

---

[25]*The New York Times,* May 7, 1989.

[26]*Ibid.*

[27]The author saw the evidence of this displeasure while he was there in August, 1989, when students at the University of Zimbabwe were staging demonstrations against it. For details, see Chapter 1 of this study.

[28]Interview with a principal of a high school, in Harare, Zimbabwe, August 6, 1989.

repressive force that the police in South Africa uses against demonstrators of apartheid is hardly a climate of openness in government. When, on January 18, 1990, the police used naked force to suppress the people who were demonstrating against the visit of the British cricket team to South Africa, the determination of the South African government to entrench both an oppressive system and rigidity became fully known.

Another important outcome of educational innovation is the need to improve manpower to sustain the strength of the economy. Once educational innovation has been established, an effort must be made to attract more students to become teachers. This can be done by improving conditions of service, including salary and benefits. To achieve this objective an increase in the number of training schools must be initiated. Short-term solutions to the problem of the supply of teachers must also be initiated, such as the one that Zimbabwe inaugurated at the time of its independence in 1980, when it recruited teachers from all over the world to fill the need.

To enable the teachers to fulfill their responsibilities fully, they must receive the support of other staff members and members of the community. All these factors combine to create a new environment which enables the teachers to prepare their students to enter employment . This is also how educational innovation plays an important role in the development of manpower. Indeed, in many countries of the Third World, one of the most critical constraints inhibiting economic development, which, in effect, becomes more critical unless there are substantial changes in education, is the serious shortage of skilled manpower. The seriousness of the shortage of skilled manpower will be more profoundly felt with the passage of time unless educational innovation is designed to eliminate it.

To ensure adequate manpower as an outcome of educational innovation two critical factors must be taken into consideration. These are supply and demand. To assess the adequacy of supply through knowledge of existing system, political accountability is necessary. This demands ability to project economic growth rate and the percentage of trained people required to man various sectors of employment aggregate. The rate of unemployment, a serious problem in all countries of Southern Africa, should offer some insights about which areas, both educational development and economic development should receive more attention and emphasis. This creates demand.[29]

The balance between supply and demand is a factor of economic growth that is often a product of educational innovation. The process of making these decisions requires political accountability because both are inseparable from the political process. This national endeavor can best be initiated through educational innovation itself. This suggests the conclusion that without educational innovation, there is no manpower, and without manpower there is no economic growth, without economic growth, national independence and development cannot take place.

Yet another critical outcome of educational innovation is the improvement of health services and housing. The important thing to remember is that the healthier the citizens the happier they become, and the happier they become the more productive

---

[29]Zimbabwe: *Transitional National Development Plan*, Vol. 1, November, 1982, p. 9.

citizens the happier they become, and the happier they become the more productive they become. But it would be wrong to assume that good health comes on its own; it must be the result of careful planning. Proper nutrition requires education. Knowledge of the importance of a balanced diet and the proper care of food is the result of good educational programs. The disparity that exists between rural health care and urban health care along with the inadequacy of medical facilities and technology, are conditions that can be resolved by educational innovation. Housing problems have their roots in the problems of socioeconomic development of the nation[30] and the failure of meaningful educational reform. Granted that it takes time to resolve the problems left behind by the colonial governments, nations of Southern Africa must realize that reform of the educational system can go a long way in assisting to find solutions to many problems they face today.

Summary and Conclusion

The discussion in this chapter leads to two basic conclusions. The first is that the concept of educational innovation is an underlying imperative of national development when it is directed towards the development of the individual. Without the development of the individual, there is no national development. Two critical factors have been identified and discussed in this chapter relative to the educational development of the individual as an outcome of educational innovation. These are the concept of self and freedom of choice. Unless these remain central to any effort directed towards seeking an improvement of education, it would lose the purpose for which it is initiated.

The second conclusion is that when educational innovation is designed to benefit the individual, it is society itself that ultimately benefits more. Therefore, it is in the best interest of the nation to remain sensitive to the need to protect and promote the educational interests of the individual in order that society may benefit. Economic self-sufficiency, manpower development, a decent standard of living and political participation are the insurance policy that creates a happy and progressive society. Nations of Southern Africa must endeavor to ensure educational innovation to preserve these important pillars of their development.

---

[30] *Ibid.*

8

THE CHALLENGE OF EDUCATIONAL INNOVATION AND NATIONAL DEVELOPMENT: SUMMARY, CONCLUSION, AND IMPLICATIONS

Education under apartheid is a crime against humanity -- Nelson Mandela, February 12, 1990

The thrust for national development in Southern Africa cannot be undertaken without meeting the challenge of educational innovation - A Zimbabwean education, August 10, 989

Introduction: Innovation in the Apartheid Setting

The announcement made on February 2, 1990, in the South African parliament by F. W. de Klerk, the president Nelson Mandela, after spending twenty - seven years in Victor Verster Prison would soon be released unconditionally and that the ANC and other political parties would be legalized once more since they were outlawed in 1964. Mandela's actual release occurred on February 11. What Mandela said in Cape Town soon after his release underscores the importance of what this study has attempted to present, and that is: change becomes innovation when it is directed towards improving the conditions governing human life. With direct reference to the destructive influence of apartheid, Mandela spoke to the thousands who came to welcome him, saying:

> I stand before you, not a prophet, but as a humble servant. Your efforts have made it possible for me to be here today. Our resort to the armed struggle in 1960 was merely a defensive action against the violence of apartheid. Our armed struggle still exists today. We have no option but to continue. We call on our white compatriots to join us in the process of eradicating apartheid.[1]

An examination of the application of apartheid evinces the determination of the Africans to end it in all its forms. Not only is there complete racial segregation, but the government also believes that white students must be educated to fill positions of political dominance. As a result, in 1984, for example, the government of South

---

[1]Nelson Mandela, in a statement made in Cape Town soon after his release from Victor Verster Prison, SABC, February 11, 1990.

Africa spent ten times as much on white education as it did on black education.[2] In the same year student-teacher ratio was 24:1 for whites and 47:1 for Africans. In 1979, only 5,000 Africans were enrolled in institutions of higher education out of a total population of 22 million compared to 11,825 white students out of a total population of 4.3 million.[3]

It is no wonder that the Africans have been demanding nothing less than the eradication of apartheid. This demand is only one of many conditions which must be eliminated in order to set South Africa on the road to genuine innovation and progress. Because it is not possible to initiate innovation under apartheid, its eradication would constitute the first step towards educational innovation as a prerequisite of the transformation of South Africa. South Africa will continue to resist this call at the peril of its own development and national strife.

Southern Africa at the Crossroads: The Need for Innovation

In deciding to release Nelson Mandela, the de Klerk government must have fully recognized that it was time for change, and that apartheid would be maintained at the peril of maintaining a devastating national conflict and isolation from the world community. Neither the world community nor the Africans of South Africa could accept the continuation of the violence of apartheid any longer. Speaking in Soweto on his reception on February 12, 1990, Mandela expressed the determination of the Africans to end apartheid.

With special reference to education, Mandela warned, "The educational crisis in our country is a crisis in politics. Education under apartheid is a crime against humanity."[4] In Chapter 1 the conclusion was reached that the problems of national development in Southern Africa cannot be resolved until solutions to the problems of educational innovation can be found. This is the reality and the perspective that a prominent educator in Zimbabwe had in mind when he concluded, "The thrust for national development in Southern Africa cannot be undertaken without meeting the challenge of educational innovation. Educational innovation is the foundation upon which national developmental programs are built."[5]

The release of Nelson Mandela must also be seen in the context of fundamental change that has been taking place elsewhere in Southern Africa. On May 12, Mobuto Sese Seko announced that Zairians were now free to form other political parties and to exercise freedom of speech, provided they operated under his control and direction as he had outlined in 1971. When the students at the University of Zaire demanded that he resign from office to make room for change and innovation, Seko resorted to his characteristic repressive approach. It is not possible for both Seko and the apartheid government to come to terms with the call for fundamental change

---

[2]The U.N.: *A Crime Against Humanity: Questions and Answers on Apartheid in South Africa.* New York, 1984, p. 16.

[3]*Ibid.* p. 17

[4]Nelson Mandela, speaking in Soweto during a reception held in his honor, February 12, 1990, SABC.

[5]An African educator in Zimbabwe, during an interview with the author, August 10, 1989.

without recognizing that innovation is an imperative of national development. Since both represent a status quo, both have become major problems in a regional endeavor to initiate innovation. There is no question that when the international community and the Africans recognize the violence of both apartheid and Seko's high-handedness as problems of regional development, they are actually acknowledging them as major handicaps to innovation.

South Africa's active involvement in the brutal civil wars in Angola and Mozambique along with the opposition activities brought about by dissident elements in Zimbabwe, and its periodic raids into neighboring countries in military pursuit of ANC guerrillas combine to distabilize the region and place it at a crossroads. Also South Africa's successful efforts to weaken SADCC so that the black countries in Southern Africa continue to depend on it for economic survival, have caused enormous difficulties for the region as a whole. From 1987 to 1989, when the apartheid government was pressured to accept the U.N.'s terms contained in Resolution 435 of 1978 for the independence of Namibia on March 21, 1990, came the realization that the South African government had to come to terms with the Africans if the whites ever hoped to have a meaningful future.

The fact of the matter is that the de Klerk government could not come to terms with the Africans in South Africa without persuading the Afrikaners to come to terms with their neighbors. But South Africa would not come to terms with its neighbors without ceasing its distabilizing activity in the region. The increase in sales of firearms by 60% among the whites in April 1990 is an action that does nothing to resolve the problems caused by apartheid. South Africa's conscious decision to stop its aid to Afonzo Dhlamini's Renamo in Mozambique and to Jonas Savimbi's UNITA in Angola would constitute a set of elements essential for regional peace. Above all, de Klerk and his government must persuade their fellow Afrikaners to accept the reality that it is in their own best interest to accept without further delay the principle of majority rule under the universal practice of one person, one vote.

This is the view that this author expressed when he wrote a letter to de Klerk on February 15, 1990, saying:

> It is very important for you to lift the state of emergency in order to allow the Africans to place their confidence in your sincerity to negotiate in good faith. To try to negotiate with them under the influence of the state of emergency is to try to have them function with their hands tied on their back. It is vitally important for the whites of South Africa to recognize that the principle of majority rule must prevail. History shows that whenever a minority rules over the majority, abuse of power and oppression become inevitable.

> The support that South Africa has been giving to Jonas Savimbi and Renamo in Mozambique has also created a violent situation in all of Southern Africa. Regional peace is important for South Africa itself and its action to stop periodic raids into front-line states can go a long way in resolving major problems.[6]

---

[6]The author, in a letter to F. W. de Klerk, February 15, 1990. On March 12, 1990, S. P. Basson, de Klerk's Administrative Secretary, wrote to "acknowledge receipt of your letter."

The massive demonstrations that were staged throughout South Africa on February 17, 1990, the first time that political demonstrations have been allowed and in which thousands of Africans participated, were in demand of fundamental change to accommodate the aspirations of all people. That the demonstrators demanded equal political rights, better housing, better salary, better work conditions, and an end to apartheid in education underscores the need for rapid innovation in South Africa. The refusal of the government to recognize the importance of extending these basic human rights is what has placed the country and the region at the crossroads. The simple fact that Africans are not allowed to vote in national elections, that they cannot hold public office outside the Bantustan Homelands is the basis of their legitimate demand for rapid change.

By coincidence, there were massive demonstrations in Washington, D. C. on the same day. It was not surprising that the demonstrators demanded President George Bush to ensure that the U.S.A. would not lift economic sanctions against South Africa until apartheid has been dismantled and a non-racial society has been created. That they also demanded President Bush to withdraw his invitation to de Klerk to visit the White House for discussions suggests the conclusions that Americans understand the imperative need for fundamental change before South Africa is readmitted into the international community. There is no doubt that these events suggest only one thing: innovation in all aspects of national life in South Africa is necessary to avoid a major national disaster.

The need for educational innovation in South Africa, like any other country in Southern Africa, is stressed by the facts themselves. In 1990 only 10% of the students were white, and yet the government spent more than ten times more on education for whites than it did for that of Africans. There were forty - seven black students per teacher while there were thirty white students per teacher. This ratio had deteriorated considerably from what it was in 1979. That the demonstrations staged by African teachers all over South Africa on February 25, 1990, were aimed at fundamental change in this situation shows the seriousness with which they viewed the need for innovation. It is not possible for South Africa to resist the call for this kind of change without doing an irreparable damage to the country.

The Colonial Period and Educational Innovation

The decade between 1970 and 1980 witnessed a spiraling demand for more and better education in Africa than at any other period in the history of the continent. However, the decade between 1980 and 1990 witnessed the emergence of new attitudes towards educational innovation to make change in the political and socioeconomic system possible. During the decade of 1960 and 1970 the African nations were still struggling to shake off the effects of European colonial rule as they attempted to carve for themselves a new national identity. But the African nations quickly realized that the thrust for educational innovation was more complex than they had thought because the influence of the colonial period was stronger than they thought. Indeed, during that decade and beyond, the African nations were attempting to educate their people to fit into social structures that are no longer in existence today. The difficult choices that nations of Southern Africa had to make in education and the priorities that they had to establish as a strategy for the future development of education were, in effect, forced upon them by economic forces that were beyond their control.

There is no question that the problems that these nations have been facing can be traced to the establishment of the colonial governments in the nineteenth century. It has been concluded that as an outcome of the Berlin Conference of 1885, European nations placed more importance on the securing of raw materials than on the development of the Africans to facilitate the creation of better human relationships for the future to suit the social conditions of a new era. For this reason the colonial governments considered it essential to limit educational opportunity for Africans so that they could be more effectively controlled politically by training them to function as laborers.

This strategy suggests that from their inception, the colonial governments did not encourage the development of education among the Africans because they knew that their ability to acquire it would enable them to acquire elements of critical thinking and so help them recognize the injustice of the colonial systems themselves. Therefore, the denial of equal educational opportunity to the Africans became the green pastures in which the milk cows of colonialism grazed. As the colonial government became more solidly established, the need to train the Africans to function as laborers became more profoundly felt. In Southern Africa as a whole the views that Cecil John Rhodes, Paul Kruger, Leopold II, Antonio Salazar and Daniel Malan expressed towards the need to restrict the educational advancement of the Africans suggest that as economic conditions changed the need to change the system of education became apparent.

But, because the colonial governments considered change in the way that it was intended to ensure their effective control, the Africans were trained only in terms of a desire to make them more efficient laborers. Therefore, this kind of change cannot be regarded as innovation, even though the colonial governments themselves considered it an improvement because it was an improvement in the effectiveness of the machinery of control, not in the conditions of the Africans. Therefore, the denial of equal educational opportunity to the Africans presented to the colonial governments a formidable problem. In colonial Zimbabwe, for example, when free and compulsory education was extended to white students in 1935, the Africans struggled against great difficulties in their effort to gain meaningful education.

After the Second World War a general political consciousness among the Africans all over the continent created a new situation that colonial governments did not anticipate. When the Africans began to recognize the injustice of the colonial systems and demanded change, not only in education, but also in other important areas of their life, the colonial governments were reluctant to respond affirmatively. The more the Africans were denied equal educational opportunity, the more they demanded it, and the more they demanded it, the more the colonial governments repressed them. This is also how a climate of conflict was created between the Africans and the colonial governments.

That this situation was having implications beyond the educational process is evident in the new environment that emerged in which political manifestations of education became a new factor of their relationships.[7] Once political manifestations of education became the new *modus operandi* of relationships between the Africans and the colonial governments, the struggle for equal educational opportunity took a back seat while the struggle for political rights became their major focus to make educational innovation possible.[8] This is precisely the strategy adopted by the Africans of South Africa today. It is equally true that the educational policy of the colonial governments in Southern Africa failed to develop a system of communication that would have become the basis of resolving national problems because the colonial governments saw the education of the Africans only as it was intended to prepare them to serve the purposes of the colonial society.

One reaches three conclusions about the formulation and implementation of the educational policy of the colonial governments in Southern Africa. The first is that not only did these policies have the effect of trying to control the rise of African nationalism, but they also had an adverse effect on the Africans' reaction to Western culture itself. The second conclusion is that the overall effect of the colonial educational policy is the emergence of an action that not only continued to isolate the colonial governments from a rapidly developing trend of thinking among the Africans that equality of both educational opportunity and socioeconomic opportunity were essential to national development, but also made it unlikely for the colonial governments to see the conflict that was emerging between the two sides from the point of view of the Africans.

The third conclusion is that because the emergence of new attitudes among the Africans against the policies of the colonial governments originated primarily as a result of their contact with missionaries, the colonial governments tried to enlist them on their side of the growing conflict. Indeed, in Angola and Mozambique, the Catholic church supported the policies of the Portuguese government. In South Africa, the Dutch Reformed church came out squarely on the side of the government. But, realizing that it was pursuing a wrong policy, the church decided to shift its policy from supporting the government to supporting the Africans because the Africans themselves had convinced them of the rightness of their cause.

That this shift of policy by the church was crucial in the ensuing struggle for independence added a critical dimension in the political landscape that would soon come into existence. The decision of some of the members[9] of the Dutch Reformed Church in 1985 to oppose apartheid is one major reason why de Klerk and his government decided to announce their intention to initiate change. But when, in April, 1990, de Klerk announced that the advent of an African majority government

---

[7]Dickson A. Mungazi, *Education and Government Control in Zimbabwe: A Study of the Commissions of Inquiry, 1908-1974*. New York: Praeger Publishers, 1990, p. 69.

[8]*Ibid.* p. 70.

[9]Led by Rev. Bass Naude, these members of the Dutch Reformed Church rejected the biblical reasons on which the church supported apartheid, that black and white had nothing in common and so were unequal even before God. See the documentary film, *The Cry of Reason* for example, for details.

was not envisaged in the kind of change he had in mind, the course of innovation that the people of South Africa had hoped would be initiated with his announcement of February 2, suffered a severe setback. This means that while some members of the Dutch Reformed Church played a critical role in forcing de Klerk to see the imperative of change, there were others who exerted on him strong pressure not to yield to demands for the kind of change that the Africans wanted to see as a prerequisite of innovation. Therefore, the action of taking sides in the controversy surrounding the need for change added a new twist in the conflict between the Africans and the government.

This critical situation suggests that educational innovation during the colonial period could not be accomplished without corresponding change in the political and socioeconomic systems. The unrepresentative character of the colonial society, such as exists in South Africa today, did not permit the Africans to play a significant role in its operations and functions. But what is even more disturbing is that in their resistance to efforts to help them perceive the need to bring about a genuine innovation in both the social system and in education, the colonial governments themselves became the ultimate victims of their own policies. This is undoubtedly the fate that awaits the government of South Africa in its resistance to efforts to assist it to see the need to end apartheid. Those members of the Dutch Reformed Church who have made a call for change cannot be blamed for supporting the Africans in their struggle for political independence as a prerequisite of educational innovation.

In 1963, William H. Lewis put the struggle for meaningful change in Africa in the context of the conditions created by the colonial systems, saying:

> This is a time of testing in Africa. The old signposts are being torn down. The hallmarks of colonialism are disappearing. In the crucible of social change new human formations are beginning to take shape. In some respects this is a supremacy of important transitional period, one signifying the end of innocence. Now, in the throes of national building and modernization, Africa is fashioning new values, identities and orientation.[10]

What is important in Lewis' observation about the need for change in Africa during the colonial period is that the need is still felt in African nations today. At this point in the history of Southern Africa, if one looks back to the dramatic events of 1963, one would have to conclude that it was almost unquestionable that the closing phase of the colonial period would leave behind a trail of legacy that, by 1990, would still stand in the way of meaningful change. Today, the practice of one-party systems of government, the system of president for life and political repression are among the most devastating forms of that legacy. In this kind of setting the African leaders themselves must be aware of the damage they are inflicting on a national effort towards change by holding on to outdated institutional structures.

Apart from the cultural, political and social consequences resulting from the policies pursued by the colonial governments in Africa, there have been serious economic consequences which have had an enormous impact on the efforts of emerging nations of Southern Africa to change the systems to ensure innovation.

---

[10]William H. Lewis, *Emerging Africa*. Washington, D.C.: Public Affairs Press, 1963, p. 5.

Because the most important reason European nations embarked on a colonial adventure in Africa was economic, it would be unrealistic to think that after years of pursuing economic policies that placed the Africans at a disadvantage, the effect would suddenly disappear at the time African countries became independent.[11] It is this reality that nations of Southern Africa must take into consideration in their effort to improve the conditions of life of their people to ensure national development.

A conclusion has also been reached in this study that economic development and educational innovation are closely related. There is a belief among some leaders of nations of Southern Africa that the economic problems of their nations originated from the system of monopoly which, in essence, meant that the colonial governments controlled major aspects of the economy. These leaders, therefore, wrongly conclude that nationalization of major industries is the answer to all their economic problems. They are not able to see all the adverse effects of nationalization - corruption by government officials themselves, rampant inflation, decline of the currency, stagnation in economic productivity and a lack of incentives are only a few of the many problems of nationalization that African leaders are not able to solve in order to invest in educational innovation.

The African leaders also fail to realize that the colonial governments were assured of markets and that exploitation of the African labor sustained the economy. The substitution of the system of monopoly during the colonial period with a system of nationalization after it offers no viable alternative solution to the problems of economic development in Southern Africa. The African governments cannot engage in either a system of monopoly or nationalization without oppressing their own people. The development of the economy is such a delicate operation that it has to be approached in a deliberate and careful manner. A balance has to be maintained between national policies that provide a dynamic advancement of the economic and the freedom of the people to engage in those economic activities that are central to their own interests as a prerequisite of national development. These are the elements that demand meaningful social change.

In 1960, Harold Macmillan, the British Prime Minister from 1957 to 1963, put the case for fundamental social change in Africa in the context of the influence of events that had global implications. Speaking to the joint session of the South African parliament in Cape Town, Macmillan warned the colonial governments of the consequences of refusing to accept change saying:

> In the twentieth century, especially since the end of the war in 1945, the process which gave birth to the nation states of Europe have been replicated all over the world. We have seen the awakening of national consciousness among people who for centuries lived in dependence upon some other power. The wind of change is blowing through the continent of Africa. Whether we like it or not, this growth of national consciousness is a political fact. We must accept it as a fact, and our national policies must take account of it. Its causes are to be found in the pushing

11*Ibid.* p. 7.

forward of the frontiers of knowledge in the service of human needs and in the spread of education.[12]

The importance of Macmillan's speech lay, not in the results that he anticipated would ensue from the positive response of the colonial establishments, but in awakening a new level of consciousness among the Africans that this was a period of change. They, therefore, regarded the speech as an invitation to mobilize themselves in response to a popular call to initiate the process for fundamental change. For the Africans of 1960 the call for change signalled the beginning of a new era in their perception about themselves as a group of people with a destiny and in shaping new directions to the kind of future that they had always wanted and hoped since 1945. They, therefore, regarded the colonial rule and all that it represented as something that must have no part in influencing that future.

The Thrust for Educational Innovation in Emerging Southern Africa

In their struggle for self, the Africans recognized the importance of shaping developmental policies despite the fact that they were not yet ready to assume their full role in an industry-based economy. The major assumption of this approach is that national political independence was a necessary condition for development. This strategy had the important feature of taking the increased political consciousness into consideration. It was quite obvious to the Africans that no economic development could take place to benefit the people in countries that were still under colonial rule. The knowledge that political institutions must be transformed along the lines that would serve the needs of the people to strengthen the economy, and so make it possible to ensure their advancement , is what the Africans recognized as the basis of the challenge of educational innovation.

But, in order to ensure an effective educational innovation to suit the needs of the emerging Southern Africa, the Africans also recognized that fundamental change had to be initiated in important features of education itself, such as organization, administration, and planning. In most countries of Southern Africa, change in the administration of education has not kept pace with rapidly moving events. The growth of school population, increase in spending for education and planning for the future are all aspects of the administration of education that must be taken into account to ensure innovation.[13] It is important to remember that seeking to improve the administration of education does not mean increased bureaucracy. It is equally true to say that no country in Southern Africa has sufficient financial resources to do all the things that need to be done to improve education. Therefore, in seeking to improve the administrative component of educational innovation, nations of Southern Africa must be aware of the need to ensure careful financial planning to avoid duplication and waste. To ensure an effective system of administration of

[12]Harold Macmillan, "Commonwealth Independence and Interdependence," a speech given to the Joint Session of the South African Parliament, Cape Town, February 3, 1960. By courtesy of the British Embassy, Harare, Zimbabwe.

[13]Botswana, *The Report of the National Commission on Education*, 1977, p. 185.

education, emerging nations of Southern Africa need to observe three basic principles. The first is that participation and consultation at all levels must form the thrust for change. This will help determine how the schools will be run, the courses offered and the general conduct of the school personnel. There must be consultation in the formulation and the implementation of policy in all its dimensions to ensure that the people are involved in their own educational development. Unless those responsible for the thrust for educational innovation take this principle into account, their efforts may yield limited results.

The second principle is to regard education as a unified system which, while intended to serve the needs of local students to suit local conditions, must embrace the thrust for national development as a secondary objective. This involves taking national issues into account, which, when properly addressed by the educational process, will give breadth and new meaning to national purpose. A unified system will necessitate coordination of all school activity, formal and informal, academic and vocational. Approach to a unified system will enable those undertaking educational innovation to set educational objectives that are consistent with larger national goals. It will also enable those in positions of responsibility to define arrangements to fulfill those objectives and to ensure proper progression.

The third principle is that nations of Southern Africa must endeavor to innovate education "in terms of both the learning outcomes and the efficiency with which they use resources."[14] To establish this objective professional efficiency is needed in managing the course of innovation in order to realize the relationship that must exist between investment, planning and educational outcomes. The utilization of specialists in various segments of education, such as financial outlay, must not be delegated to individuals who have had no professional training and experience because educational innovation is far too important to be undertaken by amateurs. It must be emphasized that in observing these principles, nations of Southern Africa must realize that they entail the practice of democracy in that those who are a part of the process in innovation are intimately affected by a national program and must, therefore, be a part of its formulation and implementation.

To serve the purpose for which it is designed, this principle must be built into the national constitution itself or into the fabric of the electoral and educational processes. While local bodies may, in their respective areas of responsibility, exercise proper authority procedures in implementing policy must take national implications into account to ensure maximum benefits of the process of innovation itself. It is only by observing principles of democratic behavior in all its dimensions that educational innovation becomes meaningful. Naming a permanent body to oversee educational innovation, to advice on planning, to coordinate programs, and to resolve problems would enhance the prospects of success in this national endeavor. The fact of the matter is that once innovation has been undertaken, it must be carried out until positive results begin to show.

In embracing these essential elements of democracy in an endeavor towards educational innovation, nations of Southern Africa must constantly remain aware that

---

[14]*Ibid.* p. 186

throughout human history, "it is actually the people who have constituted a dynamic motivation force behind cultural, social and economic development "[15] as a result of educational innovation. This suggests the conclusion that the development of the people must become both the focus of educational innovation and the major means of achieving it. Any national policy that does not take both into account is void of any real meaning. This also suggests that the people must be educated in such a manner that makes them adequately prepared to utilize the educational opportunity that results from innovation.

It has also been stated that the transformation of Southern Africa must seek to reduce the enormous differences that exist between rural areas and urban areas. Throughout the region the people fall into two groups: the rural people, most of whom are engaged in subsistence agriculture, and the people who reside in urban areas. About 80% of the people are rural. This means that without viable means of economic activity, the development of rural areas is at best haphazard. With 80% of the population denied a viable means of economic development, the emerging nations of Africa are forced to have a false sense of progress. When their resources are directed towards the development of 20% of the population in urban areas,[16] the countries of Southern Africa cannot prosper with this serious imbalance between urban conditions and rural conditions. The fact of the matter is that government leaders tend to neglect rural areas because they are less involved in national politics. Change in this situation would demand fundamental change in the economic system. This would necessitate change in the educational system that would mean eliminating differences in the nature of conditions between urban areas and rural areas. Unless emerging nations of Southern Africa make a concerted effort to eliminate rural-urban differences, they will continue to experience the scourge of underdevelopment.

It is also in the best interest of the nations of Southern Africa to recognize that their societies are composed of people of different levels of educational attainment. In addition to the rural population consisting mainly of peasants, there are also the working class, intellectuals and professionals, such as teachers, medical doctors, nurses and writers. The important thing to remember is that educational innovation will make it possible for people of varied talents and interests to choose their own careers and give their nations a widely distributed range of services. This is how nations everywhere ensure their own advancement.

As part of a developmental strategy the nations of Southern Africa need to understand that the advancement of their interests and talents must entail mobilizing natural resources to finance educational innovation. Because this cannot be done where the educational process is weak and objectives are poorly stated and plans inadequately outlined, the governments must provide an adequate institutional encouragement that is essential for the establishment of national organizations in which popular participation is open to all. This collective action enables participants to identify areas of focus to ensure innovation. This would make it possible to create new socioeconomic structures in which people can utilize national resources and

---

[15]Zimbabwe: *Transitional National Development Plan,* Vol. 1, 1982, p. 18.
[16]*Ibid.* p. 19

harness new deposits of energy for the benefit of all. Educational innovation, to serve its proper purpose, must be initiated in the context of these realities.

As a product of socioeconomic growth, educational innovation must at all times be anchored on principles relative to the ultimate aspirations of the people in an environment of established democratic values "set in a dynamic framework of a developing economy"[17] cast in a setting of free trade with minimum government control. This provides motivation and incentives for the flow of capital needed for investment to diverse industry. The exploitation of national resources, however, must be undertaken in the context of national commitment to preserve the environment and a fair system of distribution of resources. Legislation must be passed, such as Zimbabwe did in 1985, to make corruption a criminal offence. Free trade and private enterprise also enhance the flow of capital where there is no abuse. It is here where the government can play a critical role.

The citizens of any country who enter the labor force as a result of an educational system that has embraced principles of innovation will understand and operate under the reality of the emerging relationship that exists between and among different socioeconomic classes and of the exercising their freedom of choice of careers. Again, this provides an opportunity for collective action to correct the inadequacy that exists in the present system of education without class conflict. While most nations of Southern Africa have found it hard to remove the legacy of the colonial system of education, their persistent efforts to state new objectives would result in an education that would assist in removing adverse effects of the nations themselves . Acknowledging this situation provides an incentive towards educational innovation as a critical stage towards social change.

Implications

Once this environment comes into existence, the citizens also begin to see the importance of four simple factors that are essential to both education and working conditions. The first is the establishment of new levels of communication skills and adjustable minimum wages that must be undertaken with clear purpose of providing incentives to the pursuit of education. The second is providing a healthy work environment. This not only increases productivity, but also generates a healthy climate of collegiality among workers. The third factor is respecting the workers' demands for flexibility in scheduling work hours. This allows a degree of control and adjustment of time slots. The fourth factor is respecting the principle of collective bargaining. This allows both management and the workers an opportunity to understand the concerns and appreciate the problems that the other side is experiencing. This means that conflicts are resolved in mutually amicable tension and periodic strikes which disrupt productivity are avoided. This suggests that educational innovation affords benefits that would otherwise be lost to efforts towards national development.

---

[17]*Ibid.* p. 20

To fulfill national objectives based upon the observance of these principles, the nations of Southern Africa must endeavor to restructure the national ministry of education in order to give it a new and innovative role. It must then provide real, not symbolic, leadership based upon clearly identified educational objectives. It must try to recruit individuals with high moral principles, thorough knowledge of issues in education and commitment to national values and purposes. When placed under proper leadership settings, these individuals collectively facilitate the process of formulating educational programs consistent with those objectives. In this context, staff development must be directed towards new teaching strategies, scheduling harmonious operations of all levels of education and proper handling of all levels of school personnel. A special curriculum unit must be created to ensure that it continues to serve the needs of the students in order to serve the developmental needs of the nation.

In 1988, Zimbabwe attempted to launch such an initiative. In that year, President Mugabe outlined some essential elements of that level of innovation when he stated:

> A master plan for education will be unveiled to aim at expanding the facilities and the capacities of all existing institutions, as well as creating new ones. A total of forty million dollars has been set aside for expanding the facilities. Planning is in progress to inaugurate a special curriculum board which will involve experts from both the public and the private sectors in order to research and develop new courses of study which will be geared to meeting the whole spectrum of pupil abilities, aptitudes and interests.[18]

This new course of study, when fully in place, would prepare students to undertake courses at the college level to enable them to be productive citizens in post-school careers in different areas of national life. But in all his enthusiasm to bring about change in the educational systems that would mean innovation, Mugabe neglected to address some important related areas of that endeavor: the required trained personnel, strategies for implementation, expected outcomes and the social, political, cultural and economic factors that must be taken into account to ensure success. For some reason, the government of Zimbabwe, like that of any other country in Southern Africa, did not realize that for innovation to be successful it has to be initiated with all these factors in mind.

The failure of the government of Zimbabwe to take all relevant factors into consideration in making an effort to initiate educational innovation is perhaps why, in 1989, there was a political dark cloud in this educational silver lining as the government faced new problems of credibility caused by a declining economy and charges of corruption by some government officials.[19] When members of the government renewed their talk of introducing a one-party system, the situation took on dimensions of a major national crisis which the plans for educational innovation that Mugabe had announced on the shelf.

---

[18]Robert Mugabe, "Policy Statement Number 20, " June 28, 1988. By courtesy of the Zimbabwe Ministry of Information.

[19]*The New York Times,* December 10, 1989

The national crisis in Zimbabwe caused by a combination of political events and the announcement of new plans to innovate education in 1988 must be understood in the context of the announcement of educational plans that the government made at the inception of independence on April 18, 1980. Speaking on May 18, 1980, during the opening of the first session of parliament, President Canaan Banana[20] went to great lengths to outline what he called a new educational program initiated by the government, saying, among other things, that the government would spend $300 million on educational innovation in the 1981 fiscal year. Banana went on to add:

> In the field of education, it is the intention of the government to pursue vigorously the reopening of the many schools in the rural areas which were closed as a result of the war and to introduce free education on a phased basis beginning with the primary sector.[21]

Failure to take a number of critical factors into consideration led to government inability to meet the goals that Banana had outlined. When, in 1983, Mugabe outlined a new scheme to reach 100% literacy rate by 1988, there was an added loss of credibility because, while these programs cost considerable amount of tax funds, there was little evidence to point to tangible outcomes. This is precisely why the announcement of new educational plans in 1988 was received throughout Zimbabwe with measured skepticism. This situation evinces the accuracy of the conclusion that was reached in this study, and that is: failure to initiate adequate planning to ensure successful educational innovation would erode away the credibility and confidence of the people. However, this does not mean that Zimbabwe has failed in its efforts to initiate successful innovation, rather, it means that it seems to understand its importance and will continue to work out a formula that will ensure its success.

The discussion in this chapter and in this study suggests three implications of educational innovation for Southern Africa. The first is that its primary intent is to ensure the development of the individual in a larger social context. Development of the individual means self-actualization. This includes self-sufficiency, security in one's personhood and fulfillment of those goals that are unique to the individual. It means the promotion of one's interests consistent with one's talent. It means freedom to set goals and objectives and to establish priorities. It means ability to generate an environment that gives one freedom of choice to pursue study programs of one's interests. It is only when one's educational needs have become fulfilled that one plays a role in helping one's society fulfill its needs.[22] This is how the elements of national development are put in place. The underlying principle in the relationship between these elements is that there must be successful educational innovation to make it possible.

The second implication is that a truly independent nation can only arise from a truly independent population. Truly independent population can only emerge from

---

[20]Banana was president of Zimbabwe from 1980 to 1989 when Mugabe assumed that office.

[21]Zimbabwe: Government Policy Number 5, a Presidential Directive, May 18, 1980. By courtesy of the Zimbabwe Ministry of Information.

[22]Dickson Mungazi, "Educational Innovation in Zimbabwe: Possibilities and Problems," in *The Journal of Negro Education,* Vol. 52, No. 2, 1985.

educated individuals. Many nations of Africa, including Southern Africa, have yet to realize this truth. Without an educated population, nations will always be oppressed by a combination of forces such as social ills, racial bigotry, tribal or ethnic conflict and political dissent, all of which Southern Africa has experienced. One reaches the conclusion, therefore, that educational innovation is in the best interest of the nations themselves. The important thing for nations of Southern Africa to keep in mind is that educational innovation cannot be imposed from outside because it requires a collective action based upon common interests and a system of communication of ideas among the people. About this important principle of educational innovation, Paulo Freire concludes that "ability to communicate ideas of self-consciousness"[23] forms an essential part of an education designed to ensure self-fulfillment as an important step towards creating an environment of national development. This means that cooperative efforts must constitute a viable channel to successful educational innovation.

The third implication is that the greatest threat to successful innovation in all of Southern Africa comes from the government decisions to institute one-party systems of government. Government leaders seem to neglect the fact that in Africa the philosophy of one-party government has shown evidence to prove that it robs the people of a genuine desire to promote ideas of individuality as a condition of national development and replaces their confidence for the future with an abyss of despair. What has been discussed about Zimbabwe substantiates the accuracy of this conclusion. In this kind of social and political setting, the educational process has only peripheral meaning because individual incentive and self-motivation which are important characteristics of human achievement, are rendered meaningless by the government's desire to have its own philosophy and policy prevail at the expense of the goals and objectives of the individual.

Therefore instituting a one-party system of government is often an indication that the government has something either to hide or to fear in its own people. Thus, the introduction of a one-party system of government cannot be considered a step in the direction of national development. After forty-five years in office, the Nationalist Party of South Africa has found this to be true the hard way. While the Nationalist Party has ruled supreme since 1948, both the educational process and human interactions suffered a severe setback. It is therefore important that the nations of Southern Africa that have adopted a one-party system of government, such as Zambia, Malawi, South Africa, Mozambique, Angola, change course and that those nations, such as Botswana and Zimbabwe, that are multi-party democracies never adopt it. The sustenance of democracy is too important to be tempered with because the survival of nations and the course of educational innovation depend on it if waves of national conflict are to be avoided. No matter how government officials see it, one-party system of government is nothing less than a dictatorship. This is why, for example, massive demonstrations staged against the government of Kenneth Kaunda in Zambia led to an attempted military coup in June, 1990. Since he took office in October, 1964, Kaunda has not only instituted a one-party rule, but has also

---

[23]Paulo Freire, *Pedagogy of the Oppressed*, p. 62.

alienated Zambians by creating a political environment that has denied Zambians a role in the affairs of their country. Nations of Southern Africa, be well advised and be wise!

APPENDICES

Appendix 1

The Rudd Concession: A Colonial Deception (October 30, 1888)

Know all men by these presents that whereas Charles Dunell Rudd, of Kimberly, Rochfort Maguire, of London, and Francis Robert Thompson, of Kimberly, hereinafter called the grantees, have covenanted and agreed, and do hereby covenant and agree to pay to me, my heirs and successors the sum f one hundred pounds sterling British currency on the first day of every lunar month, and further to deliver at my Royal Kraal one thousand Martini-Henry breech-loading rifles, together with one thousand round of suitable ball cartridge, five hundred of the said rifles, and fifty thousand of the said cartridges to be ordered from England forthwith and delivered with reasonable despatch and the remainder of the said rifles and cartridges to be delivered as soon as the said grantees shall have commenced to work mining machinery within my territory, and further to deliver on the Zambezi River a steamboat with guns suitable for defensive purposes upon the said river, or in lieu of the same steamboat, should I so elect, to pay me the sum of five hundred pounds sterling British currency of the execution of the present, I, Lobengula, King of Matabeleland, Mashonaland, and other adjoining territories, in the exercise of my sovereign powers, and in the presence and with the consent of my Council of *Indunas*,[1] do hereby grant and assign unto the said grantees, their heirs, representatives, and assigns, jointly and severally, the complete and exclusive charge over all metals and minerals situated and contained in my kingdoms, principalities, and dominions, together with full power to do all things they may deem necessary to win and procure the same, and to hold, collect, and enjoy the profits and revenues, if any, derived from the said metals and minerals subject to the aforesaid payment, and whereas I have been much molested of late by diverse persons, seeking and desiring to obtain grants and concessions of land and mining rights in my territories, I do hereby authorize the said grantees, their heirs, representatives, and assigns, to take all necessary and lawful step to exclude from my kingdoms, principalities, and dominions, all persons seeking land, metals, or mining rights herein, and I do hereby undertake to render them such needful assistance as they may from time to time require for the exclusion of such persons and to grant no concession of land or mining rights form or after this date without their consent and concurrence, provided that if at any time the said monthly payment of one hundred pounds shall be in arrears for a period of three months then this grant shall cease and determine from the date of the last ade payment, and further provided that nothing contained in these

---

[1]*Indunas* is a Ndebele word that means councillors

presents shall extend to or affect a grant made by me of certain mining rights in a portion of my territory south of the Ramokaban River, which grant is commonly known as the Tati Concession. This given under my hand this thirtieth day of October in the year of our Lord, eighteen hundred and eighty-eight at my Royal Kraal.

Lobengula, X his mark   C. D. Rudd,

                                  Rochfort Maguire

F. R. Thompson

Source: Courtesy of the Zimbabwe National Archives

Appendix 2

U.S. Policy in Southern African:
An American Dilemma

Dickson Mungazi, 1988

Introduction

From 1981 to 1988 the crisis in southern Africa placed the policy of the Reagan administration in a difficult situation; it knew the right elements that constituted a good policy, but it was caught between two conflicting positions that it found hard to resolve. The administration desired to halt possible Communist expansion in Africa and yet it claimed to seek the promotion of human rights.

Since the end of World War II, the Africans persistently and clearly enunciated uncompromising principles of self-determination and independence as being fundamental to their future. In the Atlantic Charter of August 14, 1941, President Franklin Roosevelt and Prime Minister Winston Churchill recognized the importance of Western support of these principles when they stated that "[We] respect the right of all people to choose the form of government under which they will live and wish to see sovereign rights and self-determination restored to those who have been forcibly deprived of them."

Historical Precedence: The Kennedy-Johnson Years

It would appear that in defining and pursuing its policy in southern Africa, the Reagan administration seems to go against historical precedence. Let us examine the background evidence that leads to this conclusion.

On assuming office on January 20, 1961, John F. Kennedy recognized the need to balance his call for a "new frontier" with his call for freedom of all people as "the wave of the future." Kennedy viewed the momentum that the civil rights movement was gaining in the United States from the perspective of the struggle for self-determination in countries still under colonial domination, especially Africa. He did not think that it was possible to separate the two.

Kennedy's decision to support both movements was his ultimate frontier; the conquest of space had meaning only in the context of the conquest of human injustice and oppression. This is why Kennedy regarded opposition from such individuals as George Wallace and Ross Burnett to his efforts toward racial integration as a challenge to the concept of a new generation of Americans who believed that their destiny was invariably intertwined with that of the struggle of the world's oppressed masses.

Kennedy's belief that :"democracy is more than a form of government, it is also a way of life, variegated and full of growth" enabled him to redefine the concept of human rights in terms of the emerging values of human existence and interaction. This is why he inaugurated the Peace Corps program, to send a message of hope, to both the oppressed people of Africa and to their oppressors. It said that unless human freedom was a condition governing human life, it would have little meaning to anyone.

By helping the Africans to help themselves, Kennedy stated, during his second State of the Union address, "Our basic goal remains the same, a peaceful world community of free and independent states free to choose their own future..." This is the principle that Americans would understand and support. This is also the principle that created a dilemma for them during the Reagan administration because since Kennedy outlined it in 1961, it lost its meaning in the wake of conflicting policy positions of the Reagan government.

Kennedy's message had a tremendous influence on the Africans' struggle to end colonialism, a fact that played a major role in his restructuring of the the state department, headed by Dean Rusk, in order to give meaning to that struggle. Nowhere did Kennedy imply that U.S. policy in Africa would be influenced by the need to halt possible Communist expansion there. Rusk therefore put together an impressive team of dedicated young Americans who shared the enthusiasm of their leaders. These young men and women felt that they were called upon to help reshape American policy toward Africa and they took their assigned task seriously and in the spirit in which Kennedy outlined it. Among them was G. Mennen Williams, assistant secretary of state with special responsibility for U.S. policy in Africa.

The belief that Africa presented a special challenge to the spirit of the "new frontier" enabled Williams to define U.S. African policy in terms of what was right for the Africans, not in terms of how best to serve U.S. interests. In defining such a policy, Williams shared Rusk's and Kennedy's belief that it would also serve the interests of the United states. And in defining the policy as "Africa for the Africans," Williams, Rusk, and Kennedy became partners in promoting a dynamic new policy of human rights, which made them, "unwilling to witness the undoing of human rights around the world." Kennedy's statement that "We pledge our best efforts to help the Africans, not because the Communists may be doing it, but because it is right" has become a sober reminder of days gone by..

The focal point of the policy of "Africa for the Africans" was that "governments derive their just power from the consent of the governed." The fact that the colonial governments in Africa were displeased with this policy helps to explain why it had a chilling effect on relationships between them and the United States from 1961 to 1963. Unfortunately, the enthusiasm that Vice President Lyndon Johnson showed during a visit to Senegal in April 1961, about the importance of U.S. policy in Africa from 1964 to 1968 because the Kennedy-Johnson administration had demonstrated the wisdom of a policy based on what was right for Africa, not on how best to promote U.S. interests.

The tragedy that brought the Kennedy administration to a sudden end also impaired the Johnson administration's ability to pursue the policy it had defined. To suggest that there was a void in U.S. policy in Africa from 1968 to 1972 is to conclude that during the Nixon-Ford years entirely new policy elements came into being. These elements radically altered the direction of a new policy to the pursuit of what was right for Africa was also right for the United States, but what was right for the United States was not necessarily right for Africa. How should the United States resolve this serious conflict?

Kennedy's belief was replaced by what the United States must do to halt the possibility of Communist influence. In this regard, the elements of a conflicting policy were put in place and became a legacy that the Reagan administration utilized at the peril of developing good relationships with the Africans. This helps to explain why in 1985, for example, Bishop Desmond Tutu carried on a crusade to reverse the Reagan administration policy in the absolute conviction that it was totally incompatible with that of earlier administrations.

The Nixon-Ford Years: Creating an American Dilemma

The change in administration from Johnson to Nixon witnessed a major policy change at a critical period in Africa. On January 2, 1970, Henry Kissinger, then chairman of the National Security Council and adviser to Nixon, recommended the relaxation of the policy that sought political isolation and economic restrictions on the white-ruled countries of southern Africa. Indeed, in arguing that "The whites are in Africa to stay, the only way that change can come is through them," the Nixon administration extended an open invitation to the colonial regimes to stay where they were. They perceived this position as encouragement to entrench themselves deeper in the colonial systems and to refuse any changes that would accommodate the aspirations of the Africans.

The fundamental question running through the minds of both the Africans and the Americans was: What direction would U.S. policy take in the future? The answer began to emerge in 1966 when Gulf Oil discovered new deposits in Angola, and again in 1972. Thus a new alliance came into being between Marcello Caetano, the Portuguese dictator who had succeeded Antonio Salazar in 1968, and the Nixon administration. When President Ford dispatched Kissinger to southern Africa in September 1976, the situation had turned into a major regional crisis. The war in Zimbabwe was deteriorating, the struggle in Namibia was intensifying, Soweto had exploded, and the civil war in Angola was reaching a critical stage. U.S. policy had done nothing to resolve these problems.

Kissinger and his associates at the state department were completely confused by events that they did not fully understand in a region that was increasingly becoming volatile. Although Julius Nyerere of Tanzania tried to help Kissinger understand the nature and complexity of the problems that he faced, Kissinger seemed never to fully comprehend the seriousness of the situation. This handicapped his ability to formulate a viable U.S. policy, and this is why, for example, the Geneva conference that he tried to work out between the warring parties in Zimbabwe in 1976 was a total failure.

The dilemma of the Kissinger policy is that in failing to resolve the enormous problems that existed in southern Africa, U.S. credibility in black Africa was at best being put into question. In seeking to place U.S. interests above those of the Africans, the Nixon administration was perceived as formulating a policy that was aimed at assisting the colonial regimes. The ping-pong diplomacy that had yielded some measured success in China appeared to be in disarray.

When Donald Easum, chief adviser to Kissinger, told a press conference in Dar-es-Salaam in November 1974, that the U.S. policy was designed "to foster change in southern Africa, and not to preserve the status quo," the Africans responded with measured skepticism and pronounced disbelief. The events leading to Watergate and Nixon's pardon by Ford totally engulfed the remaining period of the administration to the extent that it was not possible for either Kissinger or Ford himself to define an effective policy in southern Africa.

Carter's Policy: A New Perspective on Morality and Human Rights

Skepticism and disbelief among the Africans during the Nixon-Ford years became the main reason why the Carter administration added the principle of morality and redefined the concept of human rights. A southern Baptist whose own life was profoundly shaped by old-fashioned religious values, Jimmy Carter believed that the threat to U.S. interests in Africa came from various forms of oppression and racism, not from Communist expansion and influence.

Carter's views became clear as the crisis in southern Africa continued to increase. In a letter to this author dated June 27, 1977, Andrew Young, Carter's ambassador to the UN, put the policy of his administration into perspective when he explained its focus: ". . . a deep and fervent belief that all human beings are entitled to enjoy basic rights and fundamental freedom. . . and that racial injustice should be dealt with forthrightly wherever it exists." This was a central commitment of the U.S. policy in southern Africa. There was no mention of the need to halt possible Communist expansion, not because it believed that it would be accomplished differently.

Three days later, on July 1, 1977, Secretary of State Cyrus Vance added, "We have expressed to the South African government our firm belief in the benefits of a progressive transformation of the South African society. This would mean an end to racial discrimination." On June 7, 1979, when a critical debate in the U.S. Senate indicated that it might lead to a vote authorizing the termination of economic sanctions against the Smith regime in Zimbabwe, Carter's definition of morality and human rights came to the fore when he stated, "The black citizens, who constitute 96% of the population of Zimbabwe, never had a chance to vote for or against the constitution under which the elections were held . . ."

This pleased the Africans and helped to restore their confidence in U.S. ability to design a policy that demanded justice and fairness as a criterion of morality and basic human rights. Carter appeared to know exactly what was right for the Africans as being synonymous with what was right for the United States. Morality was a universal human value, not a prerogative quality of any one particular racial or cultural group.

One reaches two important conclusions regarding the policy of the Carter administration in southern Africa. The first is that the introduction of morality as an essential element of foreign policy elevated the concept of human rights to a level where the crisis could be viewed from its proper perspective. What came out of this new reality is that the application of morality and the observation of human rights combined to produce the desired elements of a just society based on a political system in which the citizens would freely play a decisive role in the affairs of their country.

This is an environment that eliminates the possibility of a Communist threat. In short, Carter recognized that morality in foreign policy would enable both the Africans and the United States itself to recognize that what was good for Africa was also good fro the United States. This reality could come only from a good policy.

The second conclusion is that because the combination of human rights and morality in foreign policy generates a new level of mutual trust and confidence between the government and the people, internal strife and conflict have no medium of expression as violence is no longer justified on any basis. Political freedom becomes an absolute condition of ending racial discrimination in all its forms.

The absence of racial discrimination, in the context of the situation in southern Africa, is a prerequisite for eliminating a Communist threat. This is how Carter believed U.S. interests in southern Africa would be protected. Morality and respect of human rights become the cornerstone of a free society, in which corruption by government official and dissent by the citizens are replaced by mutual trust between them. If Ferdinand Marcos and Baby Doc Duvalier had operated under these principles, they would not have lost their positions of power and probably would have played a constructive role in the development of their countries.

Reagan's Policy of Constructive Encouragement: An American Dilemma

In January 1981, when Americans thought that their government had formulated a policy to restore African confidence in U.S. ability to promote its own national interests by seeking to promote those of the Africans, they were surprised to learn that the Reagan administration operated under a different set of beliefs. Not only did the administration return to the days of John Foster Dullies, which equated African demand for majority rule and socialism with anticapitalism but it also questioned the philosophy that was central to the policy of the Carter administration

To conclude that the policy of the Reagan administration became an American dilemma is to suggest that it created new problems out of its thinking that halting possible Communist influence in southern Africa was far more important to U.S.

interests than ending political oppression. Indeed, only one month after Reagan took office, Jeane Kirkpatrick, U.S. ambassador to the UN, readily admitted that the administration regarded halting Communist influence in southern Africa as a more important objective to sustaining U.S. interests than ending racial oppression. This view was shared by Alexander Haig, Jr., Reagan's secretary of state and a former NATO commander who was inclined to view the problems of southern Africa from a perspective of its strategic importance to the interests of the United States.

If Americans wondered whether the views expressed by Kirkpatrick and Haig were their own or the official government policy, Reagan himself erased any doubt. During a television interview on March 3, 1981, the president defended the views expressed by Kirkpatrick and Haig. With special reference to apartheid in South Africa, Reagan rhetorically asked, "Can we abandon a country that has stood beside us in every war we have fought, a country that is essential to the free world and in its production of the minerals that we all must have?"

The policy of the Reagan administration placed emphasis on ending Communist influence in southern Africa rather than ending the racial policies of the white minority regimes, which pleased the South African government. This is evident in how Prime Minster Botha responded. In concluding that Reagan had reversed a U.S. policy of two decades, he went into a state of jubilation when he said that the U.S. president was "more friendly to South Africa than Richard Nixon and Jerry Ford," He was confirming what *Die Vanderland*, a daily Afrikaans newspaper, had stated in an editorial, "The U.S. will not leave South Africa in the lurch. . ."

Botha's praise of the Reagan administration's policy must be understood in the context of his desire to have his government exploit Western fears of Soviet influence in the region, just as Marcos had done in the Philippines for 20 years. This is why the South African government sees the policy of "constructive engagement" as a tacit support of apartheid. This is also why since 1981 Botha has persistently refused to ease oppression of blacks.

On October 29, 1983, Dennis Brutus, a South African exile who was tortured by his government, put into proper perspective the influence that the policy of constructive engagement had on South Africa's refusal to dismantle apartheid. He said, "The horrors of apartheid ar connected to the extent to which the U.S. government has become an ally of that oppressive system. What does the policy of constructive engagement mean? It means the U.S. can stand by and say to the oppressor, 'I am here to assist you in your process of oppression.' That is how we perceive the policy of constructive engagement . . . "

What became more disturbing about the constructive engagement policy is that the Reagan administration nullified the Clark Amendment of 1976 in order to have a free hand in pursuing its policy. When Jonas Savimbi visited the United States in January 1986, seeking military aid for his 10-year effort to topple the MPLA government that took office in Angola in 1975, leading members of the Republican party received him in Washington as though he were a head of state. Kirkpatrick encouraged the United States to given him "real helicopters, real ground-to-air missiles, real weapons." When Savimbi responded by saying, "I consider the President of South Africa as my friend," he received loud applause. This is precisely what Brutus meant when he said that the Reagan administration was an ally of South Africa, announced that the United States would indeed provide the military aid that Savimbi had requested.

This is the setting in which one must view the policy of constructive engagement. It is true that the Reagan administration not only abandoned the principle of morality and human rights in its policy in southern Africa, but also took a new position of military involvement in seeking the end of the system of government that it disliked, especially in Angola. There is nothing constructive in giving Savimbi "real weapons." Brutus was quite correct in saying that constructive engagement means active assistance to South Africa.

The dilemma that this policy posed for Americans during the Reagan years was explained to this author on January 30, 1986, by an American: "During the Carter Administration we were made to understand that we were the champions of human rights, and that moral principles, justice, and respect of human dignity, especially in countries still under colonial domination, would help ensure our interests. Now we are made to understand that supporting South Africa and giving Savimbi military aid are in our national interests. . . . The current U.S. policy in southern Africa has now become an American dilemma for all of us, to support South Africa and abandon our claim to being the champions of human freedom, or to question the policy of our government and so encourage those who oppose it and cause confusion in the highly sensitive areas of U.S. policy in southern Africa. I hope that other Americans see the seriousness of this dilemma . . ."

Questions and Observations On the Reagan Policy

Brutus put this dilemma in the context and the perspective of the effect of the constructive engagement policy when he said, on October 29, 1983, "What surprises us is that the U.S. is often in collision with the perpetrators of apartheid, not because of the fundamental disagreement about its structure and effect, but about how it can be sustained." This suggests that some fundamental questions regarding the policy of constructive engagement, as practiced by the Reagan administration, must be asked.

First, to what extent was the Reagan administration willing to support the struggle against racism and the oppression of apartheid in South Africa and Namibia? Before he was murdered by the police in September 1977, Steve Biko had expressed the view that many Africans shared and one that was central to the oppression of apartheid when he said that the fundamental principle of apartheid ". . .is the realization that the most potent weapon in the hands of the oppressor is the mind of the oppressed . . ." Is the policy of constructive engagement seeking to end that oppression or indirectly to sustain it because the South African regime claims to be the champion in the struggle against Communist expansion?

Second, did the Reagan administration feel that it had to make a choice between ending racial oppression and ending the threat of Communist influence in southern Africa? Is it not possible that seeking to end racial oppression was and still is a viable method of protecting U.S. interests in the region? The reversal of Kennedy-

Johnson and Carter policies was resented by the Africans themselves. Did the Reagan administration consider the real possibility that by supporting both South Africa and Savimbi with military materials, the United States was seen clearly on the side of the oppressor, and so lost its positive image as the champion of human freedoms?

Third, in considering the strategic and mineral importance of southern Africa as more important to U.S. interests than the promotion of human rights, did the Reagan administration believe that it would have a positive influence on the tragic events that have been unfolding in the region?

Fourth, on January 2, 1986, Bishop Desmond Tutu warned the Botha regime that the "whites of South Africa will not be free till the Blacks are free." Is this not a more realistic approach to the policy than constructive engagement? Since the end of the World War II, there has been a new and universal thinking that the oppressor is not free until the oppressed are free. Why did the Reagan administration not examine the relevance of this idea to its policy in southern Africa?

These questions lead to the conclusion that for the policy of constructive engagement to have real meaning and serve a good purpose, the Reagan administration should have ceased to view the situation in southern Africa from the perspective of making a choice between ending possible Communist influence and ending racial oppression. It should have worked from the perspective of making a choice between ending possible Communist influence and ending racial oppression. It should have worked from the perspective that its desire to do what is right for Africa is synonymous with what is right for the United States. In this way both the United States and the Africans could have joined hands in promoting the fundamental objectives central to human rights. And then what chance would the Communists have?

The main reason why some African nations turn to socialism is that they see the unwillingness of Western nations especially the United States, to break from the policies of the past in the feat that their own interests would be threatened. With an investment of $14.6 billion in South Africa alone, the United States could play a genuinely constructive role in resolving the enormous problems that exist there for the benefit of all. Minor changes to the application of apartheid will not do; only a total dismantling of the system will avert the disaster that such people as Bishop Tutu and Winnie Mandela have been saying is inevitable.

Whereas the policy of constructive engagement was indeed engaging, it was far from being constructive. It should have, therefore, been reevaluated in terms of the effects it had on the deterioration of the situation in all of southern Africa. In the era of *glasnost*, the current leadership in the Soviet Union would have cooperated in such an endeavor because it knows that solution of the problems so southern Africa is in its own interest. Besides Reagan and Gorbachev seemed to have a personal friendship that would have helped in their coooperation in supporting a policy that would help transform southern Africa into a region in which the interests of both super powers would be sustained by sustaining those of all the people of the region. That Reagan failed to take this reality to help resolve problems of Namibia, Angola,

Mozambique, and South Africa suggests limited ability in working out a policy that would work.

The Bush Policy

The release of Nelson Mandela from prison, where he spent 27 years for opposing apartheid, and the declaration by F.D. de Klerk, the President of South Africa who succeeded Pieter Botha, that his government was reversing its ban placed on ANC in 1960 and of his intention to hold talks with it an effort to find solutions to the problems of South Africa, presented the Bush Administration with a new opportunity to to redefine U.S. policy towards Southern Africa. However, the visit of the U.S. Secretary of State to South Africa in March 1990 did not appear to shape new directions in U.S. policy apart from securing de Klerk's pledge not to reverse the course he had initiated to dismantle apartheid.

While this happening, the principal rivalry of the U.S. in terms of policy towards Southern Africa, the Soviet Union under Mikhail Gorbachev, was initiating a major reform of the Soviet political and socioeconomic system under *glasnost* and *perestroika*. In this context, the Soviet Union was in no position to play the political power game of the cold war period. It is surprising that apparent confusion was evident in the policy position of the U.S.A. under President George Bush. In 1991, on the one hand, Bush suggested that since de Klerk had indicated that apartheid would be dismantled, sanctions, which the U.S. Congress imposed against the opposition of President Reagan, should be removed. On the other hand, the Congress took their position that sanctions should not be removed until apartheid had been dismantled. The difference of opinion between the Congress and President Bush did not resolve policy position of the U.S.A.

When the Soviet Union requested experts from the U.S. to go an assist in the method of distribution of food, it was clear that the U.S.A. had nothing to fear in terms of Soviet policy in southern Africa. In fact, Gorbachev had indicated that if South dismantled apartheid, it would open new channels of cooperation between the two countries. Knowing that the Soviet Union would not initiate such a relationship without taking the interests of the Southern Africa as a region, the U.S. should have come forth more strongly than it had done in the past to demand an end to the scourge of apartheid in order to shape new directions in regional development. The crisis caused by the conflict between supporters of Inkatha and ANC, in which violence has ruled supreme, has cast a shadow of doubt as to de Klerk's sincerity to dismantle apartheid. In this tragedy, President Bush seemed more preoccupied with the plight of the Kurds in Iraq than he was with U.S. policy toward Southern Africa. As 1991 came to an end, the U.S. policy makers seemd to be in no pisition to chart a new course in U.S. policy.

Appendix 3

The Freedom Charter of South Africa

(Klipton, June 26, 1955)

Introduction

The Freedom Charter was adopted at the Congress of the People, held in Klipton, near Johannesburg, June 25-26, 1955. The Congress was convened by the African National Congress, together with the South African Indian Congress, the South African Coloured People's Organization, and the Congress of Democrats, an organization of whites who supported the liberation movement. It was attended by 2,888 delegates from throughout South Africa, and was perhaps the most representative gathering ever held in the country.

The Charter was adopted by four sponsoring organizations as their policy, and became a manifesto of their struggle for freedom. A year later, some 156 leaders of these organizations were arrested and charged with high treason. They were subsequently acquitted after a trial that lasted more than four years. But the ANC and the Congress of Democrats were soon banned, whereas the other two organizations were effectively prevented from legal operation by the banning of their leaders. One of the, Nelson Mandela, has been in prison since 1964.

We the People

We the people of South Africa, declare for all our country and the world to know:

1.that South Africa belongs to all who live in it, black and white, and that no government can justly claim authority unless it is based on the will of all the people.

2.that our people have been robbed of their birthright to land, liberty and peace by a form of government founded on injustice and inequality.

3.that our country will never be prosperous or free until all our people live in brotherhood, enjoying equal rights and opportunities.

4.that only a democratic state, based on the will of all the people, can secure to all their birthright without distinction of colour, race, sex or belief.

And therefore, we the people of South Africa, black and white together--equal, countrymen and brothers--adopt this Freedom Charter. And we pledge ourselves to strive together, sparing neither strength nor courage, until the democratic changes set out here have been won.

The People Shall Govern

Every man and woman shall have the right to vote for and to stand as a candidate for all bodies which make laws. All the people shall be entitled to take part in the administration of the country. the rights of the people shall be the same, regardless of race, colour or sex. All bodies of minority rule, advisory boards, councils and authorities shall be replaced by democratic organs of self-government.

All National Groups Shall Have Equal Rights

There shall be equal status in the bodies of state, in the courts and in the schools for all national groups and races. All people shall have equal rights to use their own languages,and to develop their own folk culture and customs. All national groups shall be a punishable crime. The people shall share in the country's wealth. All *apartheid* laws and practices shall be set aside.

The People Shall Share in the Country's Wealth

The national wealth of the country, the heritage of all of South Africans, shall be restored to the people. The mineral wealth beneath the soil, the banks and monopoly industry shall be transferred to the ownership of the people as a whole.

All other industry and trade shall be controlled to assist the well-being of the people. All the people shall have equal rights to trade where they choose, to manufacture and to enter all trades, crafts and professions.

The Land Shall be Shared Among Those Who Work It

Restrictions of landownership on a racial basis shall be ended, and all the land redivided amongst those who work it, to banish famine and land hunger. The state shall help the peasants with implements, seed, tractors and dams to save the soil and assist the tillers.

Freedom of movement shall be granted to all who work on the land. All shall have the right to occupy land wherever they choose. The people shall not be robbed of their cattle and forced labour and farm prisons shall be abolished.

All the People Shall be Equal Before the Law

No one shall be imprisoned, deported or restricted without a fair trial. No one shall be condemned by the order of any government official. The courts shall be representative of all the people. Imprisonment shall be only for serious crimes against the people,a and shall aim at re-education, not vengeance.

The police force and army shall be open to all on an equal basis and shall be the helpers and protectors of the people. all laws which discriminate on grounds of race, colour or belief shall be replaced.

All Shall Enjoy Equal Human Rights

The law shall guarantee to all their rights to speak, to organize, to meet together, to preach, to worship, and to educate their children. The privacy of the house from police raids shall be protected by law.

All the people shall be free to travel without restriction from countryside to town, from province to province and from South Africa abroad. Pass Laws, permits,a dn all other laws restricting these freedoms, shall be abolished.

There Shall be Work and Security

All the people who work shall be free to form unions, to elect their officers and to make wage agreements with their employers. The state shall recognize the rights and duty of all to work, and to draw full unemployment benefits. Men and women of all races shall receive equal pay for equal work.

There shall be a forty-hour working week, a national minimum wage, paid annual leave, and sick leave for all working mothers. Miners, domestic workers, farm workers, and civil servants shall have the same rights as all others who work. Child labour, compound labour, the *tot* system and contract labour shall be abolished.

The Doors of Learning and of Culture Shall be Open

The government shall discover, develop and encourage national talent for the enhancement of our cultural life. All the cultural treasures of mankind shall be open to all, by free exchange of books, ideas and contact with other lands. The aim of education shall be to teach the youth to love their people and their culture, to honour human brotherhood, liberty and people.

Education shall be free, compulsory, universal and equal for all children. Higher education and technical training shall be opened to all by means of state allowances and scholarships awarded on the basis of merit. Adult illiteracy shall be ended by a mass state education plan. Teachers shall have all the rights of other citizens. The colour bar in cultural life, in sport and in education shall be abolished.

There Shall be Houses, Security and Comfort

All the people shall have the rights to live where they choose, to be decently housed, and to bring up their families in comfort and security. Unused housing space shall be made available to other people. Rent and prices shall be lowered, food plentiful and non one shall go hungry.

A preventative health scheme shall be run by the state. Free medical care and hospitalization shall be provided for all with special care for mothers and young children. Slums shall be demolished, and new suburbs built where ll have transport, roads, lighting, playing fields, *creches*, and social centres. The aged, the orphans, the disabled and the sick shall be cared for the state.

Rest, leisure and recreation shall be the right of all. Fenced locations and ghettoes shall be abolished, and laws which break families shall be repealed. South Africa shall be a fully independent state, which respects the rights and sovereignty of nations.

There Shall be Peace and Friendship

South Africa shall strive to maintain world peace and the settlement of international disputes by negotiations, not war. Peace and friendship amongst all our people shall be secured by upholding the equal rights, opportunities and status of all.

The people of the protectorates--Basutoland, Bechuanaland and Swaziland-- shall be free to decide for themselves their own future. The rights of all the people of Africa to independence and self-government shall be recognized, and shall be the basis of close cooperation. Let all who love their people and their country now say, as we say here: *These freedoms we shall fight for, side by side, throughout our lives, until we have won our liberty.*

By courtesy of the U.N. Center against *Apartheid*.

Appendix 4

The Manifesto of the Rhodesia Socialist Party: A Statement of Principles, December 12, 1971

A Socialist State

1. The state exists for the people, and the people must support the state.

2. The interdependence of the state and people must be the basis of a truly democratic system.

3. In a true democracy total equality between the races and the people is an essential ingredient of peace, especially in a country like Rhodesia where a white minority seeks a perpetual political domination of a black minority.

4. Racial segregation in any form -- housing, income, education, employment, opportunity, medical services -- invites the practice of distributive justice which is often the causes of class, social, and racial conflict.

5. The party believes that racial segregation and discrimination have long been the cause of racial conflict in Rhodesia and must be eliminated immediately.

6. A socialist state recognizes the danger inherent in a socioeconomic system that allows some people to become excessively rich and forces other people to become excessively poor.

Nationalism

1. Since World War II African nationalism has been accepted as a new reality of relations in all of Africa. But the successive colonial governments of Rhodesia have denied the Africans expression of this nationalism. UDI was intended to put a quick end to that nationalism. Now, Rhodesia is paying a heavy price for this ill-conceived action.

2. The Rhodesia Socialist party will endeavor to promote, neither African nationalism not white supremacy but a new form of nationalism that embodies the elements of human and racial cooperation based on cultural diversity as a national asset.

3.The party rejects any notion of racial and cultural superiority in human interaction and views differences in color and culture as an enrichment of the Rhodesian society.

4.The party rejects the Rhodesia Front view that political and cultural differences between the whites and the Africans cannot be reconciled. Instead of curbing the growing African nationalism, RF legislation has had the effect of indirectly promoting it. In vain RF has attempted to promote white supremacy, setting in motion a confrontation between the races.

5.The party believes that only full cooperation by all races for the common good can save Rhodesia from war. We are inclined to think that those of us who have seen two major wars do not desire to see another.

6.The party therefore rejects the extremism of both white political supremacy and African nationalism because neither makes it possible for the races to cooperate. Instead, the party seeks to promote a new form of nationalism based on common interests, mutual trust, and cooperation for the good of the country.

7.The party believes that in time Rhodesia should be renamed Zimbabwe in accordance with the wishes of the majority of people of this country.

Education

1.The prevention of a racial war is the main aim of the Rhodesia Socialist party. All thinking and fair-minded people in Rhodesia now recognize that the perpetuation of racial segregation in the educational process has been the major cause of conflict between the races.

2.The party therefore believes that because education is universal, there is no justifiable basis for maintaining the distinction between African education and white education. The whites will never feel secure as long as the Africans see that they are denied equal educational opportunity on the basis of race, and indeed, on any basis.

3.In the interest of promoting racial cooperation as the only basis of building a new national identity, racial segregation, and discrimination in the educational process, as in society itself, must be terminated immediately.

4.The party believes that there is inequality in socioeconomic opportunity between the races because there is inequality in educational opportunity.

5.Inequality in both socioeconomic opportunity and in the educational process has steadily led to the racial unrest and conflict which has become a major feature of the Rhodesia Front administration.

6.The party calls on all Rhodesians, both black and white, to come forward and support these principles as the only viable means to national peace and prosperity.

Appendix 5

IAN SMITH REVIEWS THE EDUCATRIONAL POLICYOF HIS GOVERNMENT IN ZIMBABWE

(Interview Conducted by Dickson Mungazi in Parliament Building in Harare, Zimbabwe, July 20, 1983)

Introduction:

Ian Smith was first elected to the Rhodesian parliament in 1948, the year that the Nationalist Party was returned to power in South Africa. Smith slowly paved his way to the top of the political ladder by expressing views that were consistent with those of Daniel Malan of South Africa. Unhappy with the policies of the Rhodesia United Party and of the United Federal Party, both of which Godfrey Huggins led, Smith joined the Dominion Party, which was having a considerable influence in Southern Rhodesia because he supported its strong anti - African views.

When the Federation of Rhodesia and Nyasaland was formed in 1953, Smith played a major role it shaping the policy of the DP. The end of the Federation in 1963 led to rapidly moving events which convinced him that Britain was about to grant independence to Rhodesia under the same conditions it granted independence to Ghana in 1957. When a negative reaction of the voters persisted against the DP, Smith was instrumental in having it change its name to Rhodesia Front in 1962 and helped it in drafting its election principles and policies.

Displeased with the way Winston Field was leading the RF and as prime minister following its victory in the general elections of December, 1962, Smith, on April 12, 1964, led a political coup that removed Field from the office of prime minister because he was reluctant to pursue a set of radical racial policies and because he refused to function outside the framework of the requirements stipulated by Britain.In 1961, Smith and the DP vigorously opposed the new Constitution that Edgar Whitehead and the British government had agreed upon because it provided for 15 black members in a legislature of 65 members.

It is ironic that the DP contested elections in 1962 under a constitution it opposed. As soon as Smith assumed the office of prime minister on April 13, 1964, he moved quickly to establish himself as the only political leader in the country who was capable of achieving independence on his own terms. His basic policy, *No black majority government in Rhodesia in my life-time*, became an obsession, the only thing worthwhile living for.

On November 11, 1965, Smith seized power, dismissed the governor, and declared the country independent unilaterally, setting in motion events that finally led to the war of independence and the end of the RF and the political power of Smith himself in March, 1979, and the establishment of a black government he had vowed would never become a reality in his lifetime. But when the black government was installed on April 18, 1983, Smith indicated a willingness to work under new conditions.

The Interview

Mungazi: Mr Smith, I am sure that you are aware that you are one of the major political figures who have shaped the developments in Zimbabwe, especially since 1964. I would like to thank you for taking time to give me an opportunity to record this interview. At the time you took office on April 13, 1964, what was the policy of your government towards the education of the Africans?

Smith: We recognized that there was a gap between the education of the white students ands that of the African students. This was part of our history,[2] it was not due to anything that we did. I would like to say that there was a reason for this gap. I myself can remember the young men coming from our university[3], how difficult it was for us to encourage some of our African people to send their children to school. They did not believe in education because they thought that it was something that belonged to the white man. They thought that they would lose the services of their children while they were in school, the services which the children normally rendered in the tribal trust lands.[4] But after World War II there was a sudden surge, and the Africans suddenly wanted education. Therefore, the government of Sir Godfrey Huggins[5] had a major problem in finding the money to provide the necessary facilities.

It was easier to produce the bricks and mortar than to train teachers because you realize that it takes twenty years to train teachers in sufficient numbers to meet the need. So, we were conscious of the gap, but I can assure you that we went out of our way to try to bring more educational facilities to our African people than to the white people. In fact, I can recall criticism leveled against my government about the amount of money we were voting for the education of the Africans from some white people who thought that we were spending too much of the tax payers' money for the educational development of the Africans. I want to add quickly that I disagreed

---

[2]For the influence of this history see, for example, Dickson A. Mungazi, *Colonial Education for Africans: George Stark's Policy in Zimbabwe*. New York: Praeger, 1991.
[3]Known as the University College of Rhodesia and Nyasaland from 1956 to 1979, the college had a total enrollment of 69 students in 1958 of whom 8 were Africans.
[4]Known as Native Reserves created under provisions of the Land Apportionment Act of 1929, these areas became known as tribal trust lands under the Land Tenure Act of 1969
[5]Huggins served as prime minister of colonial Zimbabwe from 1933 to 1953 and of the ill-fated Federation of Rhodesia and Nyasaland from 1953 to 1956.

with them. But, as you know, all kinds of people in a community can express mixed-up ideas. This is why there were some people who criticized by government's educational policy. Therefore, my conscience is very clear because we went out of our way to increase the amount of money were were spending on the education of the Africans because we realized how important it was.

Mungazi: At the time you assumed the office of prime minister in 1964 to the time you left in March, 1979, your government maintained two separate educational systems, one for the white students, and the other for the African students. Why was it necessary to maintain that policy and practice at a time when change in political conditions demanded an integrated educational system to minimize the possibility of conflict?

Smith: Well, we did, as you rightly say, maintain a policy which we had inherited because it had already been in existence. The main argument in favor of maintaining this policy was that the different educational standards of the two racial communities meant that the education of the Africans was not as good as that of the whites.[6] But as we gradually broke the resistance to education among the Africans, we were constantly advised by our experts in education that we had to be very careful not to integrate the two systems of education because this would lower the standards of education for white students without raising that of the African students. I have always stated as a principle that what we must be careful of, as far as changing our policy was concerned, is that we must bring the standards of African education up to the standards of the white students, which, I am quite happy to say, were the highest in Africa.

We should always avoid bringing the standards down, and I am pleased to tell you that there were many black people in education who told us that they did not want to see standards come down and that we should try to bring them up to the level of those of the education of the white students. This was the reason for maintaining two separate systems of education; we were trying to raise the standards of African education without lowering those of white education. We knew that we had done it too quickly, we would have hurt the education of both racial groups.

Mungazi: What you have just said seems to suggest that the education of the white students was used as a criterion to determine the standards of education of the Africans and that this could be done only by maintaining the two systems separately. Is this correct?

Smith: This is exactly the way we understood it from the advice we received from the experts......

---

[6]This line of thinking is similar to that which existed in the U.S.A. from 1896 to 1954 under the doctrine of separate but equal. For details see Appendix 4 of this study.

Mungazi: I am sorry to interrupt, but it is apparent that the educational policy of your government, especially from 1964 to 1966, caused you some serious political problems, and you still believed that it was necessary to maintain segregation in education. Could not your advisers and you yourself see the potential for conflict due to this segregation? At what point during your administration did you recognize that your educational policy was leading to a major racial conflict?

Smith: The period you refer to in your question was a period of political turmoil in the Federation. The whole thing was sparked by the fact that were having an argument with the British government over our independence. We wanted to get rid of colonialism, and.......

Mungazi: I am sorry to interrupt again, but the Africans wanted independence, too, and wanted to end colonialism, but they considered your government the worst form of colonialism. They wanted independence under a black majority government, while you wanted it under a white minority government. The British government wanted to grant independence under a black majority government as it had been doing since 1957 when it granted independence to Ghana. Therefore, your argument with the British government was not about the question of independence, but about a fundamental disagreement about the principle of black majority government, which you rejected. Is this not true?

Smith: This is true, you are quite right. This was the main problem between my government and the British government. However, we believed that until we had achieved independence, we would never be able to settle down because the question of independence was closely related to the educational development of the Africans. We also realized that it was part and parcel of the whole problem which we were facing in the political arena, and there were no easy answers to these problems. Now, to your question of when we first realized that our educational policy was causing us serious political problems. We had our first encounter with this problem, terrorist incursion, as we called it, across the Zambezi early in 1961. I believe that the African politicians were looking for a cause, and education seemed to appeal to the African masses more than any other issue.

This was a period of political turmoil, as I have said, and we were conscious of this fact. But we believed that the educational principles we had formulated and the policies we were pursuing were correct. We had to maintain standards and we did not want to turn an evolutionary process into a revolution because the standards would fall. Therefore, we stuck to our educational guns on the basis of the advice that was given to us, not by the politicians, but by our experts in education, that what we were doing was correct and that we should continue.

Mungazi: From 1969 to 1970, your government introduced a new and controversial policy, what was known as 5% cut in salary grants for African primary teachers.[7] This created a major political crisis that some say eventually brought your government to an end in 1979. The Africans and the church leaders joined hands in opposing this policy. Some say the crisis caused by the introduction of this policy and opposition to it combined to precipitate events that intensified the civil war beginning in December, 1972. As you know, the war continued until an agreement was reached at Lancaster House in London in December, 1979, paving way for a black majority government that you had vigorously opposed. I wonder if you would care to relate these sad events to the educational policy of your government?

Smith: Yes, what we were trying to do in 5% cut was make the money we had available for education go as far as possible. You know that these things money is the deciding factor. I remember about a trip I made to Australia some years ago. The government there told me that the big problem they had in education was the lack of money. Australia did not have a problem with the black people as were we were having, yet the government still did not have sufficient financial resources to meet all its educational needs. The Australian government told me that it did not have the money it needed, and so it had to do with the limited financial resources available.

We were facing exactly the same problem, but ours was a much more complex one because while the Australian government's immigration policy was a gradual one, we had all these people from Europe [8] and they wanted education for their children at the same time that the Africans wanted it for theirs. So, it was the art of the possible. Somewhere within the system of education somebody suggested that method of 5% cut. Remember that at that point, the education of the Africans was absolutely free.[9] So, we believed that when the Africans paid a little bit, they would appreciate education more.

So we asked them to contribute 5% of the teachers' salary grants for the primary teachers so that we would save some money for other facilities and for the development of secondary schools. In spite of the 5% cut, the money that we spent on education for the Africans was rapidly increasing each year. I cannot deny that the educational policy of my government, especially 5% cut in salary grants for African primary teachers, played a major role in the outbreak if the war. But we believed that we were doing the right thing and that political considerations did not come into the picture to influence our decisions in any way.

Mungazi: Since I returned to Zimbabwe from the U.S.A. at the beginning of this month, I have had an opportunity to interview a number of people who were close either to your government policy or to the education of the Africans, both white and black. Some of them told me that your government was apprehensive about more

---

[7]The government had been paying 100% of teachers' salaries since 1959 under provisions of Native Education Act of that year.

[8]In May, 1967 the RF placed advertisements in several newspapers in Europe inviting at least a million immigrants from Europe in an effort to offset the rapidly rising African population. Due to the increasing internal conflict, only a few responded.

[9]The actual historical fact is that white students had enjoyed free and compulsory education since 1935. but for Africans is was neither

meaningful educational opportunity for the Africans because there was a feeling among some whites that the more the Africans received more education, the more they were likely to threaten the political power that the white community considered its exclusive privilege. How do you respond to this kind of criticism?

Smith: Again, I do not deny that there were some white people who thought along the lines that you indicate in your question. I want to assure you that it was never a part of my thinking. Certainly it was not a part of the official government thinking. I had enough sense and intelligence to realize that the better educated the people of as country were, the better it would be, and it was very stupid for anyone to believe that you could control the people by denying them education. I felt quite the reverse.

I never doubted in my mind that we would have more black people in government than whites. Therefore, we believed that the best way to have the most responsible government is by educating the people who would run it. This is why we went out of our way against economic sanctions[10] to provide the Africans the best education possible.

The problems that we faced in the education of the Africans were due to economic reasons, not to the thinking that we were trying to retard their advancement. If we wanted to limit the political advancement of the Africans, we would have done so by raising the voting qualifications. We actually had the political means to do this.[11] But this would have undermined our own future because we would have never been able to suppress the Africans forever.

Mungazi: What do you think about the educational innovation of the present government in Zimbabwe? In your opinion, is the government doing the right thing and pursuing the correct educational policy?

Smith: Well, I think that the government has a tremendous task. As I look back now, perhaps we should not have been dogmatic about maintaining standards. We should have lowered them a little bit in order to educate more people. But I must add that there is also the danger of lowering standards so much that the educational process would have had little meaning. I have one criticism of the present government policy. We were told at the time of the negotiations for independence in 1979 that the whites would be allowed to keep their private schools so that they would bring more Africans students into schools of high standards.

But the concept was thrown out by the present government. The Lancaster House agreement of 1979 specifically told us that we could keep those schools in order to

---

[10]Imposed in November, 1965, by the U.N. following the unilateral declaration of independence, which both Britain and the international community considered illegal.

[11]Speaking in parliament in September, 1969, Andrew Skeen, RF spokesman said, "We in the Rhodesia Front Government are determined to control the rate of African political advancement till time and education make it a safe possibility. Moreover, we wish to have the power to retard the educational development of the Africans to slow down their political ambitions." (See Dickson A. Mungazi, *Education and Government Control in Zimbabwe*. New York: Praeger, 1990, p.39.). Where does this place Smith's remarks on this issue?

maintain standards as an incentive to keep the white people in the country. But this government turned against us. We were going to take it to court. The Minister of Education was in agreement with the principle, but he was overruled by his superiors in government. This has done a great damage to the education of our children. Without good education for their children, the whites were not willing to stay. We have lost our teachers and we have lost the confidence we once placed in the government.

Mungazi: You have just indicated in retrospect that perhaps you should not have insisted on your definition of standards because you alienated the Africans from the educational process, and that that alienation had serious political implications for your government. If you had the opportunity to start all over again, in addition to standards, what other changes would you make in your educational policy?

Smith: This is a very deep question, one that requires a great deal of thought. It is really not an easy one to answer. Perhaps among the changes that we would make would be not to insist on maintaining high educational standards. We should have allowed more Africans to receive education. We should have tried to find ways of accommodating more African students into the educational process. We should have involved the Africans in defining and implementing educational policy. We should have allowed them to express their views of what education was. We should have made it possible for them to be represented in the educational decision-making process. These are among the things that we, as a government, would do if we had the opportunity to start all over again. But I know that this will not happen. We did what we thought was best for our country and I have no regrets.

Mungazi: Give me your own philosophy of education, especially for a Third World nation like Zimbabwe.

Smith: Again this is a very deep question, and I do not presume to know everything there is to know in educational philosophy. You, as a university professor, might be in a better position to define educational philosophy than I am. However, since you asked to do so, I will give you my own philosophy. In a Third World country like Zimbabwe there are a few things more important than education. I suppose it is very good to put education ahead of things like health. But education and health go hand in hand. If people are not healthy they cannot be educated, although one would have to say that if people are not educated, they cannot be healthy.

But for a country like Zimbabwe one needs to balance the two. Over the years we in Rhodesia did our best to provide both. The country to the north of us (Zambia) had only a few university graduates at the time of its independence in 1964. But we had at least 3,000 university graduates. A nation has to be very careful to make sure that it is following a practical line of education as opposed to idealistic line of education. The reason education in Britain and the U.S.A. for example, has been so successful is that those nations have followed a practical line of education. In the emerging countries of the Third World it is even more important to follow a practical line of education.

Academic education is not the only form of education that help a Third World nation develop. In fact, academic education is not for everyone. Practical education enables one to use one's head as much as academic education does. Practical education has an advantage over academic education, it enables one to use one's hands in mustering the skills that one needs to have a respectable job and to earn a decent income. This gives one a sense of importance, self-worth and dignity. Academic education has nothing to offer in terms of practical value. A Third World nation like Zimbabwe should place more emphasis on practical education than on academic education. What is the point of providing highly academically educated people who will not find employment? Look at India. It is not inconceivable that university graduates should be paid less than, say, bus drivers.

In Third World nations there is a danger of over-emphasizing the importance of academic education at the expense of practical education. The government must carefully make its plans for the future so that properly educated people will find the employment opportunities they have trained for. This will guarantee a strong economy. That is my philosophy of education for a Third World nation like Zimbabwe.

Mungazi: I have one final question which I must ask you. At the time that Zimbabwe became independent in April 1980, many of your white colleagues in government and the white community in general decided to leave the country because they did not want to live under a black government. You , yourself, used to say that there would never be a black government in Zimbabwe in your life-time. Your entire political career was based on this policy. The black government has become a reality in your life-time. Why did you decide to stay?

Smith: Well, you are putting me on the spot (laughter). I decided to stay because Zimbabwe is my country. I was born here (1919). I have lived all my life in this country of my birth. Five generations of my family have lived in this country. As political problems grew it would have been easy for me to leave. Some people even encouraged me to leave. But I rejected these suggestions because my heart is still in this country, and I will continue to do my best to make conditions better for both black and white. This is the reason why I decided to stay.

Mungazi: Thank you for taking time from your busy schedule to record this interview.

Smith: Thank you for giving me the opportunity to review the educational policy of my government and to put some developments in the history of Zimbabwe into perspective.

Appendix 6

Northern Arizona University,
Center for Excellence in Education
Box 5774
Flagstaff, Arizona, U.S.A. 86011
Phone: (602) 523-2611/7467
February 15, 1990

Mr. F. E. de Klerk,
State President,
Government House,
Cape Town, South Africa

Dear Mr. de Klerk,

I know that you have recently been receiving letters from people who, like I, are deeply concerned about recent developments in South Africa as a result of the gallant action you have taken to avert what every one who has become familiar with the history of South Africa recognizes as a major tragedy. To the letters that you have already received I would like to add my congratulation to you and your government on your ability to recognize the urgent need to break with the past and to chart a new course to save the nation from disaster.

I am aware that you are highly sensitive to the critical nature of the need to make a fresh start against overwhelming pressures of history. In 1989 I published a book entitled *The Struggle for Social Change in Southern Africa: Visions of Liberty* (New York: Taylor and Francis, 1989), in which I conclude "For both South Africa and Southern Africa this the eleventh hour. The minutes are ticking away to a fateful explosion. Indeed, South Africa needs a Marshall Plan of its own to rescue it from the devastation of apartheid." I see your initiative as a form of the *Marshall Plan* needed to save South Africa from a national disaster.

I see convincing evidence that your initiative is an outcome of a dramatic realization that apartheid has to be dismantled immediately in order to create a national climate in which negotiations can begin. This action requires complete understanding of history. From the time that Jan van Riebeeck established a settlement at the Cape on behalf of the Dutch East India Company in 1652, through the bitter racial war of 1835, the Boer War of 1899 and the demise of Paul Kruger in 1901, the Bloemfontein Convention of 1908, the granting of independence in 1910, the founding of the ANC in 1912, the enactment of the Land Act in 1913, the victory of the Nationalist Party in the elections of 1948, the withdrawal of South Africa from the British Commonwealth of Nations in 1960, the imprisonment of Nelson Mandela in 1964, the tragic death of Dr. Hendrik Verwoerd in 1966, and the Soweto uprising in 1976, South Africa has been walking an extremely slippery national road. Your clear understanding of the need to break with the past so that the future may be meaningful for all the people of South Africa may very well see a new day for the country.

The purpose of this letter is to make some suggestions that may help facilitate the process towards peace. I make these suggestions with deep concern and as someone who has been closely studying the problems of South Africa. First, it is very important for you to lift the State of Emergency in order to allow the Africans to place their confidence in your sincerity to negotiate in good faith. To try to negotiate with them under the influence of the State of Emergency is to try to have them function with their hands tied on their back. The lifting of the State of Emergency would mean that the police would not exercise excessive force to suppress the Africans.

Second, it is imperative to hold discussions with the Africans without further delay. Conventional wisdom would suggest that participation in the discussions be held on the basis of total equality, and that you yourself should not be the chairman of it, not even any one in South Africa should chair the conference. I would suggest that someone outside South Africa would bring a greater degree of credibility among participants, such as the President of the International Court of Justice at the Hague, or a leading member of the House of Lords in Britain. Their impartiality would not be in question. No one in South Africa at this point can command the same respect as emotions are running very high on all sides.

Third, conventional wisdom also suggests that the conference should be held outside South Africa, such as at the International Convention Center in Geneva. The reason for this is that participants need to get away from the pressures imposed by their constituencies, and need to remove themselves completely from the South African scene in order to examine the problems from their proper perspective. The negotiations over the future of Zimbabwe in 1979 serve as a good example of the wisdom of this action.

Fourth, it is not enough for you to argue that by announcing your intention to hold discussions with the Africans, you turn around and argue that there is no more any excuse for violence when the international community has recognized apartheid as a system of violence. What you should have done immediately was for you to end apartheid by executive directive in order to convince the Africans of your best intentions. The notion that you can negotiate the end of apartheid sounds contradictory to the principles you have expressed for the need to hold discussions with the Africans. This action would have eliminated one major problem and the discussions would focus on the substantive issues of the new constitution. By not taking this action you implied that apartheid is a subject of negotiation when you know that the Africans would not accept its continuation.

Fifth, it is vitally important for the white people of South Africa to recognize that the principle of majority rule must prevail. Experience elsewhere in Africa would substantiate the accuracy of this conclusion. The bitter Mau-Mau movement in Kenya, the struggle in Algeria, Zimbabwe, Angola, and Mozambique must serve as examples that show that whenever a minority rules over the majority abuse of power becomes an instrument of perpetuating itself. It is because of this reality that the international community has unreservedly condemned South Africa for using the instrument of apartheid to maintain a violent system. The support that South Africa has been giving to Jonas Savimbi in Angola, dissident elements in Zimbabwe and Renamo in Mozambique has also created a violent situation in all of Southern Africa. This cannot continue and hope that peace will prevail. Regional peace is important for South Africa itself and its action to stop periodic raids into front-line states can go a long way in resolving major problems.

Best wishes in your endeavor. Indeed, the eyes of the world are on you.

Yours sincerely,

Dickson A. Mungazi,
Associate Professor.

Appendix 7

Tuynhuys   1.4
Kaapstad Tuynhuys

12 March, 1990
Cape Town

Prof. D. A. Mungazi,
P. O. Box 5774,
Flagstaff, Arizona
U.S.A. 86011

Dear Professor Mungazi,

I acknowledge receipt of your letter dated 15 February, 1990 addressed to the
State President of the Republic of South Africa.

Your letter will be brought to the President"s attention as soon as possible.

With kind regards

S.P.N. Basson,
Administrative Secretary
/cb

BIBLIOGRAPHY

BOOKS

Anglin, Douglas,[Ed.], *Conflict and Change in Southern Africa. Papers from a Scandinavian Conference.* Washington, D.C., University Press of America, 1978.

Banana, Canaan, *Theology of Promise: The Dynamics of Self-reliance.* Harare: The College Press, 1982.

Battle, M, and Charles Lyons, *Essays in African Education.* New York: Teachers College Press, 1970.

Bond- Stewart, Kathy, *Education:* Gweru: Mambo Press, 1986.

Chidzero, B. T., *Education and the Challenge of Independence.* IEUP, Geneva, 1977

Cox, Cortland, *African Liberation.* New York: Black Education Press, 1972.

Curle, Adam, *Education for Liberation.* New York: John Wiley and Sons, 1973.

Dewy, John, *Experience and Education.* New York: Collier Books, 1938.

Diffendorfer, Ralph E.[Ed.], *The World Service of the Methodist Episcopal Church.* Chicago. Methodist Council on Benevolences, 1923.

Dugard, John, *The Southwest Africa/Namibia Dispute.* Berkley: University of California Press. 1973.

Eicher, J. C., *Educational Costing and Financing in Developing Countries.* Washington, D.C.: World Bank, 1984.

Fafunwa, Babs, *History of Education in Nigeria.* London: George Allen and Unwin, 1974.

Freire, Paulo, *Pedagogy of the Oppressed.* New York: Continuum, 1983.

Gelfand, Michael, *Growing up in Shona Society.* Gweru: Mambo Press, 1979.

Henderson, Lawrence, *Angola: Five Centuries of Conflict.* Ithaca: Cornell University Press, 1979.

Hirst, Paul, *Knowledge and the Curriculum: A Collection of Philosophical Papers.* London:Poutledge and Kegan Paul, 1974.

Huddleston, Trevor, *Naught for Your Comfort.* New York.Oxford University Press, 1956.

Herbstein, Dennis, *White Man, we want to talk to you.*London: Oxford University Press, 1979.

Kaunda, Kenneth, *Zambia Shall be Free.* New Yor; Frederick Praeger, 1963.

Kimble, H. T., *Emerging Africa.* New York: Scholastic Books, 1963.

Knorr, Kenneth, *British Colonial Theories.* Toronto: University of Toronto Press, 1974.

La Guma, Alex, [Ed.], *Apartheid: Collection of Writings of South Africa by South Africans,* New York: International Publishers, 1971.

Machel, Somara, *Mozambique: Sowing the Seeds of Revolution.* Harare: Zimbabwe Publishing House, 1981.

Mson, Philip, *The Birth of a Dilemma: Conquest and Settlement of Rhodesaia.* London, 1956.

Meredith, Martin, *The First Dance of Freedom: Black Africa in the Post-War Era.* New York: Harper and Row, 1984.

Memmi, Albert, *The Colonizer and the Colonized.* Boston: Beacon Press, 1965.

Mondlane, Edwardo, The Struggle for Mozambique. Boltimore: Penguin Books, 1969.

Mungazi, Dickson A., *The Honored Crusade: Ralph Dodge's Theology of Liberation and Initiative for Social Change in Zimbabwe.* Gweru: Mambo Press, 1990.

Mungazi, Dickson, A., *Education and Government Control in Zimbabwe: A Study of the Commissions of Inquiry, 1908-1974.* New York: Praeger Publishers, 1990.

Mungazi, Dickson A., *The Struggle for Social Change in Southern Africa: Visions of Liberty*. New York: Taylor and Francis, 1989.

Mungazi, Dickson A., *To Honor the Sacred Trust of Civilization: History, Politics, and Education in Southern Africa*. Cambridge (Ma.). Schenkman Publishers, 1983.

Mungazi, Dickson A., *The Cross Between Rhodesia and Zimbabwe: Racial Conflict in Rhodesia, 1962-1979*. New York: Vantage Press, 1981.

Mungazi, Dickson A., *The Underdevelopment of African Education*. Washington. D.C, University Press of America, 1982.

O'Callaghan, Marion, *Namibia: The Effects of Apartheid on Culture and Education*. Paris: Unesco, 1979

O'Callaghan, Marion, *Rhodesia: The Effects of Apartheid on Culture and Education*. Paris, Unesco, 1979.

Prker, Franklin, *African Development and Education in Southern Rhodesia*. Columbuis: Ohio State University Press, 1960.

Piper, Alan, *South Africa in the American Mind*. News York: Carnegie, 1981.

Powers, B. A., *Religion in Tswana Chiefdom*. London: Oxford University Press, 1961.

Psacharopoulos, George, and Maureen Woodhall, *Education for Development: An Analysis of Investment Choices*. New York: Oxford University Press, 1985.

Ranger, Terrence, *Revolt in Southern Rhodesia, 1896-1897*. Evanston: Northwestern University Press, 1967.

Raphaeli, Nimroid, *Public Sector Management in Botswana*. Washington, D.C.: World Bank, 1984.

Raynor, William, *Tribe and its Successors: An Account of African Traditional Life after European Settlement in Southern Rhodesia*. New York: Frederick Praeger, 1962.

Riddell, Roger, *From Rhodesia to Zimbabwe: Education for Employment*. Gweru: Mambo Press, 1980.

Samkange, Stanlake, *What Rhodes Really Said About Africa*. Harare: Harare Publishing House, 1982.

Segai, Ronald, and Ruth First, *Southwest Africa: Travesty of Trust*. London: Deutsch, 1967.

Smith, William, *Nyerere of Tanzania*. Harare: Zimbabwe Publishing House, 1981.

Smuts, J. C., *The League of Nations: A Practical Suggestion;* New York: U;N., 1918

Southall, Aiden, *The Illusion of Tribe*. The Netherlands: R. J. Brill, 1970.

Sparrow, George, *The Rhodesian Rebellion*. London: Brighton, 1966.

Thompson, A. R., *Education and Development in Africa*. New York: St. Martins' Press, 1981.

Turner, V. W., *Schism and Continuity in an African Society*. Manchester: Manchester University Press, 1957.

Tutu, Desmond, *Crying in the Wilderness: The Struggle for Justice in South Africa*. Grand Rapids,: William Eerdmans Publishers, 1982.

Vambe, Lawrence, *The Ill-Fated People: Zimbabwe Before and After Rhodes*. Pittsburgh: Pittsburgh University Press, 1957.

Van Til, William, *Education: A Beginning*. Boston: Houghton Mifflin Company, 1974.

Watson, George, *Change in School System*. Washington, D.C. National Training Laboratories, NEA, 1967.

Weaver, Thomas, [Ed.], *To See Ourselves: Anthropology and Modern Social Issues*. Glenview.]: Scott, Foreman and Company, 1973.

Wills, A. J., *An Introduction to the History of Central Africa*. London: Oxford University Press, 1964.

GOVERNMENT DOCUMENTS AND MATERIALS

British South Africa Company Records : Earl Grey, 1896-1898: Folio: AV/1/11/1/11:547-548. Zimbabwe National Archives.

Huggins, Godfrey, (Prime Minister of Colonial Zimbabwe,1933-1952, and of the Federation of Rhodesia and Nyasaland, 1953-1956), *Education Policy in Southern Rhodesia: Notes on Certain Features,* 1939.

Huggins, Godfrey, "Rhodesia Leads the Way: Education for Europeans in Southern Rhodesia," in *Times Educational Supplement,* February 14, 1931.

Huggins, Godfrey, "Partnership in Building a Country," a political speech, December 21, 1950.

Huggins, Godfrey, "Partnership in Rhodesia and Nyasaland," a speech given during a campaign for the establishment of the Federation of Rhodesia and Nyasaland, May, 1950.

Huggins, Godfrey, "Taking Stock of African Education," an address to the Southern Rhodesia Missionary Conference, Goromonzi, August 26, 1954.

South Africa: *Proclamation over Southwest Africa,* November 27, 1918.

Southern Rhodèsia: *Legislative Debates,* 1923-1961

Southern Rhodesia: *Education Ordinance Number 18: The Appointment of Inspector of Schools,* 1899.

Southern Rhodesia: *Ordinance Number 1,* 1903.

Rhodesia: *African Education,* Ref. 738, 1973

Rhodesia: *Parliamentary Debates,* August 26, 1977, August 27, 1974, August 30, 1974.

Rhodesia: *Report of the Commission of Inquiry into Racial Discrimination* [Vincent Quenet, Chairman] Ref. 27015/36050, April 23, 1976.

Southern Rhodesia, *Annual Reports of the Director of Native Education,* 1927 - 1960.

Southern Rhodesia, *Annual Reports of the Secretary for African Education,* 1962 - 1979.

Rhodesian: *Education: An Act ,* No. 8, 1979.

Tanzania, *Education for Self-reliance.* Dar es Salaam: Government Printer., 1967.

Zambia Information Service: *Zambia in Brief.* Lusaka, 1975.

Zambia, *Educational Reform: Proposals and Recommendations*, October, 1977

Zambia: K. D. Kaunda, *Blueprint for Economic Development: A Guide on How to Clear Obstacles*. October 8, 1979.

Botswana, *Ten Years of Independence*. Gaberone, 1976

Botswana: *Report of the National Commission on Education*. Gaberone, April, 1977.

Botswana: *Education Statistics*. Gaberone: Government Printer, 1979.

Botswana: *Education for Kagisano: Supplementary Report of the National Commission on Education*. Gaberone, July, 1979.

Botswana: *Botswana Update*. Gaberone, 1982.

Mozambique, Samora Machel, The Liberation of Women as a Fundamental Necessity for Revolution," an address given at the opening of the First Conference of Mozambique Women, March 4, 1973.

Mozambique, Samora Machel, "Leadership in Collective, Responsibility is Collective," a speech given to the Joint Meeting of Frelimo Instructors, February 2, 1972.

Mozambique, Samora Machel, "Educate Men to Win the War, Create a New Society, and Develop a Country," a speech given at the Second Conference on Education and Culture, September, 1970.

South Africa, *South Africa Broadcasting Corporation on Political Rights*, Ref. SABC/TV,1/90, February 2, 1990.

Zimbabwe-Rhodesia : *Report of of the Constitutional Conference*, Ref. R2R3, London. Lancaster House, December 21, 1979

Zimbabwe: Prime Minister [Robert Mugabe, *Address to the Organization of African Unity*, Document No. 2. Freetown, Sierra Leone, July 4, 1980.

Zimbabwe: *Prime Minister Opens Economic Conference*, September 5, 1980.

Zimbabwe: *Prime Minister's New Year's Message to the Nation*, December 31, 1980.

Zimbabwe: *Annual Report of the Secretary for Education,* 1980-1989. Harare: Government Printer, 1989.

Zimbabwe: *The Prime Minister Opens an Economic Symposium,* September 11, 1980.

Zimbabwe: *Annual Digest of Statistics.* Harare: Government Printer, 1988.

Zimbabwe: *The Constitution of Zimbabwe.* Harare: Government Printer, 1985.

Zimbabwe: *Constitutional Amendment* No. 23, 1987.

Zimbabwe: B. T. Chidzero, Minister of Finance and Planning, *Budget Statement,* July 27, 1989.

Zimbabwe: Mugabe, Robert, "Literacy for All in Five Years," a Speech given in launching a national literacy Campaign, July 18, 1983.

Zimbabwe: "Not in a Thousand Years: From Rhodesia to Zimbabwe,", a documentary film, PBS, 1981

Zimbabwe: ZAPU, *Primary School Syllabus*, August, 1978.

Mozambique: Ministry of Information, *Education in Mozambique*, Maputo, 1982.

NEWSPAPERS, JOURNALS, MAGAZINES

The Economist, September 30, 1989.

The Chicago Tribune, October 1, 1981

Zimbabwe: *The Herald,* July 4, 1983, August 8, 1989.

_____,April 13, 1989, "Mozambique Looks to the World for $450 million aid."

_____, July 15, 1989, "Secondary Schools Hit by Shortage of Qualified Teachers."

_____, July 10, 1989, "Apartheid Cannot be Condoned."

_____, July 17, 1989, "Worry over Schools Zoning."

_____, July 20, 1989, "Mozambique Peace Drive a Concern."

_____, July 24, 1989, "Concept of Education with Production Explained."

_____, July 28, 1989, "University of Zimbabwe gets $400 million from Federal Republic of Germany for Developing Equipment."

_____, July 28, 1989," Nkomo's Economic Objectives are a Priority in Resettlement."

_____, August 11, 1989, "Sanctions that would Bite."

_____, August 11, 1989, "Nkomo Lectures University Students."

_____, August 12, 1989, "President Calls for Revolutionary Land Reform Programs."

_____, August 17, 1989, "Compensation for Teachers who Joined Freedom Struggle."

Zimbabwe: The Sunday Mail, August, 1989, "Teachers Form Union."

The Christian Science Monitor, September 7, 1989. "Future Leaders Learn Next-door: Namibians Study at U.N. School in Zambia."

The Los Angeles Times : Africa's Future Riding the Train to Nowhere, July 17, 1990.

The New York Times, November 16, 1989, "Students Fail Zimbabwe and Pay Heavy Price."

The New York Times, "Higher Controls Seen in Zimbabwe," December 10, 1989.

The New York Times, "The Old Men versus the Public: Africa's Iron Hands Struggle to Hang on," July 15, 1990.

Moto; Gweru. August, 1983 - August, 1989.

Time. March 5, 1990.

Time, July 9, 1990

South Africa Scan: *Facts and Reports,* 1989.

The Washington Post, August 1, 1989.

The World Almanac and Book of Facts, 1990.

Zimbabwe: Ministry of Information, Press Statements, Speeches by Government Officials on Education:

Culverwell, Joseph, Minister of State for National Scholarship, "Take Education Seriously, " Ref. 59/88/SL/BC, February 23, 1989.

Culverwell, Joseph, "U.S. Sponsored Students Graduate." Ref. 78/89/CB/MA, March 1, 1989.

Chung, Faye, Minister of Primary and Secondary Education, "Pre-school Training Graduates." Ref. 317/88/GB/SD/BJ, July 25, 1988.

Chung, Faye, "The importance of Local Production of Science Textbooks," Ref. 80/89/CB/MA. March 9, 1989.

Chung, Faye, "The Role of Booksellers in Educational Development," Ref. 223/89/CB/EM/SM, July 13, 1989

Chung, Faye, "Women are Educated Less than Men," Ref. 230/89/CB/SM/SR, July 25, 1989.

Hughes, Aminia, Deputy Minister of Transport, Be Selfless and Dedicated Teachers," Ref. 482/88/SM, October 28, 1988

Karimanzira, David, Minister of Social Services, "Educate the People on the Dangers of Agrochemicals," Ref. 399/88/EMM/CB, September 14, 1988.

Karimanzira, David, "Educate Farmers on Better Livestock Production," Ref. 472/88/EMM/SM, October 25, 1988.

Karimanzira, David, "Government to Provide More Extension Staff," Ref. 235/89/EMM/SM/SK, July 25, 1989.

Kay, Jack, Deputy Minister of Lands, Agriculture, and Rural Settlement, Zimbabwe is SADDC's Breadbasket." Ref. 384/EMM/SG, August 29, 1988.

Muchemwa, Felix, Minister of Health, "State Certificated Nurses Graduate in Masvingo." Ref. 29/80/RN/SD/BJ, July 21, 1988.

Mujuru, Joyce, Minister of Community and Cooperative Development, "Women's Role in Nation Building" Ref. 4/1/89/SG/SM, June 6, 1989.

Mutumbuka, Dzingai, Minister of Higher Education, "Marymount Teachers Graduate." Ref. 365/88/03/MM, August 20, 1988.

Mutumbuka, Dzingai, "The Role of Professional Bodies in National Development," Ref. 427/88/CB/EMM, September 22, 2988.

Mutumbuka, Dzingai, "The University of Zimbabwe Staff Development," Ref. 405/88/CB/ME, September 14, 1988.

Mutumbuka, Dzingai, "Training Institutions Play Vital Role in National Development." Ref. 447/88/CC/ES, October 7, 1988.

Mutumbuka, "The importance of Revising History," Ref. 15/89/CB/SK, January 23, 1989.

Ministry of Information, "Vacancies for Zimbabwe-Cuba Teacher Education Course," Ref. 460/88/CB/SM, October 17, 1988

Ministry of Higher Education, "Learner-Tutor Course Applications," Ref. 459/88/CB/SM, October 17, 1988.

Ministry of Public Construction and National Housing, "Three Hundred Million Dollars Boost Rural Housing," Ref. 19/89/BC/SK, January 23, 1989.

Nkomo, John, Minister of Labor, " A Call for Educational Program," Ref.356/88/SK/EM/SG, August 17, 1988.

Nyagumbo, Maurice, Minister of Political Affairs, "Zimbabwe Objects to Education of U.N. Transitional Assistance Group, " Ref. 7/89/BC/SM, January 13, 1988.

OTHER MATERIALS AND DOCUMENTS

(a) UN Documents on Namibia

United Nations, Decree Number 1: *For the Protection of the Natural Resources of Namibia.* New York, September, 1974.

United Nations, *A Trust Betrayed: Namibia.* New York:, 1974.

United Nations, *Plunder of Namibian Uranium.* New York, September, 1974.

United Nations Council for Namibia, *Meetings held in Algeria*, May 28 - June 1, 1980.

United Nations Council for Namibia, *Meetings held in Panama City,* June 2-5, 1981.

United Nations, *Objective: Justice: Walvis Bay, an Integral Part of Namibia,* a statement on the future of Namibia, April 24, 1978.

United Nations, *Nationhood Program for Namibia.* New York, 1981.

United Nations, *Namibia: A Unique UN Responsibility,* New York, December, 1981.

United Nations Council on Namibia, *Arusha Declaration and Program of Action on Namibia,* May 14, 1982.

United Nations, *United Nations Council for Namibia: What it is, what it does, how it works.* New York, March 1983.

Unesco, *International Conference in Support of the Struggle of the Namibian People for Independence,* Paris, April 25-29, 1983.

(b) On Southern Africa in General

Africa Action Committee, *Uhuru for Southern Africa.* Kinshasa, December 15, 1984.

Afro-American and African Studies, *Africana.* College Park, Maryland, Vol. 2, No. 1, 1985.

United Nations, *Program of Action Against Apartheid.* New York, October 25, 1983.

Central Committee for SWAPO, *Swapo: Political Program of the Southwest Africa People's Organization.* Lusaka, July 28-August 1, 1976.

Office on Africa Educational Fund, *The Struggle for Justice in South Africa.* Washington, D.C., February, 1984.

Washington Office on Africa, *Resources on Namibia.* Washington, D.C., March, 1982.

New York Friends Group, Inc., *South Africa: Is Peaceful Change Possible?* New York, 1984.

Ayittey, George, "In Africa Independence is a far Cry from Freedom," in *The Wall Street Hournal*, March 28, 1990.

Davidson, Basil, *Afriuca: New Nations and Problems*, a Documentary film, Arts and Entertainment, 1988.

Smuts, J.C., *The League of Nations: A Practical Suggestion*, 1918.

Watson, P. *The Struggle for Democracy*, a Documentary film, P.B.S., 1988.

The League of Nations Covenant: Article 22, January 20, 1920.

The League of Nations: *The Mandate for Southwest Africa*, May 7, 1920.

Anad, Mohamed, *Apartheid: A Form of Slavery*. New York ,U.N. No. 37/71, 1971.

ABC-TV: *20/20: The Agony of Mozambique*, March 2, 1990.

OAU, "A Communique on Mozambique," Nairobi, Kenya, August 8, 1989.

The Anglo-Rhodesian Relations: Proposals for a Settlement, Ref. Cmd/RR/46/71, November 25, 1971.

Churchill, Winston, and Franklin Roosevelt, *The Atlantic Charter*, August 14, 1941.

British Council of Missionary Society, "Violence in Southern Africa: A Christian Assessment'", a statement of policy on Southern Africa, October 28, 1970.

British Methodist Church in Zimbabwe, *The Waddilove Manifesto: The Educational Policy of the Methodist Church,* a statement of policy and principles, February 9, 1946.

Basson, S. P. N., Administrative Secretary to President F. W. de Klerk, a letter dated 12 March, 1990, addressed to Dickson A. Mungazi, Northern Arizona University , Flagstaff, in response to his dated Feberuary 15, 1990, addressed to President de Klerk.

Carlson, Brian, "American Education: A South African Perspective in the Process of Desegregation," in *Kappa Delta Phi*, Summer, 1988.

Center for Applied Research, Social Implications of the Lagos Plan of Action for Economic Development in Africa, 1980-2000. Geneva, November, 1981.

Congolese National Liberation Front (CNLF), *The Struggle for Liberation*. New York:, 1975.

Dodge, Ralph, "The Church and Political Community," an unpublished essay, 1963.

Dodge, Ralph E, "A Political Community," an unpublished essay, May, 1964.

Evans, M, *The Front-line State, South Africa and Southern African Security: Military Prospects and Perspectives*. Harare. University of Zimbabwe, 1989.

Gordimer, Nadine, *Gold and teh Gun: Crisis in Mozambique and South Africa*, a documentary film, Arts and Entertainment, 1990.

Landis, Elizabeth, "Apartheid and the Disabilities of Women in South Africa," New York :United Nations Unit on Apartheid, 1975.

Loveridge, F. G., Senior Education Officer in the Ministry of African Education, Zimbabwe, "Disturbing Realities of Western Education in Southern Africa," an address to the Rotary Club International, Harare, March 13, 1963.

Southern Rhodesia: United Federal Party, *Information Statement,* Ref. UFP/SR/9, 1961.

Maier, Karl, "Opponent May Thwart Mugabe's Bid for a One-party System," in *The Washington Post*, March 29, 1990.

Mandela, Nelson, "A Statement made in Cape Town soon after his Release from Victor Verster Prison," SABC, February 11, 1990.

Mandela, Nelson, "Speech given in Soweto during a Reception held in his honor," February 12, 1990.

Malianga, Morton, a spokesman for ZANU, "We shall Wage an all out war to Liberate Ourselves," a statement issued on April 30, 1966, following a battle between the colonial forces and the African nationalist guerrillas on April 29.

M'Bow, Amadou-Mahtar, "Unesco Director-General, "Unesco and the Promotion of Education for International Understanding," an address to the New York African Studies Association Conference, Albany New York, October 29, 1982.

McHarg, James, "Influences Contributing to Education and Culture of Native People in Southern Rhodesia," a dessertation, Duke University, 1962

Macmillan, Harold, "Commonwealth Independence and Interdependence," an address to the Joint Session of the South African Parliament,Cape Town, February 3, 1960.

McNamara, Robert, "The Challenge of Sub-Sahara Africa," in John Crawford Lectures" Washington, D.C., November 1, 1985.

Mnegi wa Dikgang, *Education with Production.* Vol.. 5, No. 2, Gaberone, June, 1987.

Morton, Donald, "Partners in Apartheid," New York Center for Social Action: United Church of Christ, 1973.

Mutumbuka, Dzingai, "Zimbabwe's Educational Challenge," Paper read at the World University Services Conference, London, December, 1979.

Mungazi, Dickson, A., "Educational Policy for Africans and Church-State Conflict During the Rhodesia Front Government in Zimbabwe" in *The National Social Sceince Journal*, Vol. 2, No. 3, June, 1990.

Mungazi, Dickson A. "Educational Innovation in Zimbabwe: Possibilities and Problems," in *The Journal of Negro Education,* Vol. 54, No. 2, 1985.

Mungazi, Dickson A. "The Application of Memmi's Theory of the Colonizer and the Colonized," in *The Journal of Negro Education,* Vol.55, No. 4, 1986.

Mungazi, Dickson A. "A Strategy for Power: Commissions of Inquiry into Education and Government Control in Zimbabwe," in *The International Journal of African Historical Studies,* Boston University, Vol. 22, No. 2, 1989.

Mungazi, Dickson A. "To Bind Ties Between the School\ and Tribal Life: Educational Policy for Africans under George Stark in Zimbabwe," in *The Journal of Negro Education*, Vol. 58, No. 4, 1989.

Mungazi, Dickson A., "Apartheid in South Africa: Origin, Meaning, and Effect," a Documentary Film, Audio-Visual Services, Education, Northern Arizona University, Ref. AC/ECC/2/90, February 22, 1990.

Mungazi, Dickson A., A letter dated February 15, 1990, addressed to President F. W. de Klerk of South Africa, on the effect of apartheid on Southern Africa.

Molotsi, Peter, Fordham University, "Educational Policies and the South African Bantustans," a paper presented at the New York Association of African Studies, Albany, New York, October 29-30, 1982.

PBS, "Not in a Thousand Years: From Rhodesia to Zimbabwe," a Documentary film, 1982.

Riddell, Roger, *From Rhodesia to Zimbabwe: Alternatives to Poverty*, A position paper. Gweru: Mambo Press, 1978.

Rubin, Leslie, "Bantustan Policy: A Fantasy and a Fraud." News York: United Nations, Unit on Apartheid, Number 12/71, 1971.

Rhodesia Front Government, *The Dynamic Expansion in African Education*, a policy statement, Ref. INF/NE/Acc.40/2710, April 20, 1966.

Smith, Arthur, Minister of Education in Rhodesia, An Interview with Geoffrey Atkins of the Rhodesia Broadcasting Service, on educational Policy for Africans, January 31, 1968.

South African Ministry of Information, "South Africa Stops Native Students from Terrirotirs from Attending its Schools," a press release, November 2, 1950.

Sullivan, Leon, "Meeting the Mandate for Change: A Progress Report on the Application of the Sullivan Principles on U.S. Companies in South Africa." New York, 1984.

Tanzania, *Education for Self-reliance*. Dar es Salaam. Government Printer, 1967.

Tanzania, *Basic Facts about Education*. Dar es Salaam. Government Printer, 1984.

Thompson Publications, *Parade*. Harare, August, 1989.

Mozambique: "Documento Informativo," Ref. Doc/Inf.01/11, Maputo, 1979.

"Prospects of a Settlement in Angola and Namibia,", a Statement by the Parties [Representives of the U.S.A, Angola, SWAPO, Cuba].

The U.N.: *A Crime Against Humanity: Questions and Answers on Apartheid*. New York: 1984.

Unesco, "Education in Africa in the Light of the Lagos Conference," Paper Number 25, 1976.

United Methodist Church, *Southern Africa*. New York: Board of Global Ministries, 1986.

United Methodist Church, *Resolution Warning the Government of Southern Rhodesia against Continued Policy of Discrimination.* Harare, 1963.

University of Cape Town, "A Call for Postdoctoral Research Fellows, 1991,", in *The Chronicle of Higher Education,* March 16, 1990.

TransAfrica, *Namibia: The Crisis in U.S. Policy Toward Southern Africa.* Washington, D.C., 1983.

World Council of Churches, Involvement in the Struggles Against Oppression in Southern Africa, 1966-1980.

World Bank, *Accelerate Development in Sub-Sahara Africa: An Agenda for Action.* Washington, D.C. World Bank, 1983.

World Bank, "Alternatives to Formal Education : Unesco Conference on Education." Harare, June 28-July 3, 1982.

Zimbabwe Conference of Catholic Bishops, *Our Mission to Teach: A Pastoral Statement on Education.* Gweru: Mambo Press, 1987.

Zimbabwe Ministry of Education, *Arra Kis: School Library News.* Harare. Vol. 6, No. 60, July, 1986.

ZANU, *Liberation Through Participation: Women in the Zimbabwean Revolution.* Harare: ZANU, 1981.

ZANU: *Zimbabwe: Election Manifesto*, 1979.

Name Index

Subject Index